C Programming

ABSOLUTE
BEGINNER'S
GUIDE

Third Edition

Greg Perry and Dean Miller

800 East 96th Street
Indianapolis, Indiana 46240

C Programming Absolute Beginner's Guide
Third Edition

ISBN-13: 978-0-7897-5198-0
ISBN-10: 0-7897-5198-4

Library of Congress Cc

Printed in the United S

First Printing: August 2

Trademarks

All terms mentioned in
marks have been appr
the accuracy of this inf
regarded as affecting t

Warning and D

Every effort has been r
as possible, but no warranty or fitness is implied. The information provided is on an "as is" basis. The authors and the publisher shall have neither liability nor responsibility to any person or entity with respect to any loss or damages arising from the information contained in this book or from the use of the programs accompanying it.

Bulk Sales

Que Publishing offers excellent discounts on this book when ordered in quantity for bulk purchases or special sales. For more information, please contact

U.S. Corporate and Government Sales
1-800-382-3419
corpsales@pearsontechgroup.com

For sales outside the United States, please contact

International Sales
international@pearsoned.com

Acquisitions Editor
Mark Taber

Managing Editor
Sandra Schroeder

Project Editor
Mandie Frank

Copy Editor
Krista Hansing Editorial Services, Inc.

Indexer
Brad Herriman

Proofreader
Anne Goebel

Technical Editor
Greg Perry

Publishing Coordinator
Vanessa Evans

Interior Designer
Anne Jones

Cover Designer
Matt Coleman

Compositor
TnT Design, Inc.

Contents at a Glance

Table of Contents

Appendixes

About the Authors

Greg Perry is a speaker and writer in both the programming and applications sides of computing. He is known for bringing programming topics down to the beginner's level. Perry has been a programmer and trainer for two decades. He received his first degree in computer science and then earned a Master's degree in corporate finance. Besides writing, he consults and lectures across the country, including at the acclaimed Software Development programming conferences. Perry is the author of more than 75 other computer books. In his spare time, he gives lectures on traveling in Italy, his second favorite place to be.

Dean Miller is a writer and editor with more than 20 years of experience in both the publishing and licensed consumer product businesses. Over the years, he has created or helped shape a number of bestselling books and series, including *Teach Yourself in 21 Days*, *Teach Yourself in 24 Hours*, and the *Unleashed* series, all from Sams Publishing. He has written books on C programming and professional wrestling, and is still looking for a way to combine the two into one strange amalgam.

Dedication

To my wife and best friend, Fran Hatton, who's always supported my dreams and was an incredible rock during the most challenging year of my professional career.

Acknowledgments

Greg: My thanks go to all my friends at Pearson. Most writers would refer to them as editors; to me, they are friends. I want all my readers to understand this: The people at Pearson care about you most of all. The things they do result from their concern for your knowledge and enjoyment.

On a more personal note, my beautiful bride, Jayne; my mother, Bettye Perry; and my friends, who wonder how I find the time to write, all deserve credit for supporting my need to write.

Dean: Thanks to Mark Taber for considering me for this project. I started my professional life in computer book publishing, and it is so gratifying to return after a 10-year hiatus. I'd like to thank Greg Perry for creating outstanding first and second editions upon which this version of the book is based. It was an honor working with him as his editor for the first two editions and a greater honor to coauthor this edition. I can only hope I did it justice. I appreciate the amazing work the editorial team of Mandie Frank, Krista Hansing, and the production team at Pearson put into this book.

On a personal level, I have to thank my three children, John, Alice, and Maggie and my wife Fran for their unending patience and support.

We Want to Hear from You!

As the reader of this book, *you* are our most important critic and commentator. We value your opinion and want to know what we're doing right, what we could do better, what areas you'd like to see us publish in, and any other words of wisdom you're willing to pass our way.

We welcome your comments. You can email or write to let us know what you did or didn't like about this book—as well as what we can do to make our books better.

Please note that we cannot help you with technical problems related to the topic of this book and may not be able to reply personally to every message we receive.

When you write, please be sure to include this book's title, edition number, and authors, as well as your name and contact information. We will carefully review your comments and share them with the authors and editors who worked on the book.

Email: feedback@quepublishing.com

Mail: Que Publishing
           800 East 96th Street
           Indianapolis, IN 46240 USA

Reader Services

Visit our website and register this book at http://informit.com/register for convenient access to any updates, downloads, or errata that might be available for this book.

INTRODUCTION

Are you tired of seeing your friends get C programming jobs while you're left out in the cold? Would you like to learn C but just don't have the energy? Is your old, worn-out computer in need of a hot programming language to spice up its circuits? This book is just what the doctor ordered!

C Programming Absolute Beginner's Guide breaks the commonality of computer books by talking to you at your level without talking down to you. This book is like your best friend sitting next to you teaching C. *C Programming Absolute Beginner's Guide* attempts to express without impressing. It talks to you in plain language, not in "computerese." The short chapters, line drawings, and occasionally humorous straight talk guide you through the maze of C programming faster, friendlier, and easier than any other book available today.

Who's This Book For?

This is a beginner's book. If you have never programmed, this book is for you. No knowledge of any programming concept is assumed. If you can't even spell C, you can learn to program in C with this book.

The phrase *absolute beginner* has different meanings at different times. Maybe you've tried to learn C but gave up. Many books and classes make C much more technical than it is. You might have programmed in other languages but are a beginner in C. If so, read on, O faithful one, because in 32 quick chapters, you'll know C.

What Makes This Book Different?

This book doesn't cloud issues with internal technical stuff that beginners in C don't need. We're of the firm belief that introductory principles have to be taught well and slowly. After you tackle the basics, the "harder" parts never seem hard. This book teaches you the real C that you need to get started.

C can be an extremely cryptic and difficult language. Many people try to learn C more than once. The problem is simply this: Any subject, whether it be brain surgery, mail sorting, or C programming, is easy if it's explained properly. Nobody can teach you anything because you have to teach *yourself*—but if the instructor, book, or video doing the teaching doesn't make the subject simple and fun, you won't want to learn the subject.

We challenge you to find a more straightforward approach to C than is offered in the *C Programming Absolute Beginner's Guide*. If you can, call one of us because we'd like to read it. (You thought maybe we'd offer you your money back?) Seriously, we've tried to provide you with a different kind of help from that which you find in most other places.

The biggest advantage this book offers is that we really *like* to write C programs— and we like to teach C even more. We believe that you will learn to like C, too.

This Book's Design Elements

Like many computer books, this book contains lots of helpful hints, tips, warnings, and so on. You will run across many notes and sidebars that bring these specific items to your attention.

 TIP   Many of this book's tricks and tips (and there are lots of them) are highlighted as a Tip. When a really neat feature or code trick coincides with the topic you're reading about, a Tip pinpoints what you can do to take advantage of the added bonus.

 NOTE   Throughout the C language, certain subjects provide a deeper level of understanding than others. A Note tells you about something you might not have thought about, such as a new use for the topic being discussed.

 WARNING   A Warning points out potential problems you could face with the particular topic being discussed. It indicates a warning you should heed or provides a way to fix a problem that can occur.

Each chapter ends by reviewing the key points you should remember from that chapter. One of the key features that ties everything together is the section titled "The Absolute Minimum." This chapter summary states the chapter's primary goal, lists a code example that highlights the concepts taught, and provides a code analysis that explains that code example. You'll find these chapter summaries, which begin in Chapter 2, "Writing Your First C Program," to be a welcome wrap-up of the chapter's main points.

This book uses the following typographic conventions:

- Code lines, variables, and any text you see onscreen appears in `monospace`.

- Placeholders on format lines appear in *`italic monospace`*.

- Parts of program output that the user typed appear in **`bold monospace`**.

- New terms appear in *italic*.

- Optional parameters in syntax explanations are enclosed in flat brackets ([ ]). You do *not* type the brackets when you include these parameters.

How Can I Have Fun with C?

Appendix B, "The Draw Poker Program," contains a complete, working Draw Poker program. The program was kept as short as possible without sacrificing readable code and game-playing functionality. The game also had to be kept generic to work on all C compilers. Therefore, you won't find fancy graphics, but when you learn C, you'll easily be able to access your compiler's specific graphics, sound, and data-entry routines to improve the program.

The program uses as much of this book's contents as possible. Almost every topic taught in this book appears in the Draw Poker game. Too many books offer nothing more than snippets of code. The Draw Poker game gives you the chance to see the "big picture." As you progress through this book, you'll understand more and more of the game.

What Do I Do Now?

Turn the page and learn the C language.

WHAT IS C PROGRAMMING, AND WHY SHOULD I CARE?

Although some people consider C to be difficult to learn and use, you'll soon see that they are wrong. C is touted as being a cryptic programming language, and it can be—but a well-written C program is just as easy to follow as a program written in any other programming language. The demand for programmers and developers today is high, and learning C is an effective foundation to build the skills needed in a variety of fields, including app development, game programming, and so much more.

If you've never written a program in your life, this chapter is an excellent beginning because it teaches you introductory programming concepts, explains what a program is, and provides a short history of the C language. Get ready to be excited! C is a programming language rich in its capabilities.

What Is a Program?

A computer isn't smart. Believe it or not, on your worst days, you are still light-years ahead of your computer in intelligence. You can think, and you can tell a computer what to do. Here is where the computer shines: It will obey your instructions. Your computer will sit for days processing the data you supply, without getting bored or wanting overtime pay.

The computer can't decide what to do on its own. Computers can't think for themselves, so *programmers* (people who tell computers what to do) must give computers extremely detailed instructions. Without instructions, a computer is useless; with incorrect instructions, a computer will not successfully execute your desired task. A computer can no more process your payroll without detailed instructions than an automobile can start by itself and drive around the block independently. The collection of detailed expressions that you supply when you want your computer to perform a specific task is known as a *program*.

NOTE   Word processors, apps, spreadsheets, and computer games are nothing more than computer programs. Facebook is a collection of programs. Without such programs, the computer would just sit there, not knowing what to do next. A word-processing program contains a list of detailed instructions, written in a computer language such as C, that tells your computer exactly how to be a word processor. When you program, you are telling the computer to follow the instructions in the program you have supplied.

You can buy or download thousands of programs for your computer, tablet, or phone, but when a business needs a computer to perform a specific task, that business hires programmers and developers to create software that follows the specifications the business needs. You can make your computer or mobile device do many things, but you might not be able to find a program that does exactly what you want. This book rescues you from that dilemma. After you learn C, you will be able to write programs that contain instructions that tell the computer how to behave.

TIP   A computer program tells your computer how to do what you want. Just as a chef needs a recipe to make a dish, a program needs instructions to produce results. A recipe is nothing more than a set of detailed instructions that, if properly written, describes that proper sequence and the contents of the steps needed to prepare a certain dish. That's exactly what a computer program is to your computer.

Programs produce *output* when you *run* or *execute* them. The prepared dish is a recipe's output, and the word processor or app is the output produced by a running program.

WARNING   Just as when a chef gets an ingredient wrong or misses a step in a recipe, the resulting dish can be inedible; if you mistype code or skip a step, your program will not work.

What You Need to Write C Programs

Before you can write and execute a C program on your computer, you need a *C compiler*. The C compiler takes the C program you write and *builds* or *compiles* it (technical terms for making the program computer-readable), enabling you to run the compiled program when you're ready to look at the results. Luckily, many excellent free software packages are available in which you can edit and compile your C programs. A simple web search will provide a list. This book uses Code::Blocks (www.codeblocks.org).

TIP   If you run a search for "C Programming Compilers," you'll see a number of freeware options, including offerings from Borland and Microsoft. So why does this book use Code::Blocks? Because it offers versions for Windows, Macs, and Linux, so you can use a version of the software no matter what operating system you use. However, feel free to pick whichever programming environment looks best to you.

If you surf to the Code::Blocks page and read the very first sentence, you may worry a bit (or a lot):

The open source, cross platform, free C++ IDE.

Open source refers to software code that users can alter or improve. (You will not be doing this anytime soon, so put it out of your mind.) *Cross-platform* is an adjective that means the software can run on different operating systems—as a beginner, however, you need concern yourself with only your own platform. I think *free* is a term we can all get behind, and *IDE* is short for *integrated development environment,* which just means you can write, edit, and debug your programs without having to switch software to do so. We get to debugging shortly.

Don't panic about the C++ part. You can write either C or C++ programs in Code::Blocks. Finding a C compiler these days is harder. Most of the time, C compilers come bundled with an advanced version of C, known as C++. Therefore, when you look for a C compiler, you will almost always find a combination C and

C++ compiler, and often the C++ functionality is highlighted. The good news is that, after you learn C, you will already have a C++ compiler and you won't have to learn the ins and outs of a new IDE.

Figure 1.1 shows the Code::Blocks home page. To download the C/C++ IDE, click the Downloads choice under the Main section in the left column.

FIGURE 1.1

The home page for Code::Blocks. You want to focus on the Downloads option.

After you select Downloads, you are taken to a page that further discusses three options: Binaries, Source, and SVN. The latter two options are advanced, so you can ignore them. Click Binaries.

 NOTE   Two things to consider when doing this installation. First, the screen shots in the book will probably be a little different than what you see on the Internet—Code::Blocks is constantly improving the software, so the numbers (which refer to the software version) are constantly increasing. The version of Code::Blocks used in the book was 10.05, but at last check, they are up to 12.11, and the number is probably even larger by the time you read this. Second, if you are a Windows user, make sure you select the larger file to download (which has mingw in its title). That version has debugging tools that will come in handy when you become a C-soned programmer. (Get it? No? Just me then?)

The next page presents a variety of options, depending on your operating system. If you select the Windows option, choose the second option, highlighted in Figure 1.2. Having the full compiler and debugger will come in handy.

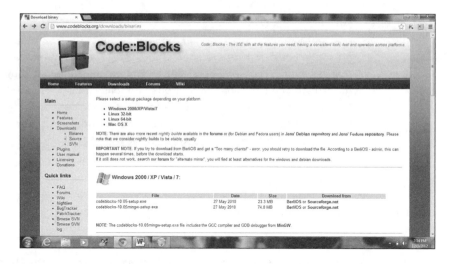

FIGURE 1.2

Selecting the Windows IDE for download. You can choose either downloading source.

After you choose to download the program, go get yourself a snack—it's a big file, so it takes several minutes to completely download. When it does, click the file and accept all defaults. (Only seasoned programmers need to tweak the installation.) Soon enough, Code::Blocks will be running on your computer. After you exit the Tip of the Day and set Code::Blocks as the associated program with all .c and .cpp files, you can also close the scripting window. You should be left with the opening screen of the software, pictured in Figure 1.3.

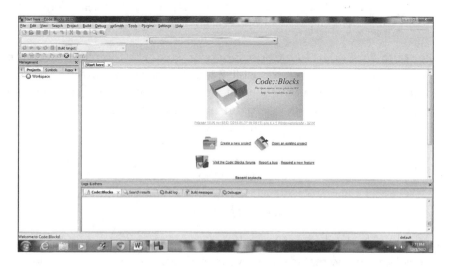

FIGURE 1.3

Welcome to your programming home!

NOTE   The C program you write is called *source code*. A compiler translates C source code into *machine language*. Computers are made up of nothing more than thousands of electrical switches that are either *on* or *off*. Therefore, computers must ultimately be given instructions in *binary*. The prefix *bi-* means "two," and the two states of electricity are called *binary states*. It's much easier to use a C compiler to convert your C programs into 1s and 0s that represent internal on and off switch settings than for you to do it yourself.

The Programming Process

Most people follow these basic steps when writing a program:

1. Decide exactly what the program should do.

2. Use an *editor* to write and save your programming language instructions. An editor is a lot like a word processor (although not usually as fancy) that lets you create and edit text. All the popular C compilers include an integrated editor along with the programming language compiler. All C program filenames end in the .c file extension.

3. Compile the program.

4. Check for program errors. If any appear, fix them and go back to step 3.

5. Execute the program.

NOTE   An error in a computer program is called a *bug*. Getting rid of errors is called *debugging* a program.

Take some time to explore Code::Blocks or whatever compiler you choose to install on your computer. A robust IDE lets you perform these five steps easily, all from within the same environment. You can compile your program, view any errors, fix the errors, run the program, and look at the results, all from within the same screen and using a uniform set of menus.

WARNING   If you have never programmed, this all might seem confusing. Relax. Most of today's C compilers come with a handy tutorial you can use to learn the basics of the compiler's editor and compiling commands.

Just in case you still don't fully understand the need for a compiler, your source code is like the raw materials that your computer needs. The compiler is like a machine that converts those raw materials to a final product, a compiled program that the computer can understand.

Using C

C is more efficient than most programming languages. It is also a relatively small programming language. In other words, you don't have to learn many *commands* in C. Throughout this book, you will learn about C commands and other elements of the C language, such as operators, functions, and preprocessor directives.

Because of the many possible versions of C, a committee known as the *American National Standards Institute (ANSI)* committee developed a set of rules (known as *ANSI C*) for all versions of C. As long as you run programs using an ANSI C compiler, you can be sure that you can compile your C programs on almost any computer that has an ANSI C compiler.

 TIP   In 1983, ANSI created the X3J11 committee to set a standard version of C. This became known as ANSI C. The most recent version of ANSI C, C11, was formally adopted in 2011.

As soon as you compile a C program, you can run the compiled program on any computer that is compatible with yours, whether or not the computer has an ANSI C compiler. "Great!" you might be saying. "But when do I get to write my first C program, let alone compile or run it?" Fear not—Chapter 2, "Writing Your First C Program," takes you on your maiden C programming voyage.

THE ABSOLUTE MINIMUM

This chapter introduced you to the C programming language and helped you select a compiler to edit, debug, and run your program. Here are a few key points to remember:

- Get a C compiler and install it on your computer.

- Get ready to learn the C programming language.

- Don't worry that C is too complex. This book breaks down C concepts into easily digestible bits. With practice, you will do just fine.

WRITING YOUR FIRST C PROGRAM

You get to see your first C program in this chapter! Please don't try to understand *every* character of the C programs discussed here. Relax and just get familiar with the look and feel of C. After a while, you will begin to recognize elements common to all C programs.

A Down-and-Dirty Chunk of Code

This section shows you a short but complete C program and discusses another program that appears in Appendix B, "The Draw Poker Program." Both programs contain common and different elements. The first program is extremely simple:

```c
/* Prints a message on the screen */
#include <stdio.h>
main()
{
    printf("Just one small step for coders. One giant leap for");
    printf(" programmers!\n");
    return 0;
}
```

Open your programming software and type in the program as listed. Simple, right? Probably not the first time you use your new compiler. When you open Code::Blocks for the first time, you will be greeted by a "Tip of the Day." These tips will come in handy later, but right now you can just get rid of it by clicking Close.

To create your program, Click the File Menu and select New. Choose Empty File from the options that appear on the submenu. Now you've got a nice clean file to start writing your seven-line program.

After you type in your program, you will need to compile or build your program. To do this, click the little yellow gear icon in the upper-left corner. If you've typed the program in exactly and had no errors, you can then run the program by clicking the green right-facing arrow next to the gear. (The next icon in that row, with a gear and arrow, will do both the compiling and running of the program, simplifying your life by reducing the number of arduous clicks you must perform from two to one.)

When you compile (or build) the program and run it, you should see something like Figure 2.1.

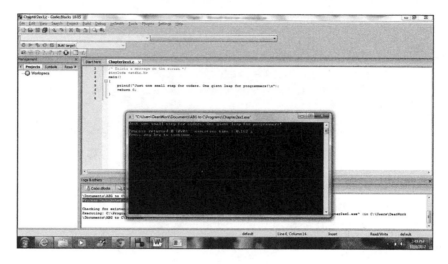

FIGURE 2.1

The output of your first program.

 NOTE   Producing that one-line message took a lot of work!
Actually, of the eight lines in the program, only two—the ones that start
with `printf`—do the work that produces the output. The other lines
provide "housekeeping chores" common to most C programs.

To see a much longer program, glance at Appendix B. Although the Draw Poker
game there spans several pages, it contains elements common to the shorter program you just saw.

Look through both the programs just discussed and notice any similarities. One
of the first things you might notice is the use of braces ({ }), parentheses (( )), and
backslashes (\). Be careful when typing C programs into your C compiler. C gets
picky, for instance, if you accidentally type a square bracket ([) when you should
type a brace.

 WARNING   In addition to making sure you don't type the
wrong character, be careful when typing code in a word processor
and then copying it to your IDE. I typed the previous program in
Word (for this book) and then copied it to Code::Blocks. When compiling the program, I received a number of errors because my quotes
on the `printf` line were smart quotes created by the word processor (to give that cool slanted look), and the compiler did not recognize them. After I deleted the quotes on the line and retyped them
in my programming editor, the code compiled just fine. So if you get
errors in programs, make sure the quotes are not the culprit.

C isn't picky about everything. For instance, most of the spacing you see in C programs makes the programs clearer to people, not to C. As you program, add blank lines and indent sections of code that go together to help the appearance of the program and to make it easier for you to find what you are looking for.

TIP Use the Tab key to indent instead of typing a bunch of spaces. Most C editors let you adjust the *tab spacing* (the number of spaces that appear when you press Tab). Some C program lines get long, so a tab setting of three provides ample indention without making lines too long.

C requires that you use lowercase letters for all commands and predefined functions. (You learn what a function is in the next section.) About the only time you use uppercase letters is on a line with #define and inside the printed messages you write.

The `main()` Function

The most important part of a C program is its main() function. Both of the programs discussed earlier have main() functions. Although at this point the distinction is not critical, main() is a C *function*, not a C command. A function is nothing more than a routine that performs some task. Some functions come with C, and some are created by you. C programs are made up of one or more functions. Each program must *always* include a main() function. A function is distinguished from a command by the parentheses that follow the function name. These are functions:

```
main() calcIt()  printf()    strlen()
```

and these are commands:

```
return while    int   if    float
```

When you read other C programming books, manuals, and webpages, the author might decide to omit the parenthesis from the end of function names. For example, you might read about the printf function instead of printf(). You'll learn to recognize function names soon enough, so such differences won't matter much to you. Most of the time, authors want to clarify the differences between functions and nonfunctions as much as possible, so you'll usually see the parentheses.

WARNING One of the functions just listed, `calcIt()`, contains an uppercase letter. However, the preceding section said you should *stay away* from uppercase letters. If a name has multiple parts, as in `doReportPrint()`, it's common practice to use uppercase letters to begin the separate words, to increase readability. (Spaces aren't allowed in function names.) Stay away from typing words in *all* uppercase, but an uppercase letter for clarity once in a while is okay.

The required `main()` function and all of C's supplied function names must contain lowercase letters. You can use uppercase for the functions that you write, but most C programmers stay with the lowercase function name convention.

Just as the home page is the beginning place to surf a website, `main()` is always the first place the computer begins when running your program. Even if `main()` is not the first function listed in your program, `main()` still determines the beginning of the program's execution. Therefore, for readability, make `main()` the first function in every program you write. The programs in the next several chapters have only one function: `main()`. As you improve your C skills, you'll learn why adding functions after `main()` improves your programming power even more. Chapter 30, "Organizing Your Programs with Functions," covers writing your own functions.

After the word `main()`, you always see an opening brace ({). When you find a matching closing brace (}), `main()` is finished. You might see additional pairs of braces within a `main()` function as well. For practice, look again at the long program in Appendix B. `main()` is the first function with code, and several other functions follow, each with braces and code.

 NOTE The statement `#include <stdio.h>` is needed in almost every C program. It helps with printing and getting data. For now, always put this statement somewhere before `main()`. You will understand why the `#include` is important in Chapter 7, "Making Your Programs More Powerful with `#include` and `#define`."

Kinds of Data

Your C programs must use data made up of numbers, characters, and words; programs process that data into meaningful information. Although many different kinds of data exist, the following three data types are by far the most common used in C programming:

- Characters

- Integers

- Floating points (also called *real numbers*)

 TIP You might be yelling "How much math am I going to have to learn?! I didn't think that was part of the bargain!" Well, you can relax, because C does your math for you; you don't have to be able to add 2 and 2 to write C programs. You do, however, have to understand data types so that you will know how to choose the correct type when your program needs it.

Characters and C

A C *character* is any single character that your computer can represent. Your computer knows 256 different characters. Each of them is found in something called the *ASCII table*, located in Appendix A, "The ASCII Table." (*ASCII* is pronounced *askee*. If you don't *know-ee*, you can just *ask-ee*.) Anything your computer can represent can be a character. Any or all of the following can be considered characters:

A   a   4   %   Q   !   +   =   ]

 NOTE The American National Standards Institute (ANSI), which developed ANSI C, also developed the code for the ASCII chart.

 TIP Even the spacebar produces a character. Just as C needs to keep track of the letters of the alphabet, the digits, and all the other characters, it has to keep track of any blank spaces your program needs.

As you can see, every letter, number, and space is a character to C. Sure, a 4 looks like a number, and it sometimes is, but it is also a character. If you indicate that a particular 4 is a character, you can't do math with it. If you indicate that another 4 is to be a number, you can do math with that 4. The same holds for the special symbols. The plus sign (+) is a character, but the plus sign also performs addition. (There I go, bringing math back into the conversation!)

All of C's character data is enclosed in *apostrophes* ('). Some people call apostrophes *single quotation marks*. Apostrophes differentiate character data from other kinds of data, such as numbers and math symbols. For example, in a C program, all of the following are character data:

'A'   'a'   '4'   '%'   ' '   '_'

None of the following can be character data because they have no apostrophes around them:

A   a   4   %   -

 TIP   None of the following are valid characters. Only single characters, not multiple characters, can go inside apostrophes.

'C is fun'

'C is hard'

'I should be sailing!'

The first program in this chapter contains the character '\n'. At first, you might not think that \n is a single character, but it's one of the few two-character combinations that C interprets as a single character. This will make more sense later.

If you need to specify more than one character (except for the special characters that you'll learn, like the \n just described), enclose the characters in *quotation marks* ("). A group of multiple characters is called a *string*. The following is a C string:

"C is fun to learn."

 NOTE   That's really all you need to know about characters and strings for now. In Chapters 4 through 6, you'll learn how to use them in programs. When you see how to store characters in variables, you'll see why the apostrophe and quotation marks are important.

Numbers in C

Although you might not have thought about it before now, numbers take on many different sizes and shapes. Your C program must have a way to store numbers, no matter what the numbers look like. You must store numbers in numeric variables. Before you look at variables, a review of the kinds of numbers will help.

Whole numbers are called *integers*. Integers have no decimal points. (Remember this rule: Like most reality shows, integers have no point whatsoever.) Any number without a decimal point is an integer. All of the following are integers:

10   54   0   −121   −68   752

WARNING   Never begin an integer with a leading 0 (unless the number *is* zero), or C will think you typed the number in *hexadecimal* or *octal*. Hexadecimal and octal, sometimes called *base-16* and *base-8*, respectively, are weird ways of representing numbers. 053 is an octal number, and 0x45 is a hexadecimal number. If you don't know what all that means, just remember for now that C puts a *hex* on you if you mess around with leading zeroes before integers.

Numbers with decimal points are called *floating-point numbers*. All of the following are floating-point numbers:

547.43   0.0   0.44384   9.1923   –168.470   .22

TIP   As you can see, leading zeroes are okay in front of floating-point numbers.

The choice of using integers or floating-point numbers depends on the data your programs are working with. Some values (such as ages and quantities) need only integers; other values (such as money amounts or weights) need the exact amounts floating-point numbers can provide. Internally, C stores integers differently than floating-point values. As you can see from Figure 2.2, a floating-point value usually takes twice as much memory as an integer. Therefore, if you can get away with using integers, do so—save floating points for values that need the decimal point.

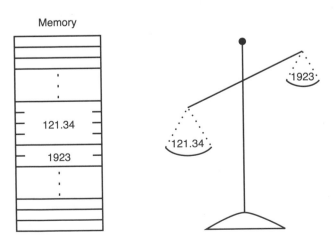

FIGURE 2.2

Storing floating-point values often takes more memory than integers.

NOTE   Figure 2.2 shows you that integers generally take less memory than floating-point values, no matter how large or small the values stored there are. On any given day, a large post office box might get much less mail than a smaller one. The contents of the box don't affect what the box is capable of holding. The size of C's number storage is affected not by the value of the number, but by the type of the number.

Different C compilers use different amounts of storage for integers and floating-point values. As you will learn later, there are ways of finding out exactly how much memory your C compiler uses for each type of data.

Wrapping Things Up with Another Example Program

This chapter's goal was to familiarize you with the "look and feel" of a C program, primarily the main() function that includes executable C statements. As you saw, C is a free-form language that isn't picky about spacing. C is, however, picky about lowercase letters. C requires lowercase spellings of all its commands and functions, such as printf().

At this point, don't worry about the specifics of the code you see in this chapter. The rest of the book explains all the details. But it is still a great idea to type and study as many programs as possible—practice will increase your coding confidence! So here is a second program, one that uses the data types you just covered:

```
/* A Program that Uses the Characters, Integers, and Floating-Point
Data Types */

#include <stdio.h>

main()
{
    printf("I am learning the %c programming language\n", 'C');
    printf("I have just completed Chapter %d\n", 2);
    printf("I am %.1f percent ready to move on ", 99.9);
    printf("to the next chapter!\n");
    return 0;
}
```

This short program does nothing more than print three messages onscreen. Each message includes one of the three data types mentioned in this chapter: a character (C), an integer (2), and a floating-point number (99.9).

NOTE   On the first `printf` statement, the `%c` tells the program where to introduce the character `'C'`. It is `%c` as an abbreviation for *character*, not because the character is a C. If you were learning the N programming language, you would still use `%c` to place the `'N'` character.

The `main()` function is the only function in the program written by the programmer. The left and right braces (`{` and `}`) always enclose the `main()` code, as well as any other function's code that you might add to your programs. You'll see another function, `printf()`, that is a built-in C function that produces output. Here is the program's output:

```
I am learning the C programming language
I have just completed Chapter 2
I am 99.9 percent ready to move on to the next chapter!
```

 TIP   Try playing around with the program, changing the messages or data. You should even try making a mistake when typing, like forgetting a semicolon (;) at the end of a line, just to see what happens when you try to compile the program. Learning from mistakes can make you a better programmer!

THE ABSOLUTE MINIMUM

This chapter familiarized you with the "look and feel" of a C program, primarily the `main()` function. The key points from this chapter include:

- A C function must have parentheses following its name. A C program consists of one or more functions. The `main()` function is always required. C executes `main()` before any other function.

- Put lots of extra spacing in your C programs, to make them more readable.

- Don't put leading zeroes before integers unless the integer is zero.

- If you use a character, enclose it in single quotes. Strings go inside quotation marks. Integers are whole numbers without decimal points. Floating-point numbers have decimal points.

3

WHAT DOES THIS DO? CLARIFYING YOUR CODE WITH COMMENTS

Your computer must be able to understand your programs. Because the computer is a dumb machine, you must be careful to spell C commands exactly right and type them in the order you want them executed. However, people also read your programs. You will change your programs often, and if you write programs for a company, the company's needs will change over time. You must ensure that your programs are understandable to *people* as well as to computers. Therefore, you should document your programs by explaining what they do.

Commenting on Your Code

Throughout a C program, you should add *comments*. Comments are messages scattered throughout your programs that explain what's going on. If you write a program to calculate payroll, the program's comments explain the gross pay calculations, state tax calculations, federal tax calculations, social security calculations, deductions, and all the other calculations that are going on.

 NOTE   If you write the program and only you will use it, you don't really need comments, right? Well, not exactly. C is a cryptic programming language. Even if *you* write the program, you aren't always able to follow it later—you might forget why you wrote a particular chunk of code, so a comment will help to decipher matters.

 TIP   Add comments as you write your programs. Get in the habit now, because programmers rarely go back and add comments later. When they must make a change later, programmers often lament about their program's lack of comments.

Another advantage is gained when commenting as you write the program instead of waiting until after you finish. While writing programs, you often refer back to statements you wrote earlier in the process. Instead of reinterpreting C code you've already written, you can scan through your comments, finding sections of code that you need faster. If you didn't comment, you would have to decipher your C code every time you looked through a piece of it.

Program *maintenance* is the process of changing a program over time to fix hidden bugs and to adapt the program to a changing environment. If you write a payroll program for a company, that company could eventually change the way it does payroll (to go from biweekly to weekly, as an example), and you (or another programmer) will have to modify the payroll program to conform to the company's new payroll procedures. Commenting speeds program maintenance. With comments, you or another programmer can quickly scan through a program listing to find the areas that need changing.

Comments are *not* C commands. C ignores every comment in your program. Comments are for people, and the programming statements residing outside the comments are for the computer.

Consider the following C statement:

```
return ((s1 < s2) ? s1 : s2);
```

You don't know C yet, but even if you did, this statement takes some study to figure out. Isn't this better?

```
return ((s1 < s2) ? s1 : s2); /* Gets the smaller of 2 values */
```

The next section explains the syntax of comments, but for now, you can see that the message between the /* and the */ is a comment.

The closer a comment is to spoken language and the further a comment is from C code, the better the comment is. Don't write a comment just for the sake of commenting. The following statement's comment is useless:

```
printf("Payroll");   /* Prints the word "Payroll" */
```

 WARNING You don't know C yet, and you *still* don't need the preceding line's comment! Redundant comments are a waste of your time, and they don't add anything to programs. Add comments to explain what is going on to people (including yourself) who might need to read your program.

Specifying Comments

C comments begin with /* and end with */. Comments can span several lines in a program, and they can go just about anywhere in a program. All of the following lines contain C comments:

```
/* This is a comment that happens to span two lines
before coming to an end */
/* This is a single-line comment */


for (i = 0; i < 25; i++)  /* Counts from 0 to 25 */
```

 NOTE Notice that comments can go on lines by themselves or before or after programming statements. The choice of placement depends on the length of the comment and the amount of code the comment describes.

The Draw Poker program in Appendix B, "The Draw Poker Program," contains all kinds of comments. By reading through the comments in that program, you can get an idea of what the program does without ever looking at the C code itself.

Don't comment every line. Usually only every few lines need comments. Many programmers like to place a multiline comment before a section of code and then insert a few smaller comments on lines that need them. Here is a complete program with different kinds of comments:

```c
/* The first code listing from Chapter 3 of The Absolute Beginner's
Guide to C
Teaching new programmer to create kick-butt code since 1994! */
/* A Dean Miller joint */
/* Filename Chapter3ex1.c */
/* Totals how much money will be spent on holiday gifts. */
#include <stdio.h>
main()
{
        float gift1, gift2, gift3, gift4, gift5; /* Variables to hold
costs. */
        float total; /* Variable to hold total amount */

/*Asks for each gift amount */
printf("How much do you want to spend on your mom? ");
scanf(" %f", &gift1);
printf("How much do you want to spend on your dad? ");
scanf(" %f", &gift2);
printf("How much do you want to spend on your sister? ");
scanf(" %f", &gift3);
printf("How much do you want to spend on your brother? ");
scanf(" %f", &gift4);
printf("How much do you want to spend on your favorite ");
printf("C Programming author? ");
scanf(" %f", &gift5);

total = gift1+gift2+gift3+gift4+gift5; /* Computes total amount
spent on gifts */
printf("\nThe total you will be spending on gifts is $%.2f", total);
return 0; /*Ends the program */
}
```

Many companies require that their programmers embed their own names in comments at the top of programs they write. If changes need to be made to the program later, the original programmer can be found to help. It's also a good idea to
include the filename that you use to save the program on disk at the beginning of
a program so that you can find a program on disk when you run across a printed
listing.

NOTE This book might comment too much in some places, especially in the beginning chapters. You are so unfamiliar with C that every little bit of explanation helps.

TIP For testing purposes, you might find it useful to *comment out* a section of code by putting /* and */ around it. By doing this, you cause C to ignore that section of code, and you can concentrate on the piece of code you're working on. Do not, however, comment out a section of code that already contains comments because you cannot embed one comment within another. The first */ that C runs across triggers the end of the comment you started. When C finds the next */ without a beginning /*, you get an error.

Whitespace

Whitespace is the collection of spaces and blank lines you find in many programs. In a way, whitespace is more important than comments in making your programs readable. People need whitespace when looking through a C program because those programs are more readable than programs that run together too much. Consider the following program:

```
#include <stdio.h>
main(){float a, b;printf("How much of a bonus did you get?
");scanf(" %f",
&a);b = .85  * a;printf("If you give 15 percent to charity, you will
still have %.2f.", b);return 0;}
```

To a C compiler, this is a perfectly good C program. You might get a headache looking at it, however. Although the code is simple and it doesn't take a lot of effort to figure out what is going on, the following program is *much* easier to decipher, even though it has no comments:

```
#include <stdio.h>
main()
{
        float a, b;

        printf("How much of a bonus did you get? ");
        scanf(" %f", &a);
```

```
    b = .85  * a;
    printf("If you give 15 percent to charity, you will still ");
    printf("have %.2f.", b);
    return 0;
}
```

This program listing is identical to the previous program, except that this one includes whitespace and line breaks. The physical length of a program does not determine readability; the amount of whitespace does. (Of course, a few comments would improve this program, too, but the purpose of this exercise is to show you the difference between no whitespace and good whitespace.)

 NOTE You might be wondering why the first line of the squeezed program, the one with the `#include`, did not contain code after the closing angle brace. After all, the point of unreadable code would seem to be made even more strong if the `#include` contained trailing code. Code::Blocks (and several other compilers) refuse to allow code after a `#include` (or any other statement that begins with a pound sign [#]).

A Second Style for Your Comments

Today's C compilers support another kind of comment that was originally developed for C++ programs. With its C99 release, the American National Standards Institute (ANSI) committee approved this new kind of comment, so you should be safe using it (unless you are using a really, really old computer and compiler!). The second style of comment begins with two slashes (//) and ends only at the end of the line.

Here is an example of the new style of comment:

```
// Another Code Example, just with a different commenting style
#include <stdio.h>
main()
{
    printf("I like these new comments!"); // A simple statement
}
```

Either style of comment works, so the code examples throughout this book take advantage of both. You should become familiar with both styles because each has its uses as you learn to write more complicated programs.

THE ABSOLUTE MINIMUM

You must add comments to your programs—not for computers, but for people. C programs can be cryptic, and comments eliminate lots of confusion. Key points to remember from this chapter include:

- The three rules of programming are comment, comment, comment. Clarify your code with abundant comments.

- For multiline comments, begin them with /*, and C considers everything after that a comment until it encounters a closing */.

- For single-line comments, you can also use //. C ignores the rest of the line after that point.

- Use whitespace and line breaks to make your programs easy to read.

IN THIS CHAPTER

- Using `printf()`
- Printing strings
- Coding escape sequences
- Using conversion characters
- Putting it all together with a code example

4

YOUR WORLD PREMIERE— PUTTING YOUR PROGRAM'S RESULTS UP ON THE SCREEN

If neither you nor anybody else could see your program's output, there would be little use for your program. Ultimately, you have to be able to view the results of a program. C's primary means of output is the `printf()` function. No actual command performs output, but the `printf()` function is a part of every C compiler and one of the most used features of the language.

How to Use `printf()`

In a nutshell, `printf()` produces output on your screen. As the sample code listings in Chapters 2, "Writing Your First C Program," and 3, "What Does This Do? Clarifying Your Code with Comments," demonstrated, `printf()` sends characters, numbers, and words to the screen. There is a lot to `printf()`, but you don't have to be an expert in all the `printf()` options (very few C programmers are) to use it for all your programs' screen output.

The Format of `printf()`

The `printf()` function takes many forms, but when you get used to its format, `printf()` is easy to use. Here is the general format of `printf()`:

```
printf(controlString [, data]);
```

Throughout this book, when you are introduced to a new command or function, you will see its basic format. The format is the general look of the statement. If something in a format appears in brackets, such as , `data` in the `printf` function just shown, that part of the statement is optional. You almost never type the brackets themselves. If brackets are required in the command, that is made clear in the text following the format. `printf()` requires a `controlString`, but the data following the `controlString` is optional.

 WARNING `printf()` doesn't actually send output to your screen, but it does send it to your computer's standard output device. Most operating systems, including Windows, route the standard output to your screen unless you know enough to route the output elsewhere. Most of the time, you can ignore this standard output device stuff because you'll almost always want output to go to the screen. Other C functions you will learn about later route output to your printer and disk drives.

 NOTE You might be wondering why some of the words in the format appear in italics. It's because they're placeholders. A placeholder is a name, symbol, or formula that you supply. Placeholders are italicized in the format of functions and commands to let you know that you should substitute something at that place in the command.

Here is an example of a `printf()`:

```
printf("My favorite number is %d", 7);  // Prints My favorite number
                                         // is 7
```

Because every string in C must be enclosed in quotation marks (as mentioned in Chapter 2), the `controlString` must be in quotation marks. Anything following the `controlString` is optional and is determined by the values you want printed.

 NOTE   Every C command and function needs a semicolon (`;`) after it to let C know that the line is finished. Braces and the first lines of functions don't need semicolons because nothing is executing on those lines. All statements with `printf()` should end in a semicolon. You won't see semicolons after `main()`, however, because you don't explicitly tell C to execute `main()`. You do, however, tell C to execute `printf()` and many other functions. As you learn more about C, you'll learn more about semicolon placement.

Printing Strings

String messages are the easiest type of data to print with `printf()`. You have to enclose only the string in quotation marks. The following `printf()` prints a message on the screen:

```
printf("You are on your way to C mastery");
```

The message `You are on your way to C mastery` appears onscreen when the computer executes this statement.

 NOTE   The string `You are on your way to C mastery` is the `controlString` in this `printf()`. There is little control going on here—just output.

The following two `printf()` statements might not produce the output you expect:

```
printf("Write code");
```

```
printf("Learn C");
```

Here is what the two `printf()` statements produce:

```
Write codeLearn C
```

 TIP   C does not automatically move the cursor down to the next line when a `printf()` executes. You must insert an escape sequence in the `controlString` if you want C to go to the next line after a `printf()`.

Escape Sequences

C contains a lot of escape sequences, and you'll use some of them in almost every program you write. Table 4.1 contains a list of some of the more popular escape sequences.

TABLE 4.1 Escape Sequences

Code	Description
\n	Newline
\a	Alarm (the computer's bell)
\b	Backspace
\t	Tab
\\	Backslash
\'	Single quote mark
\"	Double quote mark

NOTE The term *escape sequence* sounds harder than it really is. An escape sequence is stored as a single character in C and produces the effect described in Table 4.1. When C sends '\a' to the screen, for example, the computer's bell sounds instead of the characters \ and a actually being printed.

You will see a lot of escape sequences in printf() functions. Any time you want to "move down" to the next line when printing lines of text, you must type \n so that C produces a newline, which moves the blinking cursor down to the next line on the screen. The following printf() statements print their messages on separate lines because of the \n at the end of the first one:

```
printf("Write code\n");

printf("Learn C");
```

TIP The \n could have been placed at the beginning of the second line, and the same output would have occurred. Because escape sequences are characters to C, you must enclose them in quotation marks so that C knows that the escape sequences are part of the string being printed. The following also produces two lines of output:

```
printf("Write code\nLearn C");
```

Double quotation marks begin and end a string, single quotation marks begin and end a character, and a backslash signals the start of an escape sequence, so they have their own escape sequences if you need to print them. \a rings your computer's bell, \b moves the cursor back a line, and \t causes the output to appear moved over a few spaces. There are other escape sequences, but for now, these are the ones you are most likely to use.

The following program listing demonstrates the use of all the escape sequences listed in Table 4.1. As always, your best bet is to try this program and then tweak it to something you'd like to try:

```c
// Absolute Beginner's Guide to C, 3rd Edition
// Chapter 4 Example 1--Chapter4ex1.c

#include <stdio.h>

main()
{

    /* These three lines show you how to use the most popular Escape
Sequences */
    printf("Column A\tColumn B\tColumn C");
    printf("\nMy Computer\'s Beep Sounds Like This: \a!\n");
    printf("\"Letz\bs fix that typo and then show the backslash ");
    printf("character \\\" she said\n");

    return 0;
}
```

After you enter, compile, and run this code, you get the following results:

```
Column A     Column B     Column C
My Computer's Beep Sounds Like This: !
"Let's fix that typo and then show the backslash character \" she
said
```

NOTE   You should understand a few things about the previous listing. First, you must always place #include <stdio.h> at the beginning of all programs that use the printf() function—it is defined in stdio.h, so if you fail to remember that line of code, you will get a compiler error because your program will not understand how to execute printf(). Also, different C/C++ compilers might produce a different number of tabbed spaces for the \t escape sequence. Finally, it is important to note that using the \b escape sequence overwrites anything that was there. That's why the 'z' does not appear in the output, but the 's' does.

Conversion Characters

When you print numbers and characters, you must tell C exactly how to print them. You indicate the format of numbers with conversion characters. Table 4.2 lists a few of C's most-used conversion characters.

TABLE 4.2   Conversion Characters

Conversion Character	Description
%d	Integer
%f	Floating-point
%c	Character
%s	String

When you want to print a value inside a string, insert the appropriate conversion characters in the *controlString*. Then to the right of the *controlString*, list the value you want to be printed. Figure 4.1 is an example of how a printf() can print three numbers—an integer, a floating-point value, and another integer.

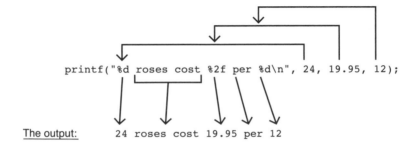

```
printf("%d roses cost %2f per %d\n", 24, 19.95, 12);
```

The output: 24 roses cost 19.95 per 12

FIGURE 4.1

printf() *conversion characters determine how and where numbers print.*

Strings and characters have their own conversion characters as well. Although you don't need %s to print strings by themselves, you might need %s when printing strings combined with other data. The next printf() prints a different type of data value using each of the conversion characters:

```
                  control string              data
printf("%s %d %f %c\n", "Sam", 14, -8.76, 'X');
```

This printf() produces this output:

```
Sam 14 -8.760000 X
```

 NOTE The string Sam needs quotation marks, as do all strings, and the character X needs single quotation marks, as do all characters.

 WARNING C is strangely specific when it comes to floating-point numbers. Even though the -8.76 has only two decimal places, C insists on printing six decimal places.

You can control how C prints floating-point values by placing a period (.) and a number between the % and the f of the floating-point conversion character. The number you place determines the number of decimal places your floating-point number prints to. The following printf() produces four different-looking numbers, even though the same floating-point number is given:

```
printf("%f  %.3f  %.2f  %.1f", 4.5678, 4.5678, 4.5678, 4.5678);
```

C rounds the floating-point numbers to the number of decimal places specified in the %.f conversion character and produces this output:

```
4.567800  4.568  4.57  4.6
```

 TIP You probably don't see the value of the conversion characters at this point and think that you can just include the information in the controlString. However, the conversion characters will mean a lot more when you learn about variables in the next chapter.

The printf() controlString controls exactly how your output will appear. The only reason two spaces appear between the numbers is that the controlString has two spaces between each %f.

Putting It All Together with a Code Example

Consider the following program listing:

```
/* Absolute Beginner's Guide to C, 3rd Edition
 Chapter 4 Example 2--Chapter4ex1.c */
#include <stdio.h>

main()
{

    /* Here is some more code to help you with printf(), Escape
Sequences, and Conversion Characters */
    printf("Quantity\tCost\tTotal\n");
    printf("%d\t\t$%.2f\t$%.2f\n", 3, 9.99, 29.97);
    printf("Too many spaces     \b\b\b\b can be fixed with the ");
    printf("\\%c Escape character\n", 'b');
    printf("\n\a\n\a\n\a\n\aSkip a few lines, and beep ");
    printf("a few beeps.\n\n\n");
    printf("%s %c.", "You are kicking butt learning", 'C');
    printf("You just finished chapter %d.\nYou have finished ", 4);
    printf("%.1f%c of the book.\n", 12.500, '%');
    printf("\n\nOne third equals %.2f or ", 0.333333);
    printf("%.3f or %.4f or ", 0.333333, 0.333333);
    printf("%.5f or %.6f\n\n\n", 0.333333, 0.3333333);


    return 0;
}
```

Enter this code and compile and run the program. You get the output in Figure 4.2.

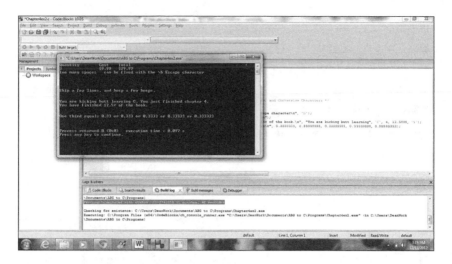

FIGURE 4.2

Output from the second listing of Chapter 4.

Notice that, because of the length of the word Quantity, the second line needed two tabs to fit the cost of the item under the Cost heading. You might not need this—you will just need to test your code to better understand how many spaces the tab escape sequence moves your cursor. Sometimes skipping one line isn't enough, but luckily, you can place multiple \n characters to jump down as many lines as you want. Finally, seeing that the % sign is a big part of conversion characters, you cannot put one in your *controlString* and expect it to print. So if you need to print a percent sign on the screen, use the %c conversion character and place it that way.

THE ABSOLUTE MINIMUM

The programs you write must be able to communicate with the user sitting at the keyboard. The `printf()` function sends data to the screen. Key points from this chapter to remember include:

- Every `printf()` requires a control string that determines how your data will look when printed.

- Don't expect C to know how to format your data automatically. You must use conversion characters.

- Use escape sequences to print newlines, tabs, quotes, and backslashes, and to beep the computer as well.

- Unless you want your floating-point numbers to print to six places after the decimal point, use the `%f` conversion character's decimal control.

5

ADDING VARIABLES TO YOUR PROGRAMS

No doubt you've heard that computers process data. Somehow you've got to have a way to store that data. In C, as in most programming languages, you store data in *variables*. A variable is nothing more than a box in your computer's memory that holds a number or a character. Chapter 2, "Writing Your First C Program," explained the different types of data: characters, strings, integers, and floating points. This chapter explains how to store those types of data inside your programs.

Kinds of Variables

C has several different kinds of variables because there are several different kinds of data. Not just any variable will hold just any piece of data. Only integer variables can hold integer data, only floating-point variables can hold floating-point data, and so on.

NOTE Throughout this chapter, think of variables inside your computer as acting like post office boxes in a post office. Post office boxes vary in size and have unique numbers that label each one. Your C program's variables vary in size, depending on the kind of data they hold, and each variable has a unique name that differentiates it from other variables.

The data you learned about in Chapter 2 is called *literal data* (or sometimes *constant data*). Specific numbers and letters don't change. The number 2 and the character 'x' are always 2 and 'x'. A lot of data you work with—such as age, salary, and weight—changes. If you were writing a payroll program, you would need a way to store changing pieces of data. Variables come to the rescue. Variables are little more than boxes in memory that hold values that can change over time.

Many types of variables exist. Table 5.1 lists some of the more common types. Notice that many of the variables have data types (character, integer, and floating point) similar to that of literal data. After all, you must have a place to store integers, and you do so in an integer variable.

TABLE 5.1 Some of the Most Common Types of C Variables

Name	Description
char	Holds character data such as 'X' and '^'
int	Holds integer data such as 1, -32, and 435125. Stores data between -2,147,483,648 and 2,147,483,647
float	Holds floating-point data such as 25.6, -145.23, and .000005
double	Holds extremely large or extremely small floating-point values

TIP In some older C compilers, int could hold only values between 32767 and -32768. If you wanted to use a larger integer, you needed to use the long int type. In most modern compilers, though, an int type can hold the same as a long int type. If you'd like to be sure with your compiler, you can use the sizeof operator, covered in Chapter 13, "A Bigger Bag of Tricks—Some More Operators for Your Programs."

WARNING You might notice that there are no string variables, although there *are* character string literals. C is one of the few programming languages that has no string variables, but as you'll see in Chapter 6, "Adding Words to Your Programs," you do have a way to store strings in variables.

The Name column in Table 5.1 lists the keywords needed when you create variables for programs. In other words, if you want an integer, you need to use the int keyword. Before completing your study of variables and jumping into using them, you need to know one more thing: how to name them.

Naming Variables

All variables have names, and because you are responsible for naming them, you must learn the naming rules. All variable names must be different; you can't have two variables in the same program with the same name.

A variable can have from 1 to 31 characters in its name. Some compilers do allow longer names, but it's better to stick with this limit, both for portability of code and to keep typing errors to a minimum. (After all, the longer the name you use, the greater the chance for a typo!) Your program's variables must begin with a letter of the alphabet, but after that letter, variable names can have other letters, numbers, or an underscore in any combination. All of the following are valid variable names:

```
myData pay94      age_limit    amount       QtlyIncome
```

 TIP C lets you begin a variable name with an underscore, but you shouldn't do so. Some of C's built-in variables begin with an underscore, so there's a chance you'll overlap one of those if you name your variables starting with underscores. Take the safe route and always start your variable names with letters—I cannot underscore this point enough! (See what I did there?)

The following examples of variable names are *not* valid:

```
94Pay        my Age      lastname,firstname
```

You ought to be able to figure out why these variable names are not valid: The first one, 94Pay, begins with a number; the second variable name, my Age, contains a space; and the third variable name, lastname,firstname, contains a special character (,).

WARNING Don't name a variable with the same name as a function or a command. If you give a variable the same name as a command, your program won't run; if you give a variable the same name as a function, you can't use that same function name later in your program without causing an error.

Defining Variables

Before you use a variable, you have to *define* it. Variable definition (sometimes called *variable declaration*) is nothing more than letting C know you'll need some variable space so it can reserve some for you. To define a variable, you only need to state its type, followed by a variable name. Here are the first few lines of a program that defines some variables:

```
main()
{
        // My variables for the program
        char answer;
        int quantity;
        float price;
/* Rest of program would follow */
```

The sample code just presented has three variables: `answer`, `quantity`, and `price`. They can hold three different types of data: character data, integer data, and floating-point data. If the program didn't define these variables, it wouldn't be able to store data in the variables.

You can define more than one variable of the same data type on the same line. For example, if you wanted to define two character variables instead of just one, you could do so like this:

```
main()
{
        // My variables for the program
        char first_initial;
        char middle_initial;
/* Rest of program would follow. */
```

or like this:

```
main()
{
```

```
        // My variables for the program
        char first_initial, middle_initial;
/* Rest of program would follow. */
```

TIP   Most C variables are defined after an opening brace, such as the opening brace that follows a function name. These variables are called *local variables*. C also lets you create *global* variables by defining the variables before a function name, such as before `main()`. Local variables are almost always preferable to global variables. Chapter 30, "Organizing Your Programs with Functions," addresses the differences between local and global variables, but for now, all programs stick with local variables.

Storing Data in Variables

The *assignment operator* puts values in variables. It's a lot easier to use than it sounds. The assignment operator is simply the equals sign (=). The format of putting data in variables looks like this:

```
variable = data;
```

The `variable` is the name of the variable where you want to store data. You must have defined the variable previously, as the preceding section explained. The `data` can be a number, character, or mathematical expression that results in a number. Here are examples of three assignment statements that assign values to the variables defined in the preceding section:

```
answer = 'B';
quantity = 14;
price = 7.95;
```

You also can store answers to expressions in variables:

```
price = 8.50 * .65;  // Gets price after 35% discount
```

You can even use other variables in the expression:

```
totalAmount = price * quantity;  /* Uses value from another variable
*/
```

TIP   The equals sign tells C this: Take whatever is on the right and stick it into the variable on the left. The equals sign kind of acts like a left-pointing arrow that says "That-a-way!" Oh, and never use commas in numbers, no matter how big the numbers are!

Let's use all this variable knowledge you've gained in a program. Open your editor, type the following program, compile it, and run it:

```
// Example program #1 from Chapter 5 of Absolute Beginner's Guide
// to C, 3rd Edition
// File Chapter5ex1.c


/* This is a sample program that lists three kids and their school
supply needs, as well as cost to buy the supplies */


#include <stdio.h>


main()
{
    // Set up the variables, as well as define a few

    char firstInitial, middleInitial;
    int number_of_pencils;
    int number_of_notebooks;
    float pencils = 0.23;
    float notebooks = 2.89;
    float lunchbox = 4.99;



    //The information for the first child
    firstInitial = 'J';
    middleInitial = 'R';

    number_of_pencils = 7;
    number_of_notebooks = 4;

    printf("%c%c needs %d pencils, %d notebooks, and 1 lunchbox\n",
            firstInitial, middleInitial,number_of_pencils,
            number_of_notebooks);
    printf("The total cost is $%.2f\n\n", number_of_pencils*pencils
    + number_of_notebooks*notebooks + lunchbox);
```

```
//The information for the second child
firstInitial = 'A';
middleInitial = 'J';

number_of_pencils = 10;
number_of_notebooks = 3;

printf("%c%c needs %d pencils, %d notebooks, and 1 lunchbox\n",
        firstInitial, middleInitial,number_of_pencils,
        number_of_notebooks);
printf("The total cost is $%.2f\n\n", number_of_pencils*pencils
+ number_of_notebooks*notebooks + lunchbox);

//The information for the third child
firstInitial = 'M';
middleInitial = 'T';

number_of_pencils = 9;
number_of_notebooks = 2;

printf("%c%c needs %d pencils, %d notebooks, and 1 lunchbox\n",
        firstInitial, middleInitial,number_of_pencils,
        number_of_notebooks);
printf("The total cost is $%.2f\n",
    number_of_pencils*pencils + number_of_notebooks*notebooks +
lunchbox);

    return 0;
    }
```

This program gives examples of naming and defining different types of variables, as well as assigning values to each. It's important to note that you can reuse a variable by just assigning a new value to the variable. You might be wondering, why keep using and reusing variables if you are just going to change the value within the code itself? Why not just skip the variables and use the values in their place? The value of variables will become more apparent after Chapter 8, "Interacting with Users," and you can get information from the user for these variables.

The Draw Poker program in Appendix B, "The Draw Poker Program," must keep track of a lot of things, and many variables are used there. At the start of most of the program's functions, you'll see a place where variables are being defined.

 TIP You can define variables and give them initial values at the same time. The previous program assigns values to the float variables `pencil`, `notebook`, and `lunchbox` when they are declared.

THE ABSOLUTE MINIMUM

This chapter covered the different types of variables in C. Because there are different kinds of data, C has different variable kinds to hold that data. Key points from this chapter include:

- Learn how to name variables because almost all of your programs will use variables.

- Always define variables before you use them

- Don't mix data types and variable types—you will get the wrong results if you do.

- If needed, you can define more than one variable on the same line.

- Don't use a comma in a number. Enter the figure 100,000 as `100000`, not `100,000`.

- When storing values in variables, use the equals sign (=), also called the assignment operator.

IN THIS CHAPTER

- Understanding the string terminator
- Determining the length of strings
- Using character arrays: listing characters
- Initializing strings

6

ADDING WORDS TO YOUR PROGRAMS

Although C doesn't have string variables, you do have a way to store string data. This chapter explains how. You already know that you must enclose string data in quotation marks. Even a single character enclosed in quotation marks is a string. You also know how to print strings with `printf()`.

The only task left is to see how to use a special type of character variable to hold string data so that your program can input, process, and output that string data.

Understanding the String Terminator

C does the strangest thing to strings: It adds a zero to the end of every string. The zero at the end of strings has several names:

- Null zero

- Binary zero

- String terminator

- ASCII 0

- \0

WARNING About the only thing you *don't* call the string-terminating zero is *zero!* C programmers use the special names for the string-terminating zero so that you'll know that a regular numeric zero or a character `'0'` is not being used at the end of the string; only the special *null zero* appears at the end of a string.

C marks the end of all strings with the string-terminating zero. You never have to do anything special when entering a string literal such as `"My name is Julie."` C automatically adds the null zero. You'll never see the null zero, but it is there. In memory, C knows when it gets to the end of a string only when it finds the null zero.

NOTE Appendix A, "The ASCII Table," contains an ASCII table (first mentioned in Chapter 2, "Writing Your First C Program"). The very first entry is labeled *null*, and the ASCII number for null is 0. Look further down at ASCII 48, and you'll see a 0. ASCII 48 is the character `'0'`, whereas the first ASCII value is the *null zero*. C puts the null zero at the end of strings. Even the string `"I am 20"` ends in an ASCII 0 directly after the character 0 in 20.

The string terminator is sometimes called \0 (*backslash zero*) because you can represent the null zero by enclosing \0 in single quotes. Therefore, '0' is the character zero, and '\0' is the string terminator. (Remember the escape sequences covered in Chapter 4, "Your World Premiere—Putting Your Program's Results Up on the Screen," that were also single characters represented by two characters—a backslash followed by a letter or another character. Now you have a backslash number to add to the collection.)

Figure 6.1 shows how the string `"Crazy"` is stored in memory. As you can see, it takes 6 bytes (a *byte* is a single memory location) to store the string, even though the string has only five letters. The null zero that is part of the string `"Crazy"` takes one of those six memory locations.

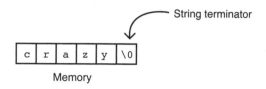

FIGURE 6.1

A *string always ends with a null zero in memory.*

The Length of Strings

The *length* of a string is always the number of characters up to, but not including, the null zero. Sometimes you will need to find the length of a string. The null zero is never counted when determining the length of a string. Even though the null zero must terminate the string (so that C knows where the string ends), the null zero is not part of the string length.

Given the definition of the string length, the following strings all have lengths of nine characters:

```
Wednesday

August 10

I am here
```

When counting the length of strings, remember that you must account for every space. So although the second string has eight letters and numbers, as well as a space in the middle, and the third string has seven letters, as well as two spaces in the middle, are all considered nine-character strings. If you chose to put three spaces between `August` and `10` in the middle example, it would become an 11-character string.

WARNING   The second string's length doesn't end at the 0 in 10 because the 0 in 10 isn't a null zero; it's a character zero.

TIP   All single characters of data have a length of 1. Therefore, both `'X'` and `"X"` have lengths of one, but the `"X"` consumes two characters of memory because of its null zero. Any time you see a string literal enclosed in quotation marks (as they all must be), picture in your mind that terminating null zero at the end of that string in memory.

Character Arrays: Lists of Characters

Character arrays hold strings in memory. An *array* is a special type of variable that you'll hear much more about in upcoming chapters. All the data types—`int`, `float`, `char`, and the rest—have corresponding array types. An array is nothing more than a list of variables of the same data type.

Before you use a character array to hold a string, you must tell C that you need a character array in the same place you would tell C that you need any other kind of variable. Use brackets (`[` and `]`) after the array name, along with a number indicating the maximum number of characters the string will hold.

An example is worth a thousand words. If you needed a place to hold month names, you could define a character array called `month` like this:

```
char month[10];  /* Defines a character array */
```

TIP   Array definitions are easy. Take away the `10` and the brackets, and you have a regular character variable. Adding the brackets with the `10` tells C that you need 10 character variables, each following the other in a list named `month`.

The reason `10` was used when defining the array is that the longest month name, `September`, has nine characters. The tenth character is for, you guessed it, the null zero.

TIP   You *always* have to reserve enough character array space to hold the longest string you will need to hold, plus the string terminator. You can define more array characters than needed, but not fewer than you need.

If you want, you can store a string value in the array at the same time you define the array:

```
char month[10] = "January";  /* Defines a character array */
```

Figure 6.2 shows you what this array looks like. Because nothing was put in the last two places of the array (January takes only seven characters plus an eighth place for the null zero), you don't know what's in the last two places. (Some compilers, however, fill the unused elements with zeroes to kind of *empty* the rest of the string.)

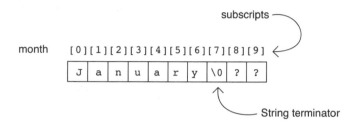

FIGURE 6.2

Defining and initializing an array named month *that holds string data.*

Each individual piece of an array is called an *element*. The month array has 10 elements. You can distinguish between them with *subscripts*. Subscripts are numbers that you specify inside brackets that refer to each of the array elements.

All array subscripts begin with 0. As Figure 6.2 shows, the first element in the month array is called month[0]. The last is called month[9] because there are 10 elements altogether, and when you begin at 0, the last is 9.

Each element in a character array is a character. The combination of characters— the array or *list* of characters—holds the entire string. If you wanted to, you could change the contents of the array from January to March one element at a time, like this:

```
Month[0] = 'M';
Month[1] = 'a';
Month[2] = 'r';
Month[3] = 'c';
Month[4] = 'h';
Month[5] = '\0'; //You must add this
```

It is vital that you insert the null zero at the end of the string. If you don't, the month array would still have a null zero three places later at Month[7]; when you attempted to print the string, you would get this:

```
Marchry
```

TIP Printing strings in arrays is easy. You use the `%s` conversion character:

```
printf("The month is %s", month);
```

If you define an array *and* initialize the array at the same time, you don't have to put the number in brackets. Both of the following do exactly the same thing:

```
char month[8] = "January";
char month[] = "January";
```

In the second example, C counts the number of characters in `January` and adds one for the null zero. You can't store a string larger than eight characters later, however. If you want to define a string's character array and initialize it but leave extra padding for a longer string later, you would do this:

```
char month[25] = "January";  /* Leaves room for longer strings */
```

Initializing Strings

You don't want to initialize a string one character at a time, as done in the preceding section. However, unlike with regular nonarray variables, you can't assign a new string to the array like this:

```
month = "April";  /* NOT allowed */
```

You can assign a string to a month with the equals sign only *at the time you define the string*. If later in the program you want to put a new string into the array, you must either assign it one character at a time or use C's `strcpy()` (*string copy*) function that comes with your C compiler. The following statement assigns a new string to the month:

```
strcpy(month, "April");  /* Puts new string in month array */
```

 NOTE In your programs that use `strcpy()`, you must put this line after the `#include <stdio.h>`:

```
#include <string.h>
```

 TIP Don't worry: `strcpy()` automatically adds a null zero to the end of the string it creates.

Now let's take everything we've covered in this chapter and put it to use in a full program. Again, it's time to fire up your editor, enter some code, and compile and run the resulting program:

```c
// Example program #1 from Chapter 6 of
// Absolute Beginner's Guide to C, 3rd Edition
// File Chapter6ex1.c

// This program pairs three kids with their favorite superhero

#include <stdio.h>
#include <string.h>

main()
{

char Kid1[12];
// Kid1 can hold an 11-character name
// Kid2 will be 7 characters (Maddie plus null 0)
char Kid2[] = "Maddie";
// Kid3 is also 7 characters, but specifically defined
char Kid3[7] = "Andrew";
// Hero1 will be 7 characters (adding null 0!)
char Hero1 = "Batman";
// Hero2 will have extra room just in case
char Hero2[34] = "Spiderman";
char Hero3[25];

    Kid1[0] = 'K';  //Kid1 is being defined character-by-character
    Kid1[1] = 'a';  //Not efficient, but it does work
    Kid1[2] - 't';
    Kid1[3] = 'i';
    Kid1[4] = 'e';
    Kid1[5] = '\0';  // Never forget the null 0 so C knows when the
                     // string ends

    strcpy(Hero3, "The Incredible Hulk");

    printf("%s\'s favorite hero is %s.\n", Kid1, Hero1);
    printf("%s\'s favorite hero is %s.\n", Kid2, Hero2);
    printf("%s\'s favorite hero is %s.\n", Kid3, Hero3);

    return 0;
}
```

As with the program that ended Chapter 5, "Adding Variables to Your Program," you might be saying, why go through all the trouble of having these variables when you could just put the names and strings right in the `printf()` statements? Again, the value of these variables will become more apparent after Chapter 8, "Interacting with Users," when you learn to get information from users.

You were already using `#include` to add the `<stdio.h>` file to all your programs that use `printf()` (as well as other common functions that you will soon be adding to your programming toolbox). Now you have a second header file, `<string.h>`, to `#include` as well. The next chapter covers `#include` in more detail.

To remind you of the different methods of declaring and initializing string variables, the `kid` and `hero` variables are each defined differently. For a fun exercise, comment out the `strcpy` line to see what your program prints on the screen when `Hero3` is used in a `printf()` without having been initialized. My output was a bizarre collection of characters—those were already sitting in the space that became that variable, so if you don't put anything in it, you'll get whatever is there now.

THE ABSOLUTE MINIMUM

If you need to store words, you need to use character arrays; C does not support a string data type. Key points from this chapter include:

- Store strings in character arrays, but reserve enough array elements to hold the longest string you'll ever store in that array.

- Don't forget that strings must end with a terminating zero.

- When writing to your array, remember that the subscripts begin at 0, not 1.

- There are three ways to place a string in a character array: You can initialize it at the time you define the array, you can assign one element at a time, or you can use the `strcpy()` function.

- If you use the `strcpy()` function in your programs, remember to add `#include <string.h>` to the beginning of your program.

7

IN THIS CHAPTER

- Including files
- Placing #include directives
- Defining constants
- Building a header file and program

MAKING YOUR PROGRAMS MORE POWERFUL WITH #include AND #define

Two types of lines you see in many C programs are not C commands at all. They are *preprocessor directives.* A preprocessor directive always begins with a pound sign (#). Preprocessor directives don't cause anything to happen at runtime (when you run your program). Instead, they work during the compiling of your program.

These preprocessor directives are used most often:

- #include
- #define

Every sample program you have written so far has used #include. This chapter finally takes the secret out of that mysterious preprocessor directive.

Including Files

`#include` has two formats, which are almost identical:

`#include <filename>`

and

`#include "filename"`

Figure 7.1 shows what `#include` does. It's nothing more than a *file merge* command. Right before your program is compiled, the `#include` statement is replaced with the contents of the filename specified after `#include`. The filename can be stated in either uppercase or lowercase letters, as long as your operating system allows for either in filenames. For example, my Windows XP implementation of Code::Blocks does not distinguish between uppercase and lowercase letters in filenames, but UNIX does. If your file is named `myFile.txt`, you might be able to use any of the following `#include` directives:

`#include "MYFILE.TXT"`

`#include "myfile.txt"`

`#include "myFile.txt"`

However, UNIX allows only this:

`#include "myFile.txt"`

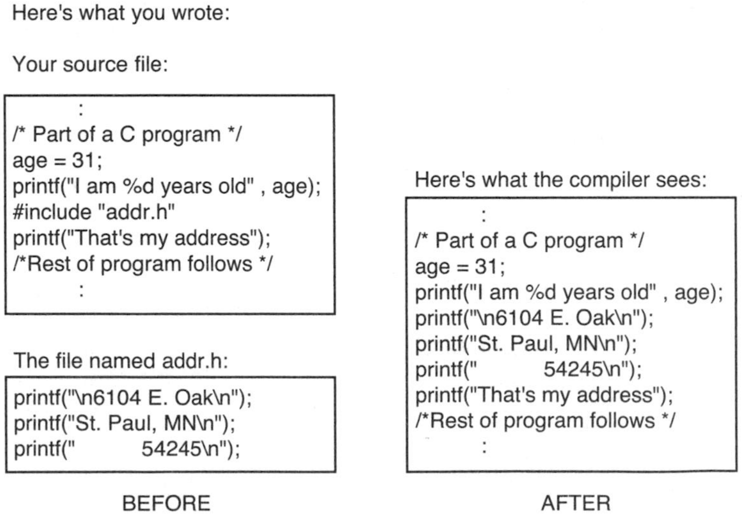

Here's what you wrote:

Your source file:

```
      :
/* Part of a C program */
age = 31;
printf("I am %d years old" , age);
#include "addr.h"
printf("That's my address");
/*Rest of program follows */
      :
```

The file named addr.h:

```
printf("\n6104 E. Oak\n");
printf("St. Paul, MN\n");
printf("       54245\n");
```

BEFORE

Here's what the compiler sees:

```
      :
/* Part of a C program */
age = 31;
printf("I am %d years old" , age);
printf("\n6104 E. Oak\n");
printf("St. Paul, MN\n");
printf("       54245\n");
printf("That's my address");
/*Rest of program follows */
      :
```

AFTER

FIGURE 7.1

`#include` *inserts a disk file into the middle of another file.*

NOTE When you've used a word processor, you might have used an #include type of command if you merged a file stored on disk into the middle of the file you were editing.

When you install your compiler, the installation program sets up a separate location on your disk (in a *directory*) for various #include files that come with your compiler. When you want to use one of these built-in #include files, use the #include format with the angled brackets, < and >.

WARNING How do you know when to use a built-in #include file? Good question! All built-in functions, such as printf(), have corresponding #include files. When this book describes a built-in function, it also tells you exactly which file to include.

You've already used two built-in functions in your programs: printf() and strcpy(). (main() is not a built-in C function; it is a function you must supply.) As a reminder, the #include file for printf() is stdio.h (which stands for *standard I/O*), and the #include file for the strcpy() function is string.h.

Almost every complete program listing in this book contains the following preprocessor directive:

```
#include <stdio.h>
```

That's because almost every program in this book uses printf(). Chapter 6, "Adding Words to Your Program," told you that whenever you use the strcpy() function, you need to include string.h.

TIP The file you include is called a *header file*. That's why most included files end in the extension .h.

When you write your own header files, use the second form of the preprocessor directive, the one that has quotation marks. When you use quotation marks, C first searches the disk directory in which your program is stored and *then* searches the built-in #include directory. Because of the search order, you can write your own header files and give them the same name as those built into C, and yours will be used instead of C's.

WARNING If you write your own header files, don't put them with C's built-in #include file directory. Leave C's supplied header files intact. There is rarely a reason to override C's headers, but you might want to add some headers of your own.

You might write your own header files when you have program statements that you frequently use in many programs. Instead of typing them in every program, you can put them in a file in your program directory and use the #include directive with the file where you want to use the statements.

Placing #include Directives

The header files you add to your programs with #include are nothing more than text files that contain C code. You will learn much more about the contents of header files later; for now, understand that a header file does two things. The built-in header files help C properly execute built-in functions. The header files you write often contain code that you want to place in more than one file.

TIP It's best to put your #include directives before main().

NOTE The Draw Poker program in Appendix B, "The Draw Poker Program," includes several header files because it uses lots of built-in functions. Notice the placement of the #include statements; they come before main().

Defining Constants

The #define preprocessor directive defines *constants*. A C constant is really the same thing as a literal. You learned in Chapter 2, "Writing Your First C Program," that a literal is a data value that doesn't change, like the number 4 or the string "C programming". The #define preprocessor directive lets you give names to literals. When you give a name to a literal, the named literal is known in C terminology as a *named constant* or a *defined constant*.

WARNING In Chapter 5, "Adding Variables to Your Programs," you learned how to define variables by specifying their data types and giving them a name and an initial value. Constants that you define with #define are *not* variables, even though they sometimes look like variables when they are used.

Here is the format of the #define directive:

#define CONSTANT constantDefinition

As with most things in C, using defined constants is easier than the format leads you to believe. Here are some sample #define directives:

```
#define AGELIMIT 21
#define MYNAME "Paula Holt"
#define PI 3.14159
```

In a nutshell, here's what #define tells C: Every place in the program that the *CONSTANT* appears, replace it with the *constantDefinition*. The first #define just shown instructs C to find every occurrence of the word AGELIMIT and replace it with a 21. Therefore, if this statement appeared somewhere in the program after the #define:

```
if (employeeAge < AGELIMIT)
```

the compiler acts as if you typed this:

```
if (employeeAge < 21)
```

even though you didn't.

 TIP   Use uppercase letters for the defined constant name. This is the one exception in C when uppercase is not only used, but recommended. Because defined constants are not variables, the uppercase lets you glance through a program and tell at a glance what is a variable and what is a constant.

Assuming that you have previously defined the constant PI, the uppercase letters help keep you from doing something like this in the middle of the program:

```
PI = 544.34;  /* Not allowed */
```

As long as you keep defined constant names in upper case, you will know not to change them because they are *constants*.

Defined constants are good for naming values that might need to be changed between program runs. For example, if you didn't use a defined constant for AGELIMIT, but instead used an actual age limit value such as 21 throughout a program, if that age limit changed, finding and changing every single 21 would be difficult. If you had used a defined constant at the top of the program and the age limit changed, you'd only need to change the #define statement to something like this:

```
#define AGELIMIT 18
```

The #define directive is not a C command. As with #include, C handles your #define statements before your program is compiled. Therefore, if you defined PI as 3.14159 and you used PI throughout a program in which you needed the value of the mathematical pi (π), the C compiler would think *you* typed 3.14159 throughout the program when you really typed PI. PI is easier to remember (and helps eliminate typing mistakes) and is clearer to the purpose of the constant.

As long as you define a constant with #define before main() appears, the entire program will know about the constant. Therefore, if you defined PI to be the value 3.14159 before main(), you could use PI throughout main() and any other functions you write that follow main(), and the compiler would know to replace PI with 3.14159 each time before compiling your program.

Building a Header File and Program

The best way to ensure that you understand header files and defined constants is to write a program that uses both. So fire up your editor and let's get typing!

First, you create your first header file:

```
// Example header program #1 from Chapter 7 of Absolute Beginner's
// Guide to C, 3rd Edition
// File Chapter7ex1.h

// If you have certain values that will not change (or only change
// rarely)
// you can set them with #DEFINE statements (so you can change them
// as needed)

// If you plan on using them in several programs, you can place them
// in a header file

#define KIDS 3
#define FAMILY "The Peytons"
#define MORTGAGE_RATE 5.15
```

When you type a header file and then save it, you need to add the .h to the end of the file to make it clear to your compiler that it is a header file, not a program. Most editors automatically add a .c to the end of your programs if you do not specify a specific extension.

Now, this is an overly simplistic header file with only a few constants set with the , statement. These are excellent examples of constants that are unlikely to change, but if they do change, it would be so much better to make the change in one place instead of having to change hundreds, if not thousands, of lines of code. If you create programs for family planning, budgeting, and holiday shopping, and you decide to have (or accidentally have) a fourth child, you can make the change in this header file, and then when you recompile all programs that use it, the change to 4 (or 5, if you're lucky enough to have twins) will roll through all your code. A family name is unlikely to change, but maybe you refinance your house and get a new mortgage rate that changes budgeting and tax planning.

A header file will not help you until you include it in a program, so here is a simple piece of code that uses your newly created .h file:

```c
// Example program #1 from Chapter 7 of Absolute Beginner's Guide to
// C, 3rd Edition
// File Chapter7ex1.c

/* This is a sample program that lists three kids and their school
supply needs, as well as cost to buy the supplies */

#include <stdio.h>
#include <string.h>
#include "Chapter7ex1.h"

main()
{
    int age;
    char childname[14] = "Thomas";

    printf("\n%s have %d kids.\n", FAMILY, KIDS);

    age = 11;
    printf("The oldest, %s, is %d.\n", childname, age);

    strcpy(childname, "Christopher");
    age = 6;
    printf("The middle boy, %s, is %d.\n", childname, age);

    age = 3;
    strcpy(childname, "Benjamin");
    printf("The youngest, %s, is %d.\n", childname, age);

    return 0;
}
```

Again, there isn't much to this code. All it does is state that a family has three children and then names each child. I promise that, as you learn new commands, statements, functions, and operators in upcoming chapters, your programs will get meatier. You might notice that one of the #define constants created in the header file, MORTGAGE_RATE, is not used in this sample program. You do not have to use every created constant if you include a header file in your program.

The program uses one variable, childname, for the name and one variable, age, for the age of three different children, with the information overwritten in each case. This is not the wisest choice—after all, there's a good chance that if you write a program that needs the names of your kids, you'll probably be using each name more than once. But in a program like this, it's a good reminder that you can overwrite and change variable names, but not constants created with a #define statement.

THE ABSOLUTE MINIMUM

C's preprocessor directives make C see code that you didn't actually type. The key concepts from this chapter include:

- Always add the proper header files, using the #include directive when using built-in functions. Use angled brackets (< and >) around the included filename when including compiler-supplied header files, and be sure to place the #include statements for these files before main().

- Use quotation marks (") around the included filename when including your own header files that you've stored in your source code's directory. You can insert your own header files with #include wherever you want the code inserted.

- Use uppercase characters in all defined constant names so that you can distinguish them from regular variable names.

IN THIS CHAPTER

- Looking at scanf()
- Prompting for scanf()
- Solving problems with scanf()

8

INTERACTING WITH USERS

printf() sends data to the screen. The scanf() function gets data from the keyboard. You must have a way to get data from your user. You can't always assign data values using assignment statements. For example, if you were writing a movie theater program for use throughout the country, you couldn't assign the cost of a ticket to a variable using the equals sign in your program because every theater's ticket price could differ. Instead, you would have to ask the user of the program in each theater location how much a ticket costs before computing a charge.

At first glance, the scanf() function might seem confusing, but it is so important to learn, to increase the power of your programs through user interactivity. To a beginner, scanf() makes little sense, but despite its strange format, it is the easiest function to use for input at this point in the book because of its close ties to the printf() function. Practice with scanf() will make your programs perfect!

Looking at `scanf()`

`scanf()` is a built-in C function that comes with all C compilers. Its header file is the same as `printf()` (`stdio.h`), so you don't have to worry about including an additional header file for `scanf()`. `scanf()` fills variables with values typed by the user.

`scanf()` is fairly easy if you know `printf()`. `scanf()` looks a lot like `printf()` because `scanf()` uses conversion codes such as `%s` and `%d`. `scanf()` is the mirror-image function of `printf()`. Often you will write programs that ask the user for values with a `printf()` and get those values with `scanf()`. Here is the format of `scanf()`:

```
scanf(controlString [, data]);
```

When your program gets to `scanf()`, C stops and waits for the user to type values. The variables listed inside `scanf()` (following the `controlString`) will accept whatever values the user types. `scanf()` quits when the user presses Enter after typing values.

Even though `scanf()` uses the same conversion characters as `printf()`, never specify escape sequences such as `\n`, `\a`, or `\t`. Escape sequences confuse `scanf()`. `scanf()` quits getting values from the user when the user presses Enter, so you don't ever specify the `\n`.

Prompting for `scanf()`

Almost every `scanf()` you write should be preceded with `printf()`. If you don't start with a `printf()`, the program stops and waits for input, and the user has no idea what to do. For example, if you need to get an amount from the user, you would put a `printf()` function like this before `scanf()`:

```
printf("What is the amount? ");  /* Prompt *//* A scanf() would
follow */
```

A `printf()` before a `scanf()` sends a *prompt* to the user. If you don't prompt the user for the value or values you want, the user has no way of knowing what values should be typed. Generally, the `printf()` requests the data from the user, and the `scanf()` gets the data that the user types.

Let's write a program with a few simple `scanf()` statements—after all, it is the best way to learn:

```
// Example program #1 from Chapter 8 of Absolute Beginner's Guide to
// C, 3rd Edition
// File Chapter8ex1.c
```

```c
/* This is a sample program that asks users for some basic data and
prints it on screen in order to show what was entered */

#include <stdio.h>


main()
{
    // Set up the variables that scanf will fill

    char firstInitial;
    char lastInitial;
    int age;
    int favorite_number;

    printf("What letter does your first name begin with?\n");
    scanf(" %c", &firstInitial);

    printf("What letter does your last name begin with?\n");
    scanf(" %c", &lastInitial);

    printf("How old are you?\n");
    scanf(" %d", &age);

    printf("What is your favorite number (integer only)?\n");
    scanf(" %d", &favorite_number);


    printf("\nYour intitials are %c.%c. and you are %d years old",
firstInitial, lastInitial, age);
    printf("\nYour favorite number is %d.\n\n", favorite_number);

    return 0;
    }
```

So those `scanf()` statements are not so bad, right? Each one is partnered with a `printf()` statement to let the user know what to type. To see how confusing `scanf()` would be without a preceding `printf()` statement, comment out any of the `printf()` statements before a `scanf()`, and recompile and run the program. You will find the prompt confusing, and you wrote the program! Think of how the user will feel.

The first two `scanf()` statements obtain character values (as you can tell from the `%c` conversion codes). The third `scanf()` gets an integer value from the keyboard and places it into a variable named age.

The variables `firstInitial`, `lastInitial`, and age will hold whatever the user types before pressing Enter. If the user types more than a single character in the first two examples, it can confuse the program and create problems for the later values.

Another point to notice about the `scanf()` statements is the spaces right before each `%c` or `%d`. The space isn't always required here, but it never hurts, and it sometimes helps the input work better when you get numbers and characters in succession. Adding the extra space is a good habit to get into now while learning `scanf()`.

Enough about all that. Let's get to the most obvious `scanf()` problem: the ampersand (&) before the three variables. Guess what? `scanf()` requires that you put the ampersand before all variables, even though the ampersand is *not* part of the variable name! Do it, and `scanf()` works; leave off the ampersand, and `scanf()` won't accept the user's values into the variables.

 TIP Make your leading `printf()` statement as descriptive as possible. In the last example, if you ask for only a favorite number, a user might enter a decimal instead of just a whole number. Who knows—maybe someone's favorite number is 3.14159.

Problems with `scanf()`

As mentioned earlier in this chapter, `scanf()` is not the easiest function to use. One of the first problems with `scanf()` is that although the user must type exactly what `scanf()` expects, the user rarely does this. If the `scanf()` needs a floating-point value, but the user types a character, there is little you can do. The floating-point variable you supply will have bad data because a character is not a floating-point value.

For now, assume that the user *does* type what is needed. Chapter 18, "Increasing Your Program's Output (and Input)," describes some ways to overcome problems brought on by scanf() (although modern-day C programmers often resort to complete data-entry routines they write, download, or purchase elsewhere that overcome C's difficult data-entry ability).

An exception to the ampersand rule does exist. If you're getting input into an array using %s, as happens when you ask users for a name to be stored in a character array, you do *not* use the ampersand.

The bottom-line rule is this: If you're asking the user to type integers, floating points, characters, doubles, or any of the other single-variable combinations (long integers and so on), put an ampersand before the variable names in the scanf(). If you are asking the user for a string to input into a character array, don't put the ampersand before the array name.

WARNING   You also wouldn't put the ampersand in front of *pointer* variables. Actually, an array is nothing more than a pointer variable, and that's why the ampersand isn't needed for arrays. We get to pointers later in this book, but if you've seen them in other languages, you know what I'm talking about. If you haven't seen a pointer variable and you don't know what this is all about, well, I promise you'll get there soon! Seriously, you'll fully understand pointers and how they are like arrays after reading Chapter 25, "Arrays and Pointers."

There's a problem with using scanf() to get character strings into character arrays that you need to know about now. scanf() stops reading string input at the first space. Therefore, you can get only a single word at a time with scanf(). If you must ask the user for more than one word, such as the user's first and last name, use two scanf() statements (with their own printf() prompts) and store the two names in two character arrays.

The following program uses scanf() statements to ask the user for a floating point (the price of a pizza), a string (a pizza topping), and several integers (number of pizza slices and the month, day, and year). Notice that the string has no ampersand, but the other variables do. The program asks for only a one-word pizza topping because scanf() isn't capable of getting two words at once.

```
// Example program #2 from Chapter 8 of Absolute Beginner's Guide to
// C, 3rd Edition
// File Chapter8ex2.c

/* This is a sample program that asks users for some basic data and
prints it on screen in order to show what was entered */

#include <stdio.h>


main()
{
    char topping[24];
    int slices;
    int month, day, year;
    float cost;

// The first scanf will look for a floating-point variable, the cost
// of a pizza
// If the user doesn't enter a $ before the cost, it could cause
// problems

    printf("How much does a pizza cost in your area?");
    printf("enter as $XX.XX)\n");
    scanf(" $%f", &cost);

// The pizza topping is a string, so your scanf doesn't need an &

    printf("What is your favorite one-word pizza topping?\n");
    scanf(" %s", topping);

    printf("How many slices of %s pizza", topping);
    printf("can you eat in one sitting?\n");
    scanf(" %d", &slices);
```

```
printf("What is today's date (enter it in XX/XX/XX format).\n");
scanf(" %d/%d/%d", &month, &day, &year);

printf("\n\nWhy not treat yourself to dinner on %d/%d/%d",
        month, day, year);
printf("\nand have %d slices of %s pizza!\n", slices, topping);
printf("It will only cost you $%.2f!\n\n\n", cost);

return (0);
}
```

The format and use of `scanf()` statements will become easier with practice. If the user wanted to enter a two-word topping, like Italian sausage, your program would need two `scanf()` statements to capture them and two variables to save the names. Later in the book, you learn some tricks to ask your users for multiple pieces of data instead of just one within a particular category.

Again, use your `printf()` statements to more effectively guide users to enter data in a format that your program needs. Try entering information incorrectly when running this program, such as leaving off the dollar sign on the pizza price or forgetting the slashes in the date, and you will see the problems you can create for your program.

 TIP   You can let the user type characters other than data values. For example, many times dates are entered with slashes or hyphens separating the day, month, and year, like this: `03/05/95`. You have to trust the user to type things just right. In the previous example, if the user doesn't type in the dollar sign before the price of the pizza, the program will not function properly. The following `scanf()` that gets a date expects the user to type the date in *mm/dd/yy* format:

```
scanf(" %d/%d/%d", &month, &day, &year);
```

The user could type `02/28/14` or `11/22/13`, but not `June 5th, 2013`, because the `scanf()` is expecting something else.

THE ABSOLUTE MINIMUM

This chapter's goal was to teach you how to ask for and get answers from the user. Being able to process user input is an important part of any language. scanf() performs data entry—that is, scanf() gets the user's input and stores that input in variables. Key concepts from this chapter include:

- Use scanf() to get data from the user by way of the keyboard, and remember to include a control string to dictate how your data will look when input.

- Before using a scanf(), use a printf() to prompt the user for the values and format you want.

- Put an ampersand (&) before nonarray variables in a scanf().

- Always add a leading space before the first control string character (as an example, " %d" contains a space before the %d) to ensure accurate character input.

CRUNCHING THE NUMBERS—LETTING C HANDLE MATH FOR YOU

Many people still break out in a cold sweat when they are told that they will have to do some math. Luckily, computers don't mind math, and as long as you enter the numbers correctly, your C program will always do your math right with the use of operators. The term *operators* might conjure images of the ladies that used to help with long-distance phone calls, but we aren't discussing those. These are C operators, which let you do math. You don't have to be a math wizard to write programs that use math operators.

Not only should you learn to recognize math operators, but you should also learn how C orders math operators. C doesn't always calculate from left to right. This chapter explains why.

Basic Arithmetic

A lot of C operators work exactly the way you expect them to. You use a plus sign (+) when you want to add, and you use a minus sign (-) when you want to subtract. An *expression* includes one or more operators. C programmers often use math expressions on the right side of the assignment operator when filling variables with values, like this:

```
totalSales = localSales + internationalSales - salesReturns;
```

C computes the answer and then stores that answer in `totalSales`.

 NOTE If you want to subtract a negative value, be sure to put a space between the minus signs, like this:

```
newValue = oldValue - -factor;
```

If you omit the space, C thinks you're using another operator, `--`, called the *decrement* operator, described in Chapter 13, "A Bigger Bag of Tricks—Some More Operators for Your Programs."

You can even put a math expression inside a `printf()`:

```
printf("In 3 years, I'll be %d years old.\n", age + 3);
```

If you want to multiply and divide, you can do so by using the * and / symbols. The following statement assigns a value to a variable using multiplication and division:

```
newFactor = fact * 1.2 / 0.5;
```

 WARNING If you put integers on *both* sides of the division symbol (/), C computes the *integer division result*. Study the following program to get familiar with integer division and regular division. The comments explain the results calculated from the divisions, but you can always double-check by compiling the program and running it yourself.

```
// Example program #1 from Chapter 9 of
// Absolute Beginner's Guide to C, 3rd Edition
// File Chapter9ex1.c

/* This is a sample program that demonstrates math operators, and
the different types of division. */
```

```c
#include <stdio.h>


main()
{
    // Two sets of equivalent variables, with one set
    // floating-point and the other integer

    float a = 19.0;
    float b = 5.0;
    float floatAnswer;

    int x = 19;
    int y = 5;
    int intAnswer;

    // Using two float variables creates an answer of 3.8
    floatAnswer = a / b;
    printf("%.1f divided by %.1f equals %.1f\n", a, b, floatAnswer);

    floatAnswer = x /y; //Take 2 creates an answer of 3.0
    printf("%d divided by %d equals %.1f\n", x, y, floatAnswer);

    // This will also be 3, as it truncates and doesn't round up
    intAnswer = a / b;
    printf("%.1f divided by %.1f equals %d\n", a, b, intAnswer);

    intAnswer = x % y; // This calculates the remainder (4)
    printf("%d modulus (i.e. remainder of) %d equals %d", x, y,
    intAnswer);

    return 0;
    }
```

The last math statement in this program might be new to you. If you need the remainder after integer division, use C's *modulus* operator (%). Given the values just listed, the following statement puts a 4 in intAnswer:

```
ansMod = x % y;   /* 4 is the remainder of 19 / 5 */
```

You now know the three ways C divides values: regular division if a float is on either or both sides of the /, integer division if an integer is on both sides of the /, and modulus if the % operator is used between two integers.

 TIP   You can't use % between anything but integer data types.

The following short program computes the net sale price of tires:

```
// Example program #2 from Chapter 9 of Absolute Beginner's Guide to
// C, 3rd Edition
// File Chapter9ex2.c


/* This program asks the user for a number of tires and price per
tire. It then calculates a total price, adding sales tax. */


// If you find you use a sales tax rate that may change, use #define
// to set it in one place
#include <stdio.h>
#define SALESTAX .07


main()
{
    // Variables for the number of tires purchased, price,
    // a before-tax total, and a total cost
    // with tax

    int numTires;
    float tirePrice, beforeTax, netSales;

    /* Get the number of tires purchased and price per tire. */
    printf("How many tires did you purchase? ");
    scanf(" %d", &numTires);
    printf("What was the cost per tire (enter in $XX.XX format)? ");
```

```
    scanf(" $%f", &tirePrice);

    /* Compute the price */

    beforeTax = tirePrice * numTires;
    netSales = beforeTax + (beforeTax * SALESTAX);

    printf("%You spent $%.2f on your tires\n\n\n", netSales);

    return 0;
    }
```

Here is a sample run of the program:

```
How many tires did you purchase? 4
What was the cost per tire (enter in $XX.XX format)? $84.99
You spent $363.76 on your tires
```

Order of Operators

As mentioned earlier in this chapter, C doesn't always compute math operations in the order you expect. The following expression explains it in a nutshell:

```
ans = 5 + 2 * 3;  /* Puts 11 in ans */
```

If you thought that C would store 21 in ans, you're reading the expression from left to right. However, C always computes multiplication before addition. It sounds crazy, but as long as you know the rules, you'll be okay. C is following the *order of operators* table. C first multiplies 2 and 3 to get 6, and then adds 5 to get 11.

Table 9.1 lists the complete order of operators. (The table includes several operators you have yet to cover—don't worry, you will learn their value throughout the book.) For each level, if your expression has more than one operator from the same level, C resolves them using the associativity direction listed. So if you do multiplication and division, C performs the operation that appears first when reading left to right, and then moves on to the next operation. When it has completed a level, it moves down to the next level. As you can see in the table, *, /, and % appear before + and -. Therefore, if C sees an expression with a combination of these operators, it evaluates *, /, and % before computing + and -.

TABLE 9.1 Order of Operators

Level	Operator	Associativity
1	( ) (parenthesis), [ ] (array element), . (structure member reference)	Left to right
2	- (negative sign), ++ (increment), - - (decrement), & (address-of), * (pointer indirection), sizeof ( ), ! (the not operator)	Right to left
3	* (multiplication), / (division), % (modulus)	Left to right
4	+ (addition), - (subtraction)	Left to right
5	< (less than), <= (less than or equal to) > (greater than), >= (greater than or equal to)	Left to right
6	== (equal to), != (not equal to)	Left to right
7	&& (logical and)	Left to right
8	¦¦ (logical or)	Left to right
9	? : (the conditional operator)	Right to left
10	=, *=, /=, %=, +=, -= (assignment operators)	Right to left
11	, (the comma operator)	Left to right

Here is a difficult expression. All the variables and numbers are integers. See if you can figure out the answer by the way C would evaluate the expression:

```
ans = 5 + 2 * 4 / 2 % 3 + 10 - 3;   /* What is the answer? */
```

Figure 9.1 shows how to solve for the answer, 13.

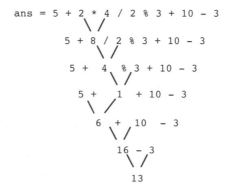

FIGURE 9.1

Solving the expression the way C would.

TIP   Don't do too much at one time when evaluating such expressions for practice. As the figure shows, you should compute one operator at a time and then bring the rest of the expression down for the next round.

If an expression such as the one in Figure 9.1 contains more than one operator that sits on the same level in the order of operators table, you must use the third column, labeled Associativity, to determine how the operators are evaluated. In other words, because *, /, and % all reside on the same level, they were evaluated from left to right, as dictated by the order of operators table's Associativity column.

You might wonder why you have to learn this stuff. After all, doesn't C do your math for you? The answer is "Yes, *but....*" C does your math, but you need to know how to set up your expressions properly. The classic reason is as follows: Suppose you want to compute the average of four variables. The following will *not* work:

```
avg = i + j + k + l / 4;  /* Will NOT compute average! */
```

The reason is simple when you understand the order of operators. C computes the division first, so l / 4 is evaluated first and then i, j, and k are added to that divided result. If you want to override the order of operators, as you would do in this case, you have to learn to use ample parentheses around expressions.

Break the Rules with Parentheses

If you need to override the order of operators, you can. As demonstrated in Table 9.1, if you group an expression inside parentheses, C evaluates that expression before the others. Because the order of operators table shows parentheses before any of the other math operators, parentheses have top precedence, as the following statement shows:

```
ans = (5 + 2) * 3;  /* Puts 21 in ans */
```

Even though multiplication is usually performed before addition, the parentheses force C to evaluate 5 + 2 first and then multiply the resulting 7 by 3. Therefore, if you want to average four values, you can do so by grouping the addition of the values in parentheses:

```
avg = (i + j + k + l) / 4;  /* Computes average */
```

TIP   Use lots of parentheses. They clarify your expressions. Even if the regular operator order will suffice for your expression, parentheses make the expression easier for you to decipher if you need to change the program later.

Assignments Everywhere

As you can see from the order of operators table, the assignment operator has precedence and associativity, as do the rest of the operators. Assignment has very low priority in the table, and it associates from right to left.

The right-to-left associativity lets you perform an interesting operation: You can assign a value to more than one variable in the same expression. To assign the value of 9 to 10 different variables, you *could* do this:

```
a = 9; b = 9; c = 9; d = 9; e = 9; f = 9; g = 9; h = 9; i = 9; j = 9;
```

but this is easier:

```
a = b = c = d = e = f = g = h = i = j = 9;
```

Because of the right-to-left associativity, C first assigns the 9 to j, then puts the 9 in i, and so on.

 NOTE C doesn't initialize variables for you. If you wanted to put 0 in a bunch of variables, a multiple assignment would do it for you.

Every C expression produces a value. The expression j = 9; does put a 9 in j, but it also results in a completed value of 9, which is available to store somewhere else, if needed. The fact that every assignment results in an expression lets you do things like this that you can't always do in other programming languages:

```
a = 5 * (b = 2);   /* Puts a 2 in b and a 10 in a */
```

Here's one last program example that uses assignments, operators, and parentheses to change the order of operators:

```
// Example program #3 from Chapter 9 of Absolute Beginner's Guide to
// C, 3rd Edition
// File Chapter9ex3.c


/* This program calculates the average of four grades and also does
some other basic math. */

#include <stdio.h>


main()
```

```c
{

    int grade1, grade2, grade3, grade4;
    float averageGrade, gradeDelta, percentDiff;

    /* The student got 88s on the first and third test,
        so a multiple assignment statement works. */
    grade1 = grade3 = 88;

    grade2 = 79;

    // The user needs to enter the fourth grade
    printf("What did you get on the fourth test");
    printf(" (An integer between 0 and 100)?");
    scanf(" %d", &grade4);

    averageGrade = (grade1+grade2+grade3+grade4)/4;

    printf("Your average is %.1f.\n", averageGrade);

    gradeDelta = 95 - averageGrade;
    percentDiff = 100 * ((95-averageGrade) / 95);
    printf("Your grade is %.1f points lower than the ", gradeDelta);
    printf("top grade in the class (95)\n");
    printf("You are %.1f percent behind ", percentDiff);
    printf("that grade!\n\n\n");

    return 0;
}
```

This program helps reinforce the use of the assignment operators, as well as the operators for addition, subtraction, multiplication, and division. You also use parentheses to set your own order of operations, including a double parentheses when calculating the percent difference between the user's grade and the top grade in the class. Keep practicing these C programs, and you will have the top grade in your programming class!

THE ABSOLUTE MINIMUM

C provides several math operators that do calculations for you. You just need to understand the order of operators to ensure that you input your numbers correctly for your desired calculations. Key concepts from this chapter include:

- Use +, -, *, and / for addition, subtraction, multiplication, and division, respectively.

- Use the modulus operator (%) if you want the remainder of an integer division.

- Remember the order of operators, and use parentheses if you need to change the order.

- Don't put two minus signs together if you are subtracting a negative number, or C will think you are using a different operator. Place a space between the two minus signs.

- Use multiple assignment operators if you have several variables to initialize.

IN THIS CHAPTER

- Saving time with compound operators
- Fitting compound operators into the order of operators
- Typecasting your variables

10

POWERING UP YOUR VARIABLES WITH ASSIGNMENTS AND EXPRESSIONS

As you can see from Table 9.1 in the last chapter, C has a rich assortment of operators. Many operators help C keep its command vocabulary small. C doesn't have many commands, but it has a lot more operators than in most other programming languages; whereas most computer programming languages have relatively few operators and lots of commands, C retains its succinct nature by providing many powerful operators.

This chapter explores a few more operators that you need as you write programs. The compound assignment operators and the typecast operator provide the vehicles for several advanced operations.

Compound Assignment

Many times in your programs, you will have to change the value of a variable. Until now, all variables have been assigned values based on constant literal values or expressions. However, often you will need to update a variable.

Suppose your program had to count the number of times a profit value went below zero. You would need to set up a *counter variable*. A counter variable is a variable that you add 1 to when a certain event takes place. Every time a profit value goes negative, you might do this:

```
lossCount = lossCount + 1;   /* Adds 1 to lossCount variable */
```

 WARNING   In math, nothing can be equal to itself plus 1. With computers, though, the previous assignment statement adds 1 to `lossCount` and then assigns that new value to `lossCount`, essentially adding 1 to the value of `lossCount`. Remember that an equals sign means to take whatever is on the right of the equals sign and store that computed value in the variable on the left.

The following simple program prints the numbers from 1 to 5 using a counter assignment statement before each `printf()` and then counts back down to 1:

```
// Example program #1 from Chapter 10 of Absolute Beginner's Guide
// to C, 3rd Edition
// File Chapter10ex1.c


/* This program increases a counter from 1 to 5, printing updates
and then counts it back down to 1. */


#include <stdio.h>


main()
{

    int ctr = 0;

    ctr = ctr + 1; // increases counter to 1
    printf("Counter is at %d.\n", ctr);
    ctr = ctr + 1; // increases counter to 2
    printf("Counter is at %d.\n", ctr);
    ctr = ctr + 1; // increases counter to 3
```

```
    printf("Counter is at %d.\n", ctr);
    ctr = ctr + 1; // increases counter to 4
    printf("Counter is at %d.\n", ctr);
    ctr = ctr + 1; // increases counter to 5
    printf("Counter is at %d.\n", ctr);
    ctr = ctr - 1; // decreases counter to 4
    printf("Counter is at %d.\n", ctr);
    ctr = ctr - 1; // decreases counter to 3
    printf("Counter is at %d.\n", ctr);
    ctr = ctr - 1; // decreases counter to 2
    printf("Counter is at %d.\n", ctr);
    ctr = ctr - 1; // decreases counter to 1
    printf("Counter is at %d.\n", ctr);

    return 0;
    }
```

The following lines show the program's output. Notice that `ctr` keeps increasing (in computer lingo, it's called *incrementing*) by 1 with each assignment statement until it reaches 5, and then decreases (called *decrementing*) by 1 with each assignment statement until it reaches 1. (Subtracting from a counter would come in handy if you needed to decrease totals from inventories as products are sold.)

```
Counter is at 1.
Counter is at 2.
Counter is at 3.
Counter is at 4.
Counter is at 5.
Counter is at 4.
Counter is at 3.
Counter is at 2.
Counter is at 1.
```

Other times, you'll need to *update* a variable by adding to a total or by adjusting it in some way. The following assignment statement increases the variable sales by 25 percent:

```
sales = sales * 1.25;  /* Increases sales by 25 percent */
```

C provides several *compound operators* that let you update a variable in a manner similar to the methods just described (incrementing, decrementing, and updating by more than 1). However, instead of repeating the variable on *both* sides of the equals sign, you have to list the variable only once. As with much of C, some examples will help clarify what is done with the compound operators.

NOTE   Chapter 15, "Looking for Another Way to Create Loops," shows you how the `for` statement makes updating variables easier.

If you want to add 1 to a variable, you can use the *compound addition* operator, `+=`. These two statements produce the same result:

```
lossCount = lossCount + 1;  /* Adds 1 to lossCount variable */
```

and

```
lossCount += 1;  /* Adds 1 to lossCount variable */
```

Instead of multiplying sales by 1.25 and then assigning it to itself like this:

```
sales = sales * 1.25;  /* Increases sales by 25 percent */
```

you can use the *compound multiplication* operator, `*=`, to do this:

```
sales *= 1.25;  /* Increases sales by 25 percent */
```

TIP   The compound operators are quicker to use than writing out the entire assignment because you don't have to list the same variable name on both sides of the equals sign. Also, the compound operators reduce typing errors because you don't have to type the same variable name twice in the same statement.

Table 10.1 lists all the compound assignment operators and gives examples of each. All the operators you've seen so far in this book, from addition through modulus, have corresponding compound operators.

TABLE 10.1   Compound Assignment Operators

Compound Operator	Example	Equivalent Statement
`*=`	`total *= 1.25;`	`total = total * 1.25;`
`/=`	`amt /= factor;`	`amt = amt / factor;`
`%=`	`days %= 3;`	`days = days % 3;`
`+=`	`count += 1;`	`count = count + 1;`
`-=`	`quantity -= 5;`	`quantity = quantity - 5;`

This second sample program produces the exact same result as the first program in the chapter; it just uses compound operators to increase and decrease the counter. In addition, some of the compound operator statements are located right in the printf() statements to show you that you can combine the two lines of code into one.

```c
// Example program #2 from Chapter 10 of Absolute Beginner's Guide
// to C, 3rd Edition
// File Chapter10ex2.c


/* This program also increases a counter from 1 to 5, printing up-
dates and then counts it back down to 1. However, it uses compound
operators*/

#include <stdio.h>

main()
{

    int ctr = 0;

    ctr += 1; // increases counter to 1
    printf("Counter is at %d.\n", ctr);
    ctr += 1; // increases counter to 2
    printf("Counter is at %d.\n", ctr);

    printf("Counter is at %d.\n", ctr += 1);
    ctr += 1; // increases counter to 4
    printf("Counter is at %d.\n", ctr);

    printf("Counter is at %d.\n", ctr += 1);
    ctr -= 1; // decreases counter to 4
    printf("Counter is at %d.\n", ctr);
    printf("Counter is at %d.\n", ctr -= 1);
    printf("Counter is at %d.\n", ctr -= 1);
    printf("Counter is at %d.\n", ctr -= 1);

    return 0;
}
```

Watch That Order!

Look at the order of operators table in the previous chapter (Table 9.1) and locate the compound assignment operators. You'll see that they have very low precedence. The +=, for instance, is several levels lower than the +.

Initially, this might not sound like a big deal. (Actually, maybe none of this sounds like a big deal. If so, *great!* C should be easier than a lot of people would have you think.) The order of operators table can haunt the unwary C programmer. Think about how you would evaluate the second of these expressions:

```
total = 5;
total *= 2 + 3;   /* Updates the total variable */
```

At first glance, you might think that the value of total is 13 because you learned earlier that multiplication is done before addition. You're right that multiplication is done before addition, but *compound multiplication* is done *after* addition, according to the order of operators. Therefore, the 2 + 3 is evaluated to get 5, and *then* that 5 is multiplied by the old value of total (which also happens to be 5) to get a total of 25, as Figure 10.1 points out.

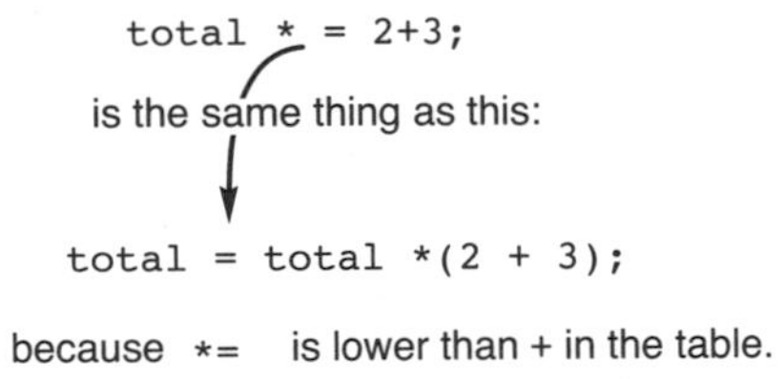

total * = 2+3;
is the same thing as this:

total = total *(2 + 3);

because *= is lower than + in the table.

FIGURE 10.1

The compound operators reside on a low level.

Typecasting: Hollywood Could Take Lessons from C

Two kinds of typecasting exist: the kind that directors of movies often do (but we don't cover that here) and also C's typecasting. A C *typecast* temporarily changes the data type of one variable to another. Here is the format of a typecast:

```
(dataType) value
```

The *dataType* can be any C data type, such as int or float. The *value* is any variable, literal, or expression. Suppose that age is an integer variable that holds 6. The following converts age to a float value of 6.0:

```
(float)age;
```

If you were using age in an expression with other floats, you should typecast age to float to maintain consistency in the expression.

TIP   Because of some rounding problems that can automatically occur if you mix data types, you'll have fewer problems if you explicitly typecast all variables and literals in an expression to the same data type.

Never use a typecast with a variable on a line by itself. Typecast where a variable or an expression has to be converted to another value to properly compute a result. The preceding typecast of age might be represented like this:

```
salaryBonus = salary * (float)age / 150.0;
```

age does *not* change to a floating-point variable—age is changed only *temporarily* for this one calculation. Everywhere in the program that age is not explicitly typecast, it is still an int variable.

WARNING   If you find yourself typecasting the same variable to a different data type throughout a program, you might have made the variable the wrong type to begin with.

You can typecast an entire expression. The following statement typecasts the result of an expression before assigning it to a variable:

```
value = (float)(number - 10 * yrsService);
```

The parentheses around the expression keep the typecast from casting only the variable number. C does perform some automatic typecasting. If value is defined as a float, C typecasts the preceding expression for you before storing the result in value. Nevertheless, if you want to clarify all expressions and not depend on automatic typecasting, go ahead and typecast your expressions.

THE ABSOLUTE MINIMUM

The goal of this chapter was to teach you additional operators that help you write C programs. You also learned to use typecasting if you want to mix variables and constants of different data types. Key concepts from this chapter include:

- Use compound assignment operators when updating variable values.

- Use compound assignment operators to eliminate a few typing errors and to decrease your program-writing time.

- Put a data type in parentheses before a variable, expression, or data value you want to typecast.

- Don't mix data types. Instead, typecast data so that it is all the same type before evaluating it.

- Don't ignore the order of operators! The compound operators have low priority in the table and are done after almost every other operator finishes.

11

THE FORK IN THE ROAD— TESTING DATA TO PICK A PATH

C provides an extremely useful statement called `if`. `if` lets your programs make decisions and execute certain statements based on the results of those decisions. By testing contents of variables, your programs can produce different output, given different input.

This chapter also describes *relational operators*. Combined with `if`, relational operators make C a powerful data-processing language. Computers would really be boring if they couldn't test data; they would be little more than calculators if they had no capability to decide courses of action based on data.

Testing Data

The C `if` statement works just like it does in spoken language: *If something is true, do one thing; otherwise, do something else.* Consider these statements:

If I make enough money, we'll go to Italy.

If the shoes don't fit, take them back.

If it's hot outside, water the lawn.

Table 11.1 lists the C relational operators, which permit testing of data. Notice that some of the relational operators consist of two symbols.

TABLE 11.1   C Relational Operators

Relational Operator	Description
==	Equal to
>	Greater than
<	Less than
>=	Greater than or equal to
<=	Less than or equal to
!=	Not equal to

NOTE   Relational operators compare two values. You always put a variable, literal, or expression—or a combination of any two of them—on either side of a relational operator.

Before delving into `if`, let's look at a few relational operators and see what they really mean. A regular operator produces a mathematical result. A relational operator produces a *true* or *false* result. When you compare two data values, the data values either produce a true comparison or they don't. For example, given the following values:

```
int i = 5;
int j = 10;
int k = 15;
int l = 5;
```

the following statements are *true:*

```
i == 1;
j < k;
k > i;
j != 1;
```

The following statements are *not* true, so they are *false:*

```
i > j;
k < j;
k == 1
```

TIP   To tell the difference between = and ==, remember that you need two equals signs to double-check whether something is equal.

WARNING   Only like values should go on either side of the relational operator. In other words, don't compare a character to a float. If you have to compare two unlike data values, use a type-cast to keep the values the same data type.

Every time C evaluates a relational operator, a value of 1 or 0 is produced. True always results in 1, and false always results in 0. The following statements assign a 1 to the variable a and a 0 to the variable b:

```
a = (4 < 10);   // (4 < 10) is true, so a 1 is put in a
b = (8 == 9);   // (8 == 9) is false, so a 0 is put in b
```

You will often use relational operators in your programs because you'll often want to know whether sales (stored in a variable) is more than a set goal, whether payroll calculations are in line, and whether a product is in inventory or needs to be ordered, for example. You have seen only the beginning of relational operators. The next section explains how to use them.

Using `if`

The `if` statement uses relational operators to perform data testing. Here's the format of the `if` statement:

```
if (condition)
{ block of one or more C statements; }
```

The parentheses around the *condition* are required. The *condition* is a relational test like those described in the preceding section. The *block of one or more C statements* is called the *body* of the `if` statement. The braces around the *block of one or more C statements* are required if the body of the `if` contains more than a single statement.

 TIP Even though braces aren't required, if an `if` contains just one statement, always use the braces. If you later add statements to the body of the `if`, the braces will be there. If the braces enclose more than one statement, the braces enclose what is known as a *compound statement.*

Here is a program with two `if` statements:

```
// Example program #1 from Chapter 11 of Absolute Beginner's Guide
// to C, 3rd Edition
// File Chapter11ex1.c


/* This program asks the user for their birth year and calculates
how old they will be in the current year. (it also checks to make
sure a future year has not been entered.) It then tells the user if
they were born in a leap year. */

#include <stdio.h>
#define CURRENTYEAR 2013

main()
{

    int yearBorn, age;

    printf("What year were you born?\n");
    scanf(" %d", &yearBorn);

    // This if statement can do some data validation, making sure
    // the year makes sense
    // The statements will only execute if the year is after the
    // current year
```

```
if (yearBorn > CURRENTYEAR)
{
    printf("Really? You haven't been born yet?\n");
    printf("Want to try again with a different year?\n");
    printf("What year were you born?\n");
    scanf(" %d", &yearBorn);
}


age = CURRENTYEAR - yearBorn;

printf("\nSo this year you will turn %d on your birthday!\n",
age);


// The second if statment uses the modulus operator to test if
// the year of birth was a Leap Year. Again, only if it is will
// the code execute

if ((yearBorn % 4) == 0)
{
    printf("\nYou were born in a Leap Year--cool!\n");
}


    return 0;
}
```

Consider a few notes about this program. If you use the current year in your program, that's a good variable to set with a #define statement before main(). That way, you can simply change that one line later if you run this program any year in the future.

The first if statement is an example of how to potentially use if as a form of data validation. The statement tests whether the user has entered a year later than the current year and, if so, executes the section of code that follows in the braces. If the user has entered a proper year, the program skips down to the line that calculates the user's age. The section in the braces reminds the reader that he or she couldn't possibly be born in the year entered and gives the user a chance to enter a new year. The program then proceeds as normal.

Here you might have noticed a limitation to this plan. If the user enters an incorrect year a second time, the program proceeds and even tells the age in negative years! A second style of conditional statements, a do...while loop, keeps hounding the user until he or she enters correct data. This is covered in Chapter 14, "Code Repeat—Using Loops to Save Time and Effort."

TIP   You can change the relational operator to not accept the data entry if the user types in a year greater than or equal to the current year, but maybe the user is helping a recent newborn!

After calculating what the user's age will be on his or her birthday this year, a second if statement tests the year of the user's birth to see whether he or she was born in a leap year by using the modulus operator. Only leap years are divisible by 4 without a remainder, so only people who were born in one of those years will see the message noting the one-in-four odds of their birth year. For the rest, that section of code is skipped and the program reaches its termination point.

NOTE   The main() function in the Draw Poker program in Appendix B, "The Draw Poker Program," asks the player which cards to keep and which cards to replace. An if is used to determine exactly what the user wants to do.

Otherwise...: Using else

In the preceding section, you saw how to write a course of action that executes if the relational test is true. If the relational test is false, nothing happens. This section explains the else statement that you can add to if. Using else, you can specify exactly what happens when the relational test is false. Here is the format of the combined if...else:

```
if (condition)
{ block of one or more C statements; }
else
{ block of one or more C statements; }
```

So in the case of if...else, one of the two segments of code will run, depending on whether the condition tested is true (in which case, the if code will run) or false (in which case, the else code will run). This is perfect if you have two possible outcomes and need to run different code for each.

Here is an example of if...else that moves the previous program to an if...else construction. In this version, the user does not have the opportunity to re-enter a year, but it does congratulate the user on coming back from the future.

```
// Example program #2 from Chapter 11 of Absolute Beginner's Guide
// to C, 3rd Edition
// File Chapter11ex2.c

/* This program asks the user for their birth year and calculates
how old they will be in the current year. (it also checks to make
sure a future year has not been entered.) It then tells the user if
they were born in a leap year. */

#include <stdio.h>
#define CURRENTYEAR 2013

main()
{

    int yearBorn, age;

    printf("What year were you born?\n");
    scanf(" %d", &yearBorn);

    // This if statement can do some data validation, making sure
    // the year makes sense
    // The statements will only execute if the year is after the
    // current year

    if (yearBorn > CURRENTYEAR)
    {
        printf("Really? You haven't been born yet?\n");
        printf("Congratulations on time travel!\n");
    }
    else
    {


        age = CURRENTYEAR - yearBorn;
```

```c
    printf("\nSo this year you will turn %d on your birthday!\n",
        age);

    // The second if statment uses the modulus operator to test
    // if the year of
    // birth was a Leap Year. Again, only if it is will the code
    // execute

    if ((yearBorn % 4) == 0)
    {
        printf("\nYou were born in a Leap Year--cool!\n");
    }
  }
  return 0;
}
```

This is largely the same program as before (with the exception that the user does not have the option of entering a second date if the first one is deemed incorrect), but something else is worth noting. The second `if` statement is embedded inside the code that executes during the `else` portion of the first `if` statement. This is known as a *nested statement,* and it is something you will probably be doing as your programs get more complicated. You can also test multiple conditions, but the `switch` statement, covered in Chapter 17, "Making the `case` for the `switch` Statement," helps you master that statement.

TIP   Put semicolons only at the end of executable statements in the body of the `if` or the `else`. Never put a semicolon after the `if` or the `else`; semicolons go only at the end of complete statements.

NOTE   As with the body of the `if`, the body of the `else` doesn't require braces if it consists of a single statement—but it's a good idea to use braces anyway.

This last program demonstrates another way to use `if` and `else`, but this time you can test for four different conditions:

```c
// Example program #3 from Chapter 11 of Absolute Beginner's Guide
// to C, 3rd Edition
// File Chapter11ex3.c
```

```
/* This program asks the user their state of happiness on a scale of
1 to 10 and then gives a custom 2-line message based on their range,
either 1-2, 3-4, 5-7, or 8-10. */

#include <stdio.h>

main()
{

    int prefer;

    printf("On a scale of 1 to 10, how happy are you?\n");
    scanf(" %d", &prefer);

    // Once the user's level of happiness is entered, a series of if
    // statements
    // test the number against decreasing numbers. Only one of the
    // four will be
    // executed.

    if (prefer >= 8)
    {
        printf("Great for you!\n");
        printf("Things are going well for you!\n");
    }
    else if (prefer >= 5)
    {
        printf("Better than average, right?\n");
        printf("Maybe things will get even better soon!\n");
    }
    else if (prefer >= 3)
    {
        printf("Sorry you're feeling not so great.\n");
        printf("Hope things turn around soon...\n");
    }
```

```
    else
    {
        printf("Hang in there--things have to improve, right?\n");
        printf("Always darkest before the dawn.\n");
    }

    return 0;
}
```

Here are two different runs of this program:

```
On a scale of 1 to 10, how happy are you?
5
Better than average, right?
Maybe things will get better soon!


On a scale of 1 to 10, how happy are you?
9
Great for you!
Things are going well for you!
```

The goal of this program is to demonstrate that if…else statements do not have to be limited to two choices. Frankly, you can set as many if…else if…else if…else conditions as you'd like. For example, you could have a custom message for every number between 1 and 10 in this program. Each test eliminates some of the possibilities. This is why the second test works only for numbers 5 through 7, even though the test is for whether the number is greater or equal to 5; numbers 8 and higher were already eliminated with the first if test.

THE ABSOLUTE MINIMUM

The goal of this chapter was to show you ways to test data and execute one set of code or another, depending on the result of that test. You don't always want the same code to execute every time someone runs your program because the data is not always the same. Key concepts from this chapter include:

- Use relational operators to compare data.

- Remember that a true relational result produces a 1, and a false relational result produces a 0.

- Use `if` to compare data and `else` to specify what to do if the `if` test fails.

- Put braces around the `if` body of code and around the `else` body of code. All the code in the braces either executes or does not execute, depending on the relational comparison.

- Don't put a semicolon after `if` or `else`. Semicolons go only at the end of each statement, inside the body of the `if` or the `else`.

JUGGLING SEVERAL CHOICES WITH LOGICAL OPERATORS

Sometimes the relational operators described in Chapter 11, "The Fork in the Road—Testing Data to Pick a Path," simply can't express all the testing conditions. For example, if you wanted to test whether a numeric or character variable is within a certain range, you would have to use two `if` statements, like this:

```
if (age >= 21)  /* See if 21 <= age <= 65 */
{ if (age <= 65)
    {
    printf("The age falls between 21 and 65.\n");
    }
}
```

Although there's nothing wrong with using nested `if` statements, they're not extremely straightforward, and their logic is slightly more complex than you really need. By using the *logical operators* you'll read about in this chapter, you can combine more than one relational test in a single `if` statement to clarify your code.

NOTE   Don't let the terms *logical* and *relational* make you think these two groups of operators are difficult. As long as you understand how the individual operators work, you don't have to keep track of what they're called as a group.

NOTE   A relational operator simply tests how two values relate (how they compare to each other). The logical operators combine relational operators.

Getting Logical

Three logical operators exist (see Table 12.1). Sometimes logical operators are known as *compound relational operators* because they let you combine more than one relational operator. (See the previous Note.)

TABLE 12.1   The Logical Operators

Logical Operator	Meaning
&&	And
||	Or
!	Not

Logical operators appear between two or more relational tests. For example, here are the first parts of three `if` statements that use logical operators:

```
if ((age >= 21) && (age <= 65)) {
```

and

```
if ((hrsWorked > 40) || (sales > 25000.00)) {
```

and

```
if (!(isCharterMember)) {
```

If you combine two relational operators with a logical operator or you use the ! (not) operator to negate a relation, the *entire* expression following the `if` statement requires parentheses. This is not allowed:

```
if !isCharterMember {   /* Not allowed */
```

Of course, there is more to the preceding `if` statements than what is shown, but to keep things simple at this point, the `if` bodies aren't shown.

Logical operators work just as they do in spoken language. For example, consider the spoken statements that correspond to the code lines just seen:

```
if ((age >= 21) && (age <= 65)) {
```

This could be worded in spoken language like this:

"If the age is at least 21 and no more than 65,..."

And the code

```
if ((hrsWorked > 40) || (sales > 25000.00)) {
```

could be worded in spoken language like this:

"If the hours worked are more than 40 or the sales are more than $25000,... "

Similarly,

```
if (!(isCharterMember)) {
```

could be worded in spoken language like this:

"If you aren't a charter member, you must..."

As you have no doubt figured out, these three spoken statements describe exactly the same tests done by the three `if` statements. You often place an *and* between two conditions, such as "If you take out the trash *and* clean your room, you can play."

 NOTE   Reread that stern statement you might say to a child. The `and` condition places a strict requirement that *both* jobs must be done before the result can take place. That's what `&&` does also. Both sides of the `&&` must be true for the body of the `if` to execute.

Let's continue with this same line of reasoning for the || (or) operator. You might be more lenient on the kid by saying this: "If you take out the trash *or* clean your room, you can play." The or is not as restrictive. One side or the other side of the || must be true (and they both can be true as well). If either side is true, the result can occur. The same holds for the || operator. One or the other side of the || must be true (or they both can be true) for the body of the `if` to execute.

The ! (not) operator reverses a true or a false condition. True becomes false, and false becomes true. This sounds confusing, and it is! Limit the number of ! operators you use. You can always rewrite a logical expression to avoid using ! by reversing the logic. For example, the following if:

```
if ( !(sales < 3000)) {
```

is exactly the same as this if:

```
if ( sales >= 3000) {
```

As you can see, you can remove the ! and turn a negative statement into a positive test by removing the ! and using an opposite relational operator.

The following program uses each of the three logical operators to test data. Two of the three conditions will be met, and their if sections of code will print; the third is not true, so the else section of code will print.

```
// Example program #1 from Chapter 12 of Absolute Beginner's Guide
// to C, 3rd Edition
// File Chapter12ex1.c


/* This program defines a series of variables and expressions and
then uses both relational and logical operators to test them against
each other. */


#include <stdio.h>



main()
{
  // set up some common integers for the program
  int planets = 8;
  int friends = 6;
  int potterBooks = 7;
  int starWars = 6;
  int months = 12;
  int beatles = 4;
  int avengers = 6;
  int baseball = 9;
  int basketball = 5;
```

```c
    int football = 11;



// This first logical statement uses the AND operator to test
// whether the cast of Friends and the Beatles would have
// enough people to make a baseball team AND the cast
// of Friends and the Avengers would have enough people
// to field a football team. If so, the statements will print.
 if ((friends + beatles >= baseball) &&
     (friends + avengers >= football))
     {
            printf("The cast of Friends and the Beatles ");
            printf("could make a baseball team,\n");
            printf("AND the cast of Friends plus the Avengers ");
            printf("could make a football team.\n");
     }
 else
 {
              printf("Either the Friends cannot make a ");
              printf("baseball team with the Fab Four, \n");
              printf("OR they can't make a Gridiron Gang with the ");
              printf("Avengers (or both!)\n");
 }
// This second logical statement uses the OR operator to test
// whether the number of Star Wars movies is less than months
// in the year OR the number of Harry Potter books is less than
// months in the year. If either statement is true,
// the statements will print.


  if ((starWars <= months) || (potterBooks <= months))
  {
    printf("\nYou could read one Harry Potter book a month,\n");
    printf("and finish them all in less than a year,\n");
    printf("OR you could see one Star Wars movie a month,\n");
    printf("and finish them all in less than a year.\n");
```

```
  }
  else
  {
    printf("Neither can happen--too many books or movies,\n");
    printf("Not enough time!\n\n");
  }


// This final logical statemnt uses the NOT operator to test
// whether the number of baseball players on a team added
// to the number of basketball players on a team is NOT
// greater than the number of football  players on
// a team. If so, the statements will print.

  if (!(baseball + basketball > football))
  {
    printf("\nThere are fewer baseball and basketball players\n");
    printf("combined than football players.");
  }
  else
  {
    printf("\nThere are more baseball and basketball players\n");
    printf("combined than football players.");
  }


  return 0;
}
```

Experiment with this program—change the conditions, variables, and operators to get different printing combinations. As mentioned before, the most confusing logical operator is the last one in the program, the not (!) operator. Most of the time, you can write a statement that avoids the use of it.

Avoiding the Negative

Suppose you wanted to write an inventory program that tests whether the number of a certain item has fallen to zero. The first part of the if might look like this:

```
if (count == 0) {
```

Because the if is true *only* if count has a value of 0, you can rewrite the statement like this:

```
if (!count) { /* Executes if's body only if count is 0 */
```

Again, the ! adds a little confusion to code. Even though you might save some typing effort with a fancy !, clearer code is better than trickier code, and if (count == 0) { is probably better to use, despite the microsecond your program might save by using !.

Using the && operator, the following program prints one message if the user's last name begins with the letters P through S, and it prints another message if the name begins with something else.

```
// Example program #2 from Chapter 12 of Absolute Beginner's Guide
// to C, 3rd Edition
// File Chapter12ex2.c


/* This program asks for a last name, and if the user has a last
name that starts with a letter between P and Q, they will be sent to
a special room for their tickets. */


#include <stdio.h>



main()
{
  // set up an array for the last name and then get it from the user

  char name[25];
  printf("What is your last name? ");
  printf("(Please capitalize the first letter!)\n");
  scanf(" %s", name);
  //For a string array, you don't need the &
```

```
if ((name[0] >= 'P') && (name[0] <= 'S'))
{
  printf("You must go to room 2432 ");
  printf("for your tickets.\n");
}
else
{
  printf("You can get your tickets here.\n");
}


  return 0;
}
```

One point about this program is worth noting. Chapter 8, "Interacting with Users," suggested that you use your `printf()` statement to clarify what data you need from the user and in what format. Reminding users to type their last name using a capital letter helps avoid possible problems. If your user's last name is Peyton, but she types it as `peyton` with a lowercase p, the program would not send the user to Room 2432 because the logical operator checks only for capitals. Now, if you wanted to check for either, you could use the following, more complicated, logical statement:

```
if ((((name[0] >= 'P') && (name[0] <= 'S')) || (name[0] >= 'p') &&
(name[0] >= 's')))
```

It's a little harder to read and follow, but such is the price of data vigilance!

 NOTE How would the program be different if the `&&` were changed to a `||`? Would the first or the second message appear? The answer is the first one. *Everybody* would be sent to Room 2432. Any letter from A to Z is either more than P or less than S. The test in the preceding program has to be `&&` because Room 2432 is available only to people whose names are between P and S.

As mentioned in the last chapter, `if` statements can be helpful when ensuring that the user has entered the proper information your program is looking for. The following section of code asks the user for a `Y` or `N` answer. The code includes an `||` to ensure that the user enters a correct value.

```
printf("Is your printer on (Y/N) ?\n");
scanf(" %c", &ans); //need an & before the name of your char variable
if ((ans == 'Y') || (ans == 'N'))
```

```
{
    // Gets here if user typed a correct answer.
    if (ans == 'N')
    {
        printf("*** Turn the printer on now. ***\n");
    }
}
else
{
    printf("You did not enter a Y or N.\n");
}
```

 TIP   You can combine more than two relational operators with logical operators, but doing too much in a single statement can cause confusion. This is a little too much:

```
if ((a < 6) || (c >= 3) && (r != 9) || (p <= 1)) {
```

Try to keep your combined relational tests simple so that your programs remain easy to read and maintain.

The Order of Logical Operators

Because logical operators appear in the order of operators table, they have priority at times, just as the other operators do. Studying the order of operators shows you that the && operator has precedence over the ||. Therefore, C interprets the following logic:

```
if (age < 20 || sales < 1200 && hrsWorked > 15) {
```

like this:

```
if ((age < 20) || ((sales < 1200) && (hrsWorked > 15))) {
```

Use ample parentheses. Parentheses help clarify the order of operators. C won't get confused if you don't use parentheses because it knows the order of operators table very well. However, a person looking at your program has to figure out which is done first, and parentheses help group operations together.

Suppose that a teacher wants to reward her students who perform well and have missed very few classes. Also, the reward requires that the students either joined three school organizations or were in two sports activities. Whew! You must admit, not only will that reward be deserved, but sorting out the possibilities will be difficult.

In C code, the following `if` statement would test true if a student met the teacher's preset reward criteria:

```
if (grade > 93 && classMissed <= 3 && numActs >= 3 || sports >= 2) {
```

That's a lot to decipher. Not only is the statement hard to read, but there is a subtle error. The || is compared last (because || has lower precedence than &&), but that || should take place before the second &&. (If this is getting confusing, you're right! Long-combined relational tests often are.) Here, in spoken language, is how the previous `if` operates without separating its pieces with proper parentheses:

If the student's grade is more than 93 and the student missed three or fewer classes and the school activities total three or more, OR if the student participated in two or more sports...

Well, the problem is that the student only has to be in sports activities to get the reward. The last two relations (separated with the ||) must be compared before the third &&. The spoken description should read like this:

If the student's grade is more than 93 and the student missed three or fewer classes and EITHER the school activities total three or more OR the student participated in two or more sports...

The following `if`, with correct parentheses, not only makes the `if` accurate, but also makes it a little more clear:

```
if ((grade > 93) && (classMissed <= 3) && ((numActs >= 3) || (sports
>= 2)) {
```

If you like, you can break such long `if` statements into two or more lines, like this:

```
if ((grade > 93) && (classMissed <= 3) &&
((numActs >= 3) || (sports >= 2)) {
```

Some C programmers even find that two `if` statements are clearer than four relational tests, such as these statements:

```
if ((grade > 93) && (classMissed <= 3)
    { if ((numActs >= 3) || (sports >= 2))
        { /* Reward the student */ }
```

The style you end up with depends mostly on what you like best, what you are the most comfortable with, and what appears to be the most maintainable.

THE ABSOLUTE MINIMUM

This chapter's goal was to teach you the logical operators. Although relational operators test data, the logical operators, && and ||, let you combine more than one relational test into a single statement and execute code accordingly. Key concepts from this chapter include:

- Use logical operators to connect relational operators.

- Use && when both sides of the operator have to be true for the entire condition to be true.

- Use || when either one side or the other side (or both) have to be true for the entire condition to be true.

- Don't overdo the use of !. Most negative logic can be reversed (so < becomes >= and > becomes <=) to get rid of the not operator.

- Don't combine too many relational operators in a single expression.

IN THIS CHAPTER

- Saying goodbye to `if...else` and hello to conditional
- Using the small-change operators: ++ and --
- Sizing up the situation

13

A BIGGER BAG OF TRICKS—SOME MORE OPERATORS FOR YOUR PROGRAMS

Have patience! You've learned about almost all the C operators. With the exception of a few more advanced operators that you'll read about in Chapter 24, "Solving the Mystery of Pointers," this chapter rounds out the order of operators table and explains *conditional operators*, *increment operators*, and *decrement operators.*

C operators sometimes substitute for more wordy commands that you would use in other programming languages. Not only can an assortment of operators speed your program development time, but they also compile more efficiently and run faster than commands. The C operators do a lot to make C the efficient language that it is.

Goodbye `if…else`; Hello, Conditional

The conditional operator is the only C operator that requires *three* arguments. Whereas division, multiplication, and most of the others require two values to work, the conditional operator requires three. Although the format of the conditional operator looks complex, you will see that it streamlines some logic and is actually straightforward to use.

The conditional operator looks like this: `?:`. Here is its format:

`relation ? trueStatement : falseStatement;`

The `relation` is any relational test, such as age `>= 21` or `sales <= 25000.0`. You also can combine the relational operators with the logical operators you learned about in Chapter 12, "Juggling Several Choices with Logical Operators." The `trueStatement` is any valid C statement, and the `falseStatement` is also any valid C statement. Here is an example of a conditional operator:

`(total <= 3850.0) ? (total *= 1.10): (total *= 1.05);`

 TIP The parentheses are not required, but they do help group the three parts of the conditional operator so that you can see them easier.

If the test in the first set of parentheses is true, the `trueStatement` executes. If the test in the first set of parentheses is false, the `falseStatement` executes. The conditional operator you just saw does *exactly* the same thing as this `if…else` statement:

```
if (total <= 3850.0
        { total *= 1.10; }
else
        { total *= 1.05; )
```

This statement tells C to multiply `total` by 1.10 or by 1.05, depending on the result of the relational test.

Just about any `if…else` statement can be rewritten as a conditional statement. The conditional requires less typing, you won't accidentally leave off a brace somewhere, and the conditional runs more efficiently than an `if…else` because it compiles into more compact code.

 TIP The format of the conditional operator is obvious when you think of it like this: The question mark asks a question. Keeping this in mind, you could state the earlier example as follows: *Is the total <= 3850.0? If so, do the first thing; otherwise, do the second.*

C programmers don't like the redundancy you saw in the earlier use of the conditional operator. As you can see, the `total` variable appears twice. Both times, it is being assigned a value. When you face such a situation, take the assignment out of the conditional operator's statements:

```
total *= (total <= 3850.0) ? (1.10): (1.05);
```

Don't replace every single `if…else` with a conditional operator. Many times, `if…else` is more readable, and some conditional statements are just too complex to squeeze easily into a conditional operator. However, when a simple `if…else` is all that's needed, the conditional operator provides a nice alternative.

The conditional operator offers one additional advantage over `if`: The conditional often can appear in places where `if` can't go. The following `print(f)` prints a trailing `s` if the number of pears is more than 1:

```
printf("I ate %d pear%s\n", numPear, (numPear>1) ? ("s.") : ("."));
```

If the value in `numPear` is greater than 1, you'll see something like this printed:

```
I ate 4 pears.
```

But if there is only one pear, you'll see this:

```
I ate 1 pear.
```

NOTE   Maybe you're wondering why the conditional operator is `?:`, but the question mark and colon *never* appear next to each other. Well, that's just the way it is. It would be too cumbersome to go around saying that the conditional operator looks like a question mark and a colon with some stuff in between.

Here's a short program that uses the conditional operator. (Actually, it uses it eight times!) The program prompts the user for an integer and then tests whether the number is divisible by all single-digit numbers between 2 and 9:

```
// Example program #1 from Chapter 13 of Absolute Beginner's Guide
// to C, 3rd Edition
// File Chapter13ex1.c


/* This program asks for a number from 1 to 100 and tells then
whether or not their choice is equally divisible by 2 through 9. */


#include <stdio.h>
```

```
main()
{
    // Define the integer to hold the user's guess and then get it
    // from the user

int numPick;
printf("Pick an integer between 1 and 100 ");
printf("(The higher the better!)\n");
scanf(" %d", &numPick); //remember for an int, you do need the &

printf("%d %s divisible by 2.", numPick, (numPick % 2 == 0) ? ("is")
: ("is not"));
printf("\n%d %s divisible by 3.", numPick, (numPick % 3 == 0) ?
("is") : ("is not"));
printf("\n%d %s divisible by 4.", numPick, (numPick % 4 == 0) ?
("is") : ("is not"));
printf("\n%d %s divisible by 5.", numPick, (numPick % 5 == 0) ?
("is") : ("is not"));
printf("\n%d %s divisible by 6.", numPick, (numPick % 6 == 0) ?
("is") : ("is not"));
printf("\n%d %s divisible by 7.", numPick, (numPick % 7 == 0) ?
("is") : ("is not"));
printf("\n%d %s divisible by 8.", numPick, (numPick % 8 == 0) ?
("is") : ("is not"));
printf("\n%d %s divisible by 9.", numPick, (numPick % 9 == 0) ?
("is") : ("is not"));

return 0;
}
```

NOTE Although the printf() statement asks for the number to be between 1 and 100, users actually can enter any integer. If you use 362880, you'll find that it is divisible by all eight single-digit integers.

The Small-Change Operators: ++ and - -

Although the conditional operator works on three arguments, the *increment* and *decrement* operators work on only one. The increment operator adds 1 to a variable, and the decrement operator subtracts 1 from a variable. That's it. 'Nuff said. Almost....

Incrementing and decrementing variables are things you would need to do if you were counting items (such as the number of customers who shopped in your store yesterday) or counting down (such as removing items from an inventory as people buy them). In Chapter 10, "Powering Up Your Variables with Assignments and Expressions," you read how to increment and decrement variables using compound operators. Here, you learn two operators that can more easily do the same. The increment operator is ++, and the decrement operator is - -. If you want to add 1 to the variable count, here's how you do it:

```
count++;
```

You also can do this:

```
++count;
```

The decrement operator does the same thing, except that the 1 is subtracted from the variable. You can do this:

```
count--;
```

You also can do this:

```
--count;
```

As you can see, the operators can go on either side of the variable. If the operator is on the left, it's called a *prefix increment* or *prefix decrement* operator. If the operator is on the right, it's known as a *postfix increment* or *postfix decrement* operator.

 NOTE   Never apply an increment or decrement operator to a literal constant or an expression. Only variables can be incremented or decremented. You will never see this:

```
--14;   /* Don't do this! */
```

Prefix and postfix operators produce identical results when used by themselves. Only when you combine them with other expressions does a small "gotcha" appears. Consider the following code:

```
int i = 2, j = 5, n;

n = ++i * j;
```

The question is, what is n when the statements finish executing? It's easy to see what's in j because j doesn't change and still holds 5. The ++ ensures that i is always incremented, so you know that i becomes 3. The trick is determining exactly when i increments. If i increments before the multiplication, n becomes 15, but if i increments after the multiplication, n becomes 10.

The answer lies in the *prefix* and *postfix* placements. If the ++ or -- is a *prefix*, C computes it before anything else on the line. If the ++ or -- is a *postfix*, C computes it after everything else on the line finishes. Because the ++ in the preceding code is a prefix, i increments to 3 before being multiplied by j. The following statement increments i *after* multiplying i by j and storing the answer in n:

```
n = i++ * j;   /* Puts 10 in n and 3 in i */
```

Being able to increment a variable in the same expression as you use the variable means less work on the programmer's part. The preceding statement replaces the following two statements that you would have to write in other programming languages:

```
n = i * j;
i = i + 1
```

 NOTE The ++ and -- operators are extremely efficient. If you care about such things (most of us don't), ++ and -- compile into only one machine language statement, whereas adding or subtracting 1 using +1 or -1 doesn't always compile so efficiently.

Let's revisit the count up and count down program from Chapter 10, this time using the prefix increment and decrement operators. This involves even fewer lines of code than the last program; we can even cut the code to fewer lines when you learn about loops in the next chapter.

```
// Example program #2 from Chapter 13 of Absolute Beginner's Guide
// to C, 3rd Edition
// File Chapter13ex2.c


/* This program increases a counter from 1 to 5, printing updates
and then counts it back down to 1. However, it uses the increment
and decrement operators */


#include <stdio.h>


main()
{
```

```
int ctr = 0;

printf("Counter is at %d.\n", ++ctr);
printf("Counter is at %d.\n", ++ctr);
printf("Counter is at %d.\n", ++ctr);
printf("Counter is at %d.\n", ++ctr);
printf("Counter is at %d.\n", ++ctr);

printf("Counter is at %d.\n", --ctr);
printf("Counter is at %d.\n", --ctr);
printf("Counter is at %d.\n", --ctr);
printf("Counter is at %d.\n", --ctr);

return 0;
}
```

 NOTE   To understand the difference between prefix and post-fix, move all the increment and decrement operators to after the `ctr` variables (`ctr++` and `ctr--`). Can you guess what will happen? Compile it and see if you are right!

Sizing Up the Situation

You use `sizeof()` to find the number of memory locations it takes to store values of any data type. Although most C compilers now use 4 bytes to store integers, not all do. To find out for sure exactly how much memory integers and floating points are using, you can use `sizeof()`. The following statements do just that:

```
i = sizeof(int); // Puts the size of integers into i.
f = sizeof(float); // Puts the size of floats into f
```

`sizeof()` works on variables as well as data types. If you need to know how much memory variables and arrays take, you can apply the `sizeof()` operator to them. The following section of code shows you how:

```
char name[] = "Ruth Claire";
int i = 7;
printf("The size of i is %d.\n", sizeof(i));
printf("The size of name is %d.\n", sizeof(name));
```

Here is one possible output from this code:

```
The size of i is 4
The size of name is 12
```

Depending on your computer and C compiler, your output might differ because of the differences in integer sizes. Notice that the character array size is 12, which includes the null zero.

 TIP The length of a string and the size of a string are two different values. The length is the number of bytes up to but not including the null zero, and it is found via `strlen()`. The size of a string is the number of characters it takes to hold the string, including the null zero.

 NOTE Although `sizeof()` might seem worthless right now, you'll see how it comes in handy as you progress in C.

THE ABSOLUTE MINIMUM

The goal of this chapter was to round out your knowledge of C operators. Understanding these operators doesn't take a lot of work, yet the operators are powerful and substitute for complete statements in other languages. Key concepts from this chapter include:

- Use the conditional operator in place of simple `if...else` statements to improve efficiency.

- The conditional operator requires three arguments. Extra parentheses help clarify these three arguments by separating them from each other.

- Use `++` and `--` to increment and decrement variables instead of adding and subtracting 1 using assignment or the `+=` and `-=` operators.

- Don't think that a prefix and postfix always produce the same values. A prefix and postfix are identical only when a single variable is involved. If you combine `++` or `--` with other variables and expressions, the placement of the prefix and postfix is critical to get the result you want.

IN THIS CHAPTER

- Saving time by looping through code
- Using `while`
- Using `do...while`

14

CODE REPEAT—USING LOOPS TO SAVE TIME AND EFFORT

Now that you've learned the operators, you're ready to play "loop the loop" with your programs. A *loop* is simply a section of code that repeats a few times. You don't want a loop to repeat forever—that's called an *infinite loop*. The loops you write (if you write them properly—and, of course, you will) should come to a conclusion when they finish doing the job you set them up to do.

Why would you want a program to loop? The answer becomes clear when you think about the advantage of using a computer for tasks that people wouldn't want to do. Computers never get bored, so you should give them mundane and repetitive tasks; leave the tasks that require thought to people. You wouldn't want to pay someone to add a list of hundreds of payroll figures, and few people would want to do it anyway. Computer programs can do that kind of repetitive work. People can then analyze the results when the computer loop finishes calculating all the figures.

If you want to add a list of figures, print company sales totals for the past 12 months, or add up the number of students who enroll in a computer class, you need to use a loop. This chapter explains two common C loops that use the `while` command.

`while` We Repeat

The `while` statement always appears at the beginning or end of a loop. The easiest type of loop that uses `while` is called the `while` loop. (The other is called the do...while loop. You'll see it a little later.) Here is the format of `while`:

```
while (condition)

{ block of one or more C statements; }
```

The *condition* is a relational test that is exactly like the relational test *condition* you learned for `if`. The *block of one or more C statements* is called the *body* of the `while`.

The body of the `while` repeats as long as the *condition* is true. This is the difference between a `while` statement and an `if` statement: The body of the `if` executes if the *condition* is true. The body of the `if` executes only once, however, whereas the body of the `while` can execute a lot of times.

Figure 14.1 helps explain the similarities and differences between `if` and `while`. The formats of the two commands are similar, in that braces are required if the body of the `while` has more than one statement. Even if the body of the `while` contains only a single statement, you should enclose the body in braces so that the braces will still be there if you later add statements to the `while`. Never put a semicolon after the `while`'s parenthesis. The semicolon follows only the statements inside the body of the `while`.

WARNING   The two statements in Figure 14.1 are similar, but they don't do the same thing. `while` and `if` are two separate statements that do two separate things.

You *must* somehow change a variable inside the `while` loop's *condition*. If you don't, the `while` will loop forever because it will test the same *condition* each time through the loop. Therefore, you avoid infinite loops by making sure the body of the `while` loop changes something in the *condition* so that eventually the *condition* becomes false and the program continues with the statements that follow the `while` loop.

Using `if`:
```
  if(amount < 25)
    {
    printf("Amount is too small.\n");
    wrongVal++; MOVE ALONG
    }
```
Executes only one time but only then if amount is less than 25.

Using `while`:
```
  while (amount < 25)
    {
    printf("Amount is too small.\n");

    wrongVal++;

    printf("Try again...What is new amount?\n");

    scanf("%d",&amount); GO BACK
    }
```
Keeps repeating as long as amount is less than 25.

FIGURE 14.1

The `if` body executes once; the `while` body can repeat more than once.

NOTE   As with `if`, the `while` might *never* execute! If the `condition` is false going into `while` the first time, the body of the `while` doesn't execute.

Using `while`

If you want to repeat a section of code until a certain condition becomes false, `while` is the way to go. Let's revisit the counter up and down program for a fourth go-round and use `while` loops this time:

```
// Example program #1 from Chapter 14 of Absolute Beginner's Guide
// to C, 3rd Edition
// File Chapter14ex1.c


/* This program increases a counter from 1 to 5, printing updates
and then counts it back down to 1. However, it uses while loops and
the increment and decrement operators */


#include <stdio.h>
```

```
main()
{

    int ctr = 0;

    while (ctr < 5)
    {
        printf("Counter is at %d.\n", ++ctr);
    }

    while (ctr > 1)
    {
        printf("Counter is at %d.\n", --ctr);
    }

    return 0;
}
```

You might be getting a little sick of our "Counter is at..." code example, but using different statements, formats, and functions to accomplish the same task is an excellent method to show how new skills can help you execute a task differently or more efficiently.

When comparing this listing to the previous times you wrote programs to accomplish the same goal, you can see that your number of lines decreases significantly when using a loop. Previously, you needed to type five printf() statements for the count up and then type another four to count down. However, by using while loops, you need only one printf() statement in the count up loop and one in the count down loop, which streamlines the program.

The variable ctr is initially set to 0. The first time while executes, i is less than 5, so the while *condition* is true and the body of the while executes. In the body, a newline is sent to the screen and ctr is incremented. The second time the *condition* is tested, ctr has a value of 1, but 1 is still less than 5, so the body executes again. The body continues to execute until ctr is incremented to 5. Because 5 is not less than 5 (they are equal), the *condition* becomes false and the loop stops repeating. The rest of the program is then free to execute, leading to the second while loop that counts down from 5 to 1, when it eventually makes the second *condition* false and ends the loop.

TIP   If `ctr` were not incremented in the `while` loop, the `printf()` would execute forever or until you pressed Ctrl+Break to stop it.

Using do...while

`while` also can be used in conjunction with the `do` statement. When used as a pair, the statements normally are called do...while statements or the do...while loop. The do...while behaves almost exactly like the `while` loop. Here is the format of do...while:

```
do
{ block of one or more C statements; }
while (condition)
```

NOTE   The `do` and `while` act like wrappers around the body of the loop. Again, braces are required if the body has more than a single statement.

Use a do...while in place of a `while` only when the body of the loop *must execute at least one time*. The *condition* is located at the *bottom* of the do...while loop, so C can't test the *condition* until the loop finishes the first time.

Here's a quick program that uses a do...while loop. It asks the user for two numbers and then gives the resulting value if the two inputs are multiplied. It then asks the user if he or she would like to multiply two more numbers. As long as the user keeps typing *Y*, the program keeps asking for numbers to multiply. Only answering *N* breaks the loop.

```
// Example program #2 from Chapter 14 of Absolute Beginner's Guide
// to C, 3rd Edition
// File Chapter14ex2.c


/* This program will multiply two numbers and display the result for
as long as the user wants. Answering 'N' will break the loop. */


#include <stdio.h>


main()
{
```

```c
float num1, num2, result;
char choice;

do {

    printf("Enter your first number to multiply: ");
    scanf(" %f", &num1);

    printf("Enter your second number to multiply: ");
    scanf(" %f", &num2);

    result = num1 * num2;
    printf("%.2f times %.2f equals %.2f\n\n",
        num1, num2, result);
    printf("Do you want to enter another pair of numbers ");
    printf("to multiply (Y/N): ");
    scanf(" %c", &choice);
    // If the user enters a lowercase n, this if statement will
    // convert it to an N
    if (choice == 'n')
        {
            choice = 'N';
        }

} while (choice != 'N');

return 0;

}
```

Although this program is simple and straightforward, it demonstrates an effective use of a do...while loop. Again, you use the do...while construct instead of while when you want to ensure that the code within the loop executes at least once. So after getting two floating-point numbers from the user and displaying the result, the program asks the user if he or she wants to multiply two new numbers. If the user enters Y (or any character other than N), the loop begins again from the beginning.

Without the `if` statement in the loop, a lowercase n would not terminate the loop, but it seems obvious that a user who enters n is looking to terminate the loop and just forgot to use the Shift key. As mentioned earlier in the book, when programming, you cannot always count on the user entering what you want, so when you can, you should anticipate common data-entry errors and provide work-arounds. Converting a lowercase n to N is not the only way you could account for this possibility. You could also use a logical AND operator in the `while` portion of the loop, as follows:

```
} while (choice != 'N'&& choice != 'n');
```

In plain language, this is telling the program to keep running as long as the choice is not an uppercase N or a lowercase n.

TIP   Chapter 19, "Getting More from Your Strings," explains a simpler method to test for an uppercase Y or N or a lowercase y or n with a built-in function named `toupper()`.

THE ABSOLUTE MINIMUM

The goal of this chapter was to show you how to repeat sections of code. The `while` and `do...while` loops both repeat statements within their statement bodies. The difference between the two statements lies in the placement of the relational test that controls the loops. The `while` statement tests the relation at the top of the loop, and the `do...while` statement tests the relation at the bottom of the loop, forcing all its statements to execute at least once. Key concepts covered in this chapter include:

- Use `while` or `do...while` when you need to repeat a section of code.

- Make sure that the body of the `while` or `do...while` loop changes something in the *condition*, or the loop will repeat forever.

- Remember that loops differ from `if` because the body of an `if` executes only once instead of many times if the *condition* is true.

- Don't put a semicolon after the `while` *condition*'s closing parenthesis. If you do, an infinite loop will occur.

15

LOOKING FOR ANOTHER WAY TO CREATE LOOPS

Another type of C loop is called the `for` loop. A `for` loop offers more control than `while` and `do-while`. With a `for` loop, you can specify exactly how many times you want to loop; with `while` loops, you must continue looping as long as a condition is true.

C programs have room for all three kinds of loops. Sometimes one loop fits one program's requirements better than another. For example, if you wrote a program to handle customer orders as customers purchase items from the inventory, you would need to use a `while` loop. The program would process orders *while* customers came through the door. If 100 customers happened to buy things, the `while` loop would run 100 times. At the end of the day, you might want to add the 100 customer purchases to get a total for the day. You could then use a `for` loop because you would then know exactly how many times to loop.

NOTE By incrementing counter variables, you can simulate a `for` loop with a `while` loop. You also can simulate a `while` with a `for`! Therefore, the kind of loop you use ultimately depends on which kind you feel comfortable with at the time.

for Repeat's Sake!

As you can see from the lame title of this section, the `for` loop is important for controlling repeating sections of code. The format of `for` is a little strange:

```
for (startExpression; testExpression; countExpression)

{ block of one or more C statements; }
```

Perhaps a short example with actual code is easier to understand:

```
for (ctr = 1; ctr <= 5; ctr++)
{
    printf("Counter is at %d.\n", ctr);
}
```

If you are looking at the code and thinking that it's a bit familiar, you are right. This code would be the beginning of a fifth version of the count up/count down program, but one that used a `for` loop instead. Here's how this `for` statement works: When the `for` begins, the *startExpression*, which is `ctr = 1;`, executes. The *startExpression* is executed *only once* in any `for` loop. The *testExpression* is then tested. In this example, the *testExpression* is `ctr<= 5;`. If it is true—and it will be true the first time in this code—the body of the `for` loop executes. When the body of the loop finishes, the *countExpression* is executed (`ctr` is incremented).

TIP As you can see, indenting the body of a `for` loop helps separate the body of the loop from the rest of the program, making the loop more readable. (The same is true for the other kinds of loops, such as `do-while` loops.)

That's a lot to absorb in one full swoop, even in one paragraph. Let's make it easy. Follow the line in Figure 15.1, which shows the order in which `for` executes. While following the line, reread the preceding paragraph. It should then make more sense to you.

```
for(ctr=1;ctr <=10;ctr++)

   {printf("Still counting...");
   printf("%d.\n", ctr);


   }
```

FIGURE 15.1

Following the order of for.

 NOTE   The for loop's format is strange because of the embedded semicolons that are required. It is true that semicolons go only at the end of executable statements, but statements inside for loops *are* executable. For instance, the initial expression, ctr = 1;, is completed before the loop begins, as Figure 15.1 shows.

Here is the very same loop written as a while statement:

```
ctr = 1;
while (ctr <= 5)
{
       printf("Counter is at %d.\n", ctr);
       ctr++;
}
```

Here is the output of this code:

```
Counter is at 1.
Counter is at 2.
Counter is at 3.
Counter is at 4.
Counter is at 5.
```

 TIP   If you follow Figure 15.1's guiding line and read the preceding while loop, you'll see that the for and while do the same thing. The ctr = 1; that precedes the while is the first statement executed in the for.

A do-while loop can't really represent the for loop because the relational test is performed *before* the body of the for loop and after it in the do-while. As you might recall from the end of Chapter 14, "Code Repeat—Using Loops to Save Time and Effort," the do-while test always resides at the bottom of the loop.

Working with for

The for loop reads a lot like the way you speak in everyday life. Consider this statement:

For each of our 45 employees, calculate the pay and print a check.

This statement leaves no room for ambiguity. There will be 45 employees, 45 pay calculations, and 45 checks printed. To make this loop work for even more companies, the program could prompt the user to enter how many employees will need to have payroll calculations and then use that entry for the loop as follows:

```
printf("How many employees in the organization? ");
scanf(" %d", &employees);


// Loop to calculate payroll for each employee
for (i=1; i <= employees; i++;)
{
        // Calculations for each employee follow...
```

for loops don't always count *up* as the preceding two did. This for loop counts *down* before printing a message:

```
for (cDown = 10; cDown >0; cDown--)
{
        printf("%d.\n", cDown);
}
printf("Blast off!\n");
```

Here is the output of this code:

```
10
9
8
7
6
5
```

```
4
3
2
1
Blast off!
```

WARNING   If the last expression in the `for` parentheses decrements in some way, the initial value must be greater than the test value for the loop to execute. In the previous `for` statement, the initial value of `10` is greater than the *testExpression*'s `0` comparison.

You also do not have to increase or decrease your loop counter by 1. The following `for` loop counts up by threes, beginning with `1`:

```
for (i = 1; i < 18; i += 3)
{
        printf("%d ", i); // Prints 1, 4, 7, 10, 13, 16
}
```

The following code produces an interesting effect:

```
for (outer = 1; outer <= 3; outer++)
{
        for (inner = 1; inner <= 5; inner++)
        {
                printf("%d ", inner)
        }
        // Print a newline when each inner loop finishes
        printf("\n");
}
```

Here is the code's output:

```
1 2 3 4 5
1 2 3 4 5
1 2 3 4 5
```

If you put a `for` loop in the body of another loop, you are *nesting* the loops. In effect, the inner loop executes as many times as the outer loop dictates. You might need a nested `for` loop if you wanted to print three lists of your top five customers. The outer loop would move from 1 to 3, while the inner loop would print the top five customers.

Here's a full program that executes a `for` loop based on the number of movies a user has claimed to see in the current year. It asks for the name of the movie and a rating on a scale of 1 to 10. It then tells the user what movie was ranked as a favorite and what movie was the least favorite:

```c
// Example program #1 from Chapter 15 of Absolute Beginner's Guide
// to C, 3rd Edition
// File Chapter15ex1.c


/* This program will ask users how many movies they've seen this
year, and then loop through asking the name of each movie and a
rating from 1 to 10. It will remember their favorite movie and their
least favorite movie. */

#include <stdio.h>
#include <string.h>

main()
{

    int ctr, numMovies, rating, favRating, leastRating;
    char movieName[40], favorite[40], least[40];

    //initialize the favRating to 0 so any movie with any rating of
    // 1 or higher will replace it and the leastRating to 10 so any
    // movie rated 9 or lower will replace it

    favRating = 0;
    leastRating = 10;

    // Find out how many movies the user has seen and can rate
    // The loop will continue until they enter a number more than 0

    do {
        printf("How many movies have you seen this year? ");
        scanf(" %d", &numMovies);

        // If the user enters 0 or a negative number, the program
```

```
        // will remind them to enter a positive number and prompt
        // them again

        if (numMovies < 1)
        {
            printf("No movies! How can you rank them?\nTry again!\
n\n");
        }
    } while (numMovies < 1);

    for (ctr = 1; ctr <= numMovies; ctr++)
        {
            //Get the name of the movie and the user's rating

            printf("\nWhat was the name of the movie? ");
            printf("(1-word titles only!) ");
            scanf(" %s", movieName);
            printf("On a scale of 1 to 10, what would ");
            printf("you rate it? ");
            scanf(" %d", &rating);

            //Check whether it's their best-rated movie so far
            if (rating > favRating)
            {
                strcpy(favorite, movieName);
                favRating = rating;
            }

            //Check whether it's their worst-rated movie so far
            if (rating < leastRating)
            {
                strcpy(least, movieName);
                leastRating = rating;
            }
        }
```

```
        printf("\nYour Favorite Movie was %s.\n", favorite);
        printf("\nYour Least-favorite Movie was %s.\n", least);

        return 0;

    }
```

Here is a sample output from the program:

```
How many movies have you seen this year? 5

What was the name of the movie? (1-word titles only!) Veranda
On a scale of 1 to 10, what would you rate it? 7

What was the name of the movie? (1-word titles only!) Easiness
On a scale of 1 to 10, what would you rate it? 3

What was the name of the movie? (1-word titles only!) TheJuggler
On a scale of 1 to 10, what would you rate it? 5

What was the name of the movie? (1-word titles only!) Kickpuncher
On a scale of 1 to 10, what would you rate it? 8

What was the name of the movie? (1-word titles only!) Celery
On a scale of 1 to 10, what would you rate it? 8

Your Favorite Movie was Kickpuncher

Your Least-favorite Movie was Easiness
```

Now, this program is a little long, but you should be able to follow it line by line, and the comments should help as well. It also combines the use of a `do-while` loop, a `for` loop, and some data tests using `if` statements. The first `if` statement serves as a data tester. You are asking users how many movies they've seen, and the code then loops through that number of movies to get titles and ratings. If the user enters 0 (or mistakenly enters a negative number), there will be no loop, so you give the user a chance to enter a correct number with a `do-while` loop.

Assigning 0 to `favRating` and 10 to `leastRating` might seem confusing at first, but once you are in the loop getting movie names and ratings, you need a baseline to compare each movie's rating. Initially, you want the lowest possible rating for favorite so that any movie rated will become the favorite, and you want the highest possible rating for least favorite so that any movie rated will become the least favorite. This means that the first movie (in the code sample, *Veranda*) will become both the favorite and the least favorite movie of the user. But that makes sense—if you only saw one movie, it would be both the best and the worst, until you had something to compare.

When you enter additional movies, the two `if` statements in the loop see whether you liked the next movie more or less than your current top and bottom movies and make the appropriate change. In the code sample, the second movie, *Easiness*, had a rating of 3. This rating is not higher than *Veranda*'s 7, so *Veranda* remains the highest movie; now *Easiness* is the least favorite movie.

You will be able to account for a few issues with this program as you learn more about C. First is the limitation of `scanf()` when dealing with strings—it can only take one word without spaces. Obviously, most movies have multiple words in the title. When you learn additional input/output methods later in this book, you can adjust for this problem.

When you learn about other arrays, including pointer arrays, you will be able to keep all the movie names in a program like this. You will also learn how to sort data, so you can revisit this program and print a ranking of your favorite movies instead of listing just a favorite and a least favorite. The last problem also would be fixed with this listing because the program saves only one movie for each ranking; if the user enters two equal values (such as `Kickpuncher` and `Celery`, in the sample output), only one can be listed as a favorite.

THE ABSOLUTE MINIMUM

The goal of this chapter was to show you an additional way to form a loop of statements in C. The `for` statement gives you a little more control over the loop than either `while` or `do-while`. The `for` statement controls a loop with a variable that is initialized and changed according to the expressions in the `for` statement. Key concepts in this chapter include:

- Use a `for` loop when you want to increment or decrement a variable through a loop.

- Remember that the `for` loop's relational test is performed at the top of the loop.

- Use a nested loop if you want to loop a certain number of times.

- Don't forget the semicolons inside the `for` loop—`for` requires them.

- Don't use an initial value that is less than the test value if you want to count down with `for`.

16

BREAKING IN AND OUT OF LOOPED CODE

This chapter doesn't teach you how to use another kind of loop. Instead, this chapter extends the information you learned in the last two chapters. You have ways available to control the `while` loop in addition to a relational test, and you can change the way a `for` loop operates via means other than the counter variable.

The `break` and `continue` statements let you control loops for those special occasions when you want to quit a loop early or repeat a loop sooner than it would normally repeat.

Take a break

The break statement rarely, if ever, appears on a line by itself. Typically, break appears in the body of an if statement. The reason for this will be made clear shortly. Here is the format of break:

```
break;
```

 NOTE break is easy, isn't it? Yep, not much to it. However, keep in mind that break usually resides in the body of an if. In a way, if is the first part of almost every break.

break always appears inside a loop. The purpose of break is to terminate the current loop. When a loop ends, the code following the body of the loop takes over. When break appears inside a loop's body, break terminates that loop immediately, and the rest of the program continues.

Here is a for loop that normally would print 10 numbers. Instead of printing 10, however, the break causes the loop to stop after printing 5 numbers.

```
for (i=0; i < 10; i++)
{
        printf("%d ", i)
        if (i == 4)
        {
                break;
        }
}
// Rest of program would follow.
```

As a real-world example, suppose a teacher wrote a program to average the 25 students' test scores. The following program keeps a running total of the 25 students. However, if a student or two missed the test, the teacher wouldn't want to average the entire 25 student scores. If the teacher enters a -1.0 for a test score, the -1.0 triggers the break statement and the loop terminates early.

```
// Example program #1 from Chapter 16 of Absolute Beginner's Guide
// to C, 3rd Edition
// File Chapter16ex1.c
```

```c
/* This program will ask users to input test grades for the 25
students in a class and then compute an average test grade. If fewer
than 25 students took the test, the user can enter -1 as a grade
and break the loop, and only those entered grades will be used to
compute the average. */

#include <stdio.h>

main()
{

    int numTest;
    float stTest, avg, total = 0.0;

    // Asks for up to 25 tests

    for (numTest = 0; numTest < 25; numTest++)
        {
            // Get the test scores, and check if -1 was entered

            printf("\nWhat is the next student's test score? ");
            scanf(" %f", &stTest);
            if (stTest < 0.0)
            {
              break;
            }
            total += stTest;
        }

    avg = total / numTest;
    printf("\nThe average is %.1f%%.\n", avg);

    return 0;

}
```

Before discussing the program, take a look at a sample run of it:

```
What is the next student's test score? 89.9
What is the next student's test score? 92.5
What is the next student's test score? 51.0
What is the next student's test score? 86.4
What is the next student's test score? 78.6
What is the next student's test score? -1


The average is 79.7%
```

The teacher had a lot of sick students that day! If all 25 students had shown up, the `for` loop would have ensured that exactly 25 test scores were asked for. However, because only five students took the test, the teacher had to let the program know, via a negative number in this case, that she was done entering the scores and that she now wanted an average.

TIP   To print the percent sign at the end of the final average, two `%` characters have to be used in the `printf()` control string. C interprets a percent sign as a control code unless you put two of them together, as done in this program. Then it still interprets the first percent sign as a control code for the second. In other words, the percent sign is a control code for itself.

WARNING   `break` simply offers an early termination of a `while`, `do-while`, or `for` loop. `break` can't exit from `if`, which isn't a loop statement. Figure 16.1 helps show the action of `break`.

```
printf("How many numbers do you want to see?");
scanf("%d",&num);
for (i=1; i<10;i++)
          {
            printf("Counting up...%d\n" ,i);
            if (i== num)
                {break;}
          }
        /* Rest of program follows*/
```

Normal flow of the loop

If break executes

FIGURE 16.1

`break` *terminates a loop earlier than usual.*

Let's continue Working

Whereas break causes a loop to *break* early, continue forces a loop to *continue* early. (So *that's* why they're named that way!) Depending on the complexity of your for, while, or do-while loop, you might not want to execute the *entire body of the loop every iteration*. continue says, in effect, "C, please ignore the rest of this loop's body this iteration of the loop. Go back up to the top of the loop and start the next loop cycle."

 TIP   The word *iteration* is a fancy computer name for the cycle of a loop. Programmers sometimes think they will keep their jobs if they use words that nobody else understands.

The following program shows off continue nicely. The program contains a for loop that counts from 1 to 10. If the loop variable contains an odd number, the message I'm rather odd... prints, and the continue instructs C to ignore the rest of the loop body because it prints Even up! for the even numbers that are left.

```
// Example program #2 from Chapter 16 of Absolute Beginner's Guide
// to C, 3rd Edition
// File Chapter16ex2.c

/* This program loops through 10 numbers and prints a message that
   varies whether the program is odd or even. It tests for odd and
   if the number is odd, it prints the odd message and then starts
   the next iteration of the loop using continue. Otherwise, it
   prints the even message. */

#include <stdio.h>

main()
{

    int i;

    // Loops through the numbers 1 through 10

    for (i = 1; i <= 10; i++)
        {
```

```
            if ((i%2) == 1) // Odd numbers have a remainder of 1
            {
              printf("I'm rather odd...\n");
              // Will jump to the next iteration of the loop
              continue;
            }
            printf("Even up!\n");
        }


    return 0;


    }
```

Here is the program's output:

```
I'm rather odd...
Even up!
I'm rather odd...
Even up!
I'm rather odd...
Even up!
I'm rather odd...
Even up!
I'm rather odd...
Even up!
```

 NOTE As with `break`, `continue` is rarely used without a preceding `if` statement of some kind. If you *always* wanted to continue, you wouldn't have entered the last part of the loop's body. You want to use `continue` only in some cycles of the loop.

THE ABSOLUTE MINIMUM

The goal of this chapter was to teach you how to control loops better with the break and continue statements. The while, do-while, and for loops all can be terminated early with break or continued early with continue. Key concepts covered in this chapter included the following:

- Use break to terminate for, while, or do-while loops early.

- Use continue to force a new cycle of a loop.

- Don't use break or continue without some sort of relational test before them.

17

IN THIS CHAPTER

- Testing multiple cases with `switch`
- Combining `break` with `switch`

MAKING THE case FOR THE switch STATEMENT

The `if` statement is great for simple testing of data, especially if your data tests have only two or three possibilities. You can use `if` to test for more than two values, but if you do, you have to nest several `if` statements inside one another, and that can get confusing and hard to maintain.

Consider for a moment how you execute code based on a user's response to a menu. A menu is a list of options from which to select, such as this one:

```
What do you want to do?
1. Add New Contact
2. Edit Existing Contact
3. Call Contact
4. Text Contact
5. Delete Contact
6. Quit the Program
What is your choice?
```

NOTE When you create menus that ask for user input, you are creating a user interface.

It would take five `if-else` statements, nested inside one another, to handle all these conditions, as you can see here:

```
if (userAns == 1)
      {
                // Perform the Add Contact Routine
      }
else if (userAns == 2)
      {
               //Perform the Edit Contact Routine
      }
else if (userAns == 3)
      {
               //Perform the Call Contact Routine
      }
else if (userAns == 4)
      {
               //Perform the Text Contact Routine
      }
else if (userAns == 5)
      {
               //Perform the Delete Contact Routine
      }
else
      {
               //Perform the Quit Routine
      }
```

Nothing is wrong with nested `if` statements, but the C `switch` statement is clearer for multiple conditions.

Making the `switch`

The `switch` statement has one of the longest formats of any statement in C (or just about any other language). Here is the format of `switch`:

```
switch (expression)
{
        case (expression1): { one or more C statements; }
        case (expression2): { one or more C statements; }
        case (expression3): { one or more C statements; }
// This would keep going for however many case statements to test
        default: { one or more C statements; }
```

TIP   As with most statements, the actual use of `switch` is a lot less intimidating than its format leads you to believe.

The menu shown earlier is perfect for a series of function calls. The problem is that this book has not yet discussed function calls, except for a handful of built-in functions such as `printf()` and `scanf()`. The following simple program uses a `switch` statement to print an appropriate message, depending on the choice the user makes.

TIP   Ordinarily, a function call would replace the `printf()` statements you see after each `case`. After you read Chapter 31, "Passing Variables to Your Functions," you'll understand how to use function calls to perform `case` actions.

```
// Example program #1 from Chapter 17 of Absolute Beginner's Guide
// to C, 3rd Edition
// File Chapter17ex1.c


/* This program presents a menu of choices, gets the user's choice,
and then uses the switch statement to execute a line or two of code
based on that choice. (What the user wants to do is not truly
implemented -it is just a series of stubs to teach the value of the
switch statement. */


#include <stdio.h>
#include <stdlib.h>
```

```c
main()
{

    int choice;

    printf("What do you want to do?\n");
    printf("1. Add New Contact\n");
    printf("2. Edit Existing Contact\n");
    printf("3. Call Contact\n");
    printf("4. Text Contact\n");
    printf("5. Exit\n");
    do
    {

        printf("Enter your choice: ");
        scanf(" %d", &choice);
        switch (choice)
        {
            case (1): printf("\nTo add you will need the );
                      printf("contact's\n");
                      printf("First name, last name, and number.\n");
                      break;
            case (2): printf("\nGet ready to enter the name of ");
                      printf("name of the\n");
                      printf("contact you wish to change.\n");
                      break;
            case (3): printf("\nWhich contact do you ");
                      printf("wish to call?\n");
                      break;
            case (4): printf("\nWhich contact do you ");
                      printf("wish to text?\n");
                      break;
            case (5): exit(1); //Exits the program early
            default:  printf("\n%d is not a valid choice.\n", choice);
                      printf("Try again.\n");
                      break;
```

```
        }
    } while ((choice < 1) || (choice > 5));

    return 0;


}
```

The case statements determine courses of action based on the value of choice. For example, if choice equals 3, the message Which contact do you wish to call? prints. If choice equals 5, the program quits using the built-in exit() function.

 WARNING   Anytime you need to terminate a program before its natural conclusion, use the exit() function. The value you place in the exit() parentheses is returned to your operating system. Most beginning programmers ignore the return value and put either a 0 or a 1 in the parentheses. You must remember to add <stdlib.h> with the #include directive in every program that uses exit().

The do-while loop keeps the user honest. If the user enters something other than a number from 1 to 5, the ...is not a valid choice. message prints, thanks to the default keyword. C ensures that if none of the other cases matches the variable listed after switch, the default statements execute.

default works like else, in a way. else takes care of an action if an if test is false, and default takes care of an action if none of the other case conditions successfully matches the switch variable. Although default is optional (as is else), it's good programming practice to use a default to handle unexpected switch values.

 TIP   The switch variable can be either an integer or a character variable. Do not use a float or a double for the switch test.

break and switch

The switch statement shown earlier has several break statements scattered throughout the code. The break statements ensure that only one case executes. Without the break statements, the switch would "fall through" to the other case statements. Here is what would happen if the break statements were removed from the switch and the user answered with a choice of 2:

```
Get ready to enter the name of the
contact you wish to change.
Which contact do you wish to call?
Which contact do you wish to text?
```

The break keeps switch case statements from running together.

NOTE The only reason the default condition's message did not print is that the exit() function executed inside case (5).

Efficiency Considerations

case statements don't have to be arranged in any order. Even default doesn't have to be the last case statement. As a matter of fact, the break after the default statement isn't needed as long as default appears at the end of switch. However, putting break after default helps ensure that you move both statements if you ever rearrange the case statements. If you were to put default higher in the order of case statements, default would require a break so that the rest of the case statements wouldn't execute.

TIP You can rearrange the case statements for efficiency. Put the most common case possibilities toward the top of the switch statement so that C doesn't have to search down into the case statements to find a matching case.

Let's add a second program to demonstrate the switch statement, as well as a program that uses two levels of menus.

```
// Example program #2 from Chapter 17 of Absolute Beginner's Guide to
// C, 3rd Edition
// File Chapter17ex2.c


/* This program presents a menu of choices (three different decades),
gets the user's choice, and then presents a secondary menu (sports,
entertainment, and politics).
When the user makes her second choice, it prints a list of key
information from that specific decade in that specific category. */
```

```c
#include <stdio.h>
#include <stdlib.h> //Remember, if you plan to use exit(), you need
                    // this header file

main()
{

    // Despite being a long program, you only need two variables:
    // one for the first menu and one for the second

    int choice1;
    int choice2;



    // The potential decade choices

    printf("What do you want to see?\n");
    printf("1. The 1980's\n");
    printf("2. The 1990's\n");
    printf("3. The 2000's\n");
    printf("4. Quit\n");

    // The top-menu choice and the switch statement that makes the
    // resulting
    // information appear are encased in a do-while loop that
    // ensures one
    // of the 4 menu choices are made
    do
    {

        printf("Enter your choice: ");
        scanf(" %d", &choice1);
        switch (choice1)
        {
            // In the first case, the user picked the 1980s. Now it
            // time to see what specific info they need.
```

```
case (1):
{
    printf("\n\nWhat would you like to see?\n");
    printf("1. Baseball\n");
    printf("2. The Movies\n");
    printf("3. US Presidents\n");
    printf("4. Quit\n");

    printf("Enter your choice: ");
    scanf(" %d", &choice2);

    if (choice2 == 1)
    {
        printf("\n\nWorld Series Champions ");
        printf("of the 1980s:\n");
        printf("1980: Philadelphia Phillies\n");
        printf("1981: Los Angeles Dodgers\n");
        printf("1982: St. Louis Cardinals\n");
        printf("1983: Baltimore Orioles\n");
        printf("1984: Detroit Tigers\n");
        printf("1985: Kansas City Royals\n");
        printf("1986: New York Mets\n");
        printf("1987: Minnesota Twins\n");
        printf("1988: Los Angeles Dodgers\n");
        printf("1989: Oakland A's\n");
        printf("\n\n\n");
        break;
    } else if (choice2 == 2)
    {
        printf("\n\nOscar-Winning Movies in the 1980s:\n");
        printf("1980: Ordinary People\n");
        printf("1981: Chariots of Fire\n");
        printf("1982: Gandhi\n");
        printf("1983: Terms of Endearment\n");
        printf("1984: Amadeus\n1985: Out of Africa\n");
        printf("1986: Platoon\n");
```

```
            printf("1987: The Last Emperor\n");
            printf("1988: Rain Man\n");
            printf("1989: Driving Miss Daisy");
            printf("\n\n\n");
            break;
        } else if (choice2 == 3)
        {
            printf("\n\nUS Presidents in the 1980s:\n");
            printf("1980: Jimmy Carter\n");
            printf("1981-1988: Ronald Reagan\n");
            printf("1989: George Bush\n");
            printf("\n\n\n");
            break;
        } else if (choice2 == 4)
        {
            exit(1);
        } else
        {
            printf("Sorry, that is not a valid choice!\n");
            break;
        }
    }


// This case is for the 1990s.
// Unlike the top menu, there isn't a data-validation
// do-while loop

case (2):
{
    printf("\n\nWhat would you like to see?\n");
    printf("1. Baseball\n");
    printf("2. The Movies\n");
    printf("3. US Presidents\n");
    printf("4. Quit\n");

    printf("Enter your choice: ");
```

```c
    scanf(" %d", &choice2);

    if (choice2 == 1)
    {
        printf("\n\nWorld Series Champions of ");
        printf("the 1990s:\n");
        printf("1990: Cincinnati Reds\n");
        printf("1991: Minnesota Twins\n");
        printf("1992: Toronto Blue Jays\n");
        printf("1993: Toronto Blue Jays\n");
        printf("1994: No World Series\n");
        printf("1995: Atlanta Braves\n");
        printf("1996: New York Yankees\n");
        printf("1997: Florida Marlins\n");
        printf("1998: New York Yankees\n");
        printf("1999: New York Yankees\n");
        printf("\n\n\n");
        break;
    } else if (choice2 == 2)
    {
        printf("\n\nOscar-Winning Movies in ");
        printf("the 1990s:\n");
        printf("1990: Dances with Wolves\n");
        printf("1991: The Silence of the Lambs\n");
        printf("1992: Unforgiven\n");
        printf("1993: Schindler's List\n");
        printf("1996: The English Patient\n");
        printf("1997: Titanic\n");
        printf("1998: Shakespeare in Love\n");
        printf("1999: American Beauty\n");
        printf("\n\n\n");
        break;
    } else if (choice2 == 3)
    {
        printf("\n\nUS Presidents in the 1990s:\n");
        printf("1990-1992: George Bush\n");
```

```c
            printf("1993-1999: Bill Clinton\n");
            printf("\n\n\n");
            break;
    } else if (choice2 == 4)
    {
            exit(1);
    } else
    {
            printf("Sorry, that is not a valid choice!\n");
            break;
    }
}


// The section for when the user selects the 2000s
case (3):
{
    printf("\n\nWhat would you like to see?\n");
    printf("1. Baseball\n");
    printf("2. The Movies\n");
    printf("3. US Presidents\n");
    printf("4. Quit\n");

    printf("Enter your choice: ");
    scanf(" %d", &choice2);

    if (choice2 == 1)
    {
            printf("\n\nWorld Series Champions of ");
            printf("the 2000s:\n");
            printf("2000: New York Yankees\n");
            printf("2001: Arizona Diamondbacks\n");
            printf("2002: Anaheim Angels\n");
            printf("2003: Florida Marlins\n");
            printf("2004: Boston Red Sox\n");
            printf("2005: Chicago White Sox\n");
            printf("2006: St. Louis Cardinals\n");
```

```
        printf("2007: Boston Red Sox\n");
        printf("2008: Philadelphia Phillies\n");
        printf("2009: New York Yankees\n");
        printf("\n\n\n");
        break;
    } else if (choice2 == 2)
    {
        printf("\n\nOscar-Winning Movies in ");
        printf("the 2000s:\n");
        printf("2000: Gladiator\n");
        printf("2001: A Beautiful Mind\n");
        printf("2002: Chicago\n2003: The ");
        printf("Lord of the Rings: The ");
        printf("Return of the King\n");
        printf("2004: Million Dollar Baby\n");
        printf("2005: Crash\n");
        printf("2006: The Departed\n");
        printf("2007: No Country for Old Men\n");
        printf("2008: Slumdog Millionaire\n");
        printf("2009: The Hurt Locker\n");

        printf("\n\n\n");
        break;
    } else if (choice2 == 3)
    {
        printf("\n\nUS Presidents in the 2000s:\n");
        printf("2000: Bill Clinton\n");
        printf("2001-2008: George Bush\n");
        printf("2009: Barrack Obama\n");
        printf("\n\n\n");
        break;
    } else if (choice2 == 4)
    {
        exit(1);
    } else
    {
```

```
            printf("Sorry, that is not a valid choice!\n");
            break;
        }
    }
    case (4):
        exit (1);

    default:  printf("\n%d is not a valid choice.\n",
                    choice1);
              printf("Try again.\n");
              break;
    }
} while ((choice1 < 1) || (choice1 > 4));

return 0;


}
```

Now, this might look intimidating at first glance, but consider a few things. First of all, you are more than halfway through this book, so have a little faith in your C knowledge. Second, long does not mean hard—just break down the code section by section, and you'll find nothing too intimidating in this code.

This program has two levels of menus to it. At the top menu, you are asking the user to select a specific decade: the 1980s, the 1990s, or the 2000s. After the user picks 1, 2, or 3 for the chosen decade (or 4 to quit the program), a switch statement sends the program to the next level of menus. The user then gets information about sports (specifically baseball), the movies, or U.S. presidents. Within each case section of code, if and else statements test the user's entry to present the information they want to see.

You might be thinking, "Hey, the switch statement was a great idea for the top menu—why not use it for the next level of menu choices as well?" Well, although you can nest if statements in other if statements and nest for statements within other for statements, nesting switch statements is not a good idea, particularly when the default choices start overlapping. It confuses your compiler, and the program will not run.

Another note is that, in the first program, you did not enter open and closing braces for the statements after each case (*expression*): statement, but here you did. The braces are not needed, but with more complex blocks of code, the braces can help keep things clear.

TIP You can replace the repeated code sections in the second-level menus with single lines of code when you learn to write your own functions later in the book.

THE ABSOLUTE MINIMUM

The goal of this chapter was to explain the C switch statement. switch analyzes the value of an integer or character variable and executes one of several sections of code called cases. You can write equivalent code using embedded if statements, but switch is clearer—especially when your program needs to analyze a user's response to a menu and execute sections of code accordingly. Key concepts from this chapter include:

- Use switch to code menu selections and other types of applications that need to select from a variety of values.

- Use an integer or character value in switch because float and double values can't be matched properly.

- Put a break statement at the end of each case chunk of code if you don't want the subsequent case statements to execute.

- Don't use nested if statements when a switch statement will work instead. switch is a clearer statement.

IN THIS CHAPTER

- Using `putchar()` and `getchar()`
- Dealing with the newline consideration
- Getting a little faster with `getch()`

18

INCREASING YOUR PROGRAM'S OUTPUT (AND INPUT)

You can produce input and output in more ways than with the `scanf()` and `printf()` functions. This chapter shows you some of C's built-in I/O functions that you can use to control I/O. You can use these simple functions to build powerful data-entry routines of your own.

These functions offer the *primitive* capability to input and output one character at a time. Of course, you also can use the `%c` format specifier with `scanf()` and `printf()` for single characters; however, the character I/O functions explained here are a little easier to use, and they provide some capabilities that `scanf()` and `printf()` don't offer.

`putchar()` and `getchar()`

`getchar()` gets a single character from the keyboard, and `putchar()` sends a single character to the screen. Figure 18.1 shows you what happens when you use these functions. They work basically the way you think they do. You can use them just about anytime you want to print or input a single character into a variable.

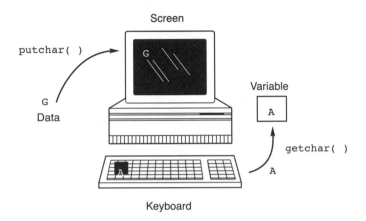

FIGURE 18.1

`getchar()` and `putchar()` input and output single characters.

TIP Always include the `stdio.h` header file when using this chapter's I/O functions, just as you do for `printf()` and `scanf()`.

The name `getchar()` sounds like "get character," and `putchar()` sounds like "put character." Looks as though the designers of C knew what they were doing!

The following program prints `C is fun`, one character at a time, using `putchar()` to print each element of the character array in sequence. Notice that `strlen()` is used to ensure that the `for` doesn't output past the end of the string.

```
// Example program #1 from Chapter 18 of Absolute Beginner's Guide
// to C, 3rd Edition
// File Chapter18ex1.c


/* This program is nothing more than a simple demonstration of the
putchar() function. */
```

```
// putchar() is defined in stdio.h, but string.h is needed for the
// strlen() function

#include <stdio.h>
#include <string.h>

main()
{
      int i;
      char msg[] = "C is fun";

      for (i = 0; i < strlen(msg); i++)
      {
            putchar(msg[i]); //Outputs a single character
      }
      putchar('\n'); // One line break after the loop is done.

      return(0);
}
```

The getchar() function returns the character input from the keyboard. Therefore, you usually assign the character to a variable or do something else with it. You can put getchar() on a line by itself, like this:

```
getchar();   /* Does nothing with the character you get */
```

However, most C compilers warn you that this statement is rather useless. The getchar() function would get a character from the keyboard, but then nothing would be done with the character.

Here is a program that gets one character at a time from the keyboard and stores the collected characters in a character array. A series of putchar() functions then prints the array backward.

```
// Example program #2 from Chapter 18 of Absolute Beginner's Guide
// to C, 3rd Edition
// File Chapter18ex2.c

/* This program is nothing more than a simple demonstration of the
getchar() function. */
```

```c
// getchar() is defined in stdio.h, but string.h is needed for the
// strlen() function

#include <stdio.h>
#include <string.h>

main()
{
      int i;
      char msg[25];

      printf("Type up to 25 characters and then press Enter...\n");
      for (i = 0; i < 25; i++)
      {
            msg[i] = getchar(); //Outputs a single character
             if (msg[i] == '\n')
             {
                  i--;
                  break;
             }
      }

      putchar('\n'); // One line break after the loop is done.

      for (; i >= 0; i--)
      {
            putchar(msg[i]);
      }

      putchar('\n');

      return(0);
}
```

NOTE   Notice that the second `for` loop variable `i` has no initial value. Actually, it does. `i` contains the last array subscript entered in the previous `getchar()` `for` loop. Therefore, the second `for` loop continues with the value of `i` left by the first `for` loop.

The `getchar()` input character typically is defined as an `int`, as done here. Integers and characters are about the only C data types you can use interchangeably without worry of typecasts. In some advanced applications, `getchar()` can return a value that won't work in a `char` data type, so you're safe if you use `int`.

Aren't you glad you learned about `break`? The program keeps getting a character at a time until the user presses Enter (which produces a newline `\n` escape sequence). `break` stops the loop.

The Newline Consideration

Although `getchar()` gets a single character, control isn't returned to your program until the user presses Enter. The `getchar()` function actually instructs C to accept input into a *buffer*, which is a memory area reserved for input. The buffer isn't released until the user presses Enter, and then the buffer's contents are released a character at a time. This means two things. One, the user can press the Backspace key to correct bad character input, as long as he or she hasn't pressed Enter. Two, the Enter keypress is left on the input buffer if you don't get rid of it.

Getting rid of the Enter keypress is a problem that all beginning C programmers must face. Several solutions exist, but none is extremely elegant. Consider the following segment of a program:

```
printf("What are your two initials?\n");
firstInit = getchar();
lastInit = getchar();
```

You would think that if the user typed *GT*, the `G` would go in the variable `firstInit` and the `T` would go in `lastInit`, but that's not what happens. The first `getchar()` doesn't finish until the user presses Enter because the `G` was going to the buffer. Only when the user presses Enter does the `G` leave the buffer and go to the program—but *then* the Enter is *still* on the buffer! Therefore, the second `getchar()` sends that Enter (actually, the `\n` that represents Enter) to `lastInit`. The `T` is still left for a subsequent `getchar()` (if there is one).

TIP   One way to fix this problem is to insert an extra
`getchar()` that captures the Enter but doesn't do anything
with it.

Here is a workaround for the initial-getting problem:

```
printf("What are your two initials?\n");
firstInit = getchar();
n1 = getchar();
lastInit = getchar();
n1 = getchar();
```

This code requires that the user press Enter between each initial. You don't have
to do anything with the `n1` variable because `n1` exists only to hold the in-between
newline. You don't even have to save the newline keypress in a variable. The following code works just like the last:

```
printf("What are your two initials?\n");
firstInit = getchar();
getchar();  // Discards the newline
lastInit = getchar();
getchar();  // Discards the newline
```

Some C compilers issue warning messages when you compile programs with
a standalone `getchar()` on lines by themselves. As long as you use these
`getchar()`s for discarding Enter keypresses, you can ignore the compiler warnings.

You also can request the two initials by requiring the Enter keypress *after* the user
enters the two initials, like this:

```
printf("What are your two initials?\n");
firstInit = getchar();
lastInit = getchar();
getchar();
```

If the user types *GP* and then presses Enter, the G resides in the `firstInit` variable and the P resides in the `lastInit` variable.

A Little Faster: `getch()`

A character input function named `getch()` helps eliminate the leftover Enter keypress that `getchar()` leaves. `getch()` is *unbuffered*—that is, `getch()` gets whatever keypress the user types immediately and doesn't wait for an Enter keypress. The drawback to `getch()` is that the user can't press the Backspace key to correct bad input. For example, with `getchar()`, a user could press Backspace if he or she typed a B instead of a D. The B would be taken off the buffer by the Backspace, and the D would be left for `getchar()` to get after the user pressed Enter. Because `getch()` does *not* buffer input, there is no chance of the user pressing Backspace. The following code gets two characters without an Enter keypress following each one:

```
printf("What are your two initials?\n");

firstInit = getch();

lastInit = getch();
```

`getch()` is a little faster than `getchar()` because it doesn't wait for an Enter keypress before grabbing the user's keystrokes and continuing. Therefore, you don't need a standalone `getch()` to get rid of the \n as you do with `getchar()`.

 WARNING `getch()` does *not* echo the input characters to the screen as `getchar()` does. Therefore, you must follow `getch()` with a mirror-image `putch()` if you want the user to see onscreen the character he or she typed. To echo the initials, you could do this:

```
printf("What are your two initials?\n");
firstInit = getch();

putch(firstInit);

lastInit = putch();

putch(lastInit);
```

The next chapter explains more built-in functions, including two that quickly input and output strings as easily as this chapter's I/O functions work with characters.

THE ABSOLUTE MINIMUM

This chapter's goal was to explain a few additional input and output functions. The functions presented here are character I/O functions. Unlike `scanf()` and `printf()`, the `getchar()`, `getch()`, `putchar()`, and `putch()` functions input and output single characters at a time. Key concepts from this chapter include:

- Use `getchar()` and `putchar()` to input and output single characters.

- Use a standalone `getchar()` to get rid of the Enter keypress if you don't want to capture it. You also can create a loop to call `getchar()` *until* the return value is \n, as shown in the sample code.

- Use `getch()` to get *unbuffered* single characters as soon as the user types them.

- Don't use a character I/O function with character variables. Use an `int` variable instead.

- Don't forget to print character input using `putch()` if you want that input echoed on the screen as the user types.

IN THIS CHAPTER

- Employing character-testing functions
- Checking whether the case is correct
- Adding case-changing functions
- Using string functions

19

GETTING MORE FROM YOUR STRINGS

This chapter shows you ways to take work off your shoulders and put it on C's. C includes many helpful built-in functions in addition to ones such as `strlen()`, `getchar()`, and `printf()` that you've read about so far.

Many more built-in functions exist than there is room for in a single chapter. This chapter explains the most common and helpful character and string functions. In the next chapter, you'll learn about some numeric functions.

Character-Testing Functions

C has several built-in *character-testing functions*. Now that you know how to use getchar() and getch() to get single characters, the character-testing functions can help you determine exactly what kind of input characters your program receives. You can set up if logic to execute certain courses of action based on the results of the character tests.

 TIP You must include the ctype.h header file at the top of any program that uses the character functions described in this chapter.

The isalpha() function returns true (which is 1 to C) if the value in its parentheses is an alphabetic character a through z (or the uppercase A through Z) and returns false (which is 0 to C) if the value in parentheses is any other character. Consider this if:

```c
if (isalpha(inChar))
{
        printf("Your input was a letter.\n");
}
```

The message prints only if inChar contains an alphabetic letter.

C has a corresponding function named isdigit() that returns true if the character in the parentheses is a number from 0 through 9. The following if prints A number if inChar contains a digit:

```c
if (isdigit(inChar))
{
        printf("A number\n");
}
```

 NOTE Do you see why these are called *character-testing* functions? Both isalpha() and isdigit() test character content and return the relational result of the test.

Is the Case Correct?

The isupper() and islower() functions let you know whether a variable contains an upper- or lowercase value. Using isupper() keeps you from having to write long if statements like this:

```
if ((inLetter >= 'A') && (inLetter <= 'Z'))
{
      printf("Letter is uppercase\n");
}
```

Instead, use isupper() in place of the logical comparison:

```
if (isupper(inLetter))
{
printf("Letter is uppercase\n");
}
```

 NOTE islower() tests for lowercase values in the same way as isupper() tests for uppercase values.

You might want to use isupper() to ensure that your user enters an initial-uppercase letter when entering names.

Here's a quick little program that gets a username and password and then uses the functions described in this chapter to check whether the password has an uppercase letter, a lowercase letter, and a number in it. If a user has all three, the program congratulates him or her for selecting a password with enough variety to make it harder to crack. If the password entered does not have all three categories, the program suggests that the user consider a stronger password.

```
// Example program #1 from Chapter 19 of Absolute Beginner's Guide
// to C, 3rd Edition
// File Chapter19ex1.c


/* This program asks a user for a username and a password. It tests
whether their password has an uppercase letter, lowercase letter,
and a digit. If it does, the program congratulates their selection.
If not, it suggests they might want to consider a password with more
variety for the sake of security. */

// stdio.h is needed for printf() and scanf()
// string.h is needed for strlen()
// ctype.h is needed for isdigit, isupper, and islower

#include <stdio.h>
#include <string.h>
```

```c
#include <ctype.h>

main()
{
        int i;
        int hasUpper, hasLower, hasDigit;
        char user[25], password[25];

    // Initialize all three test variables to 0 i.e. false

        hasUpper = hasLower = hasDigit = 0;

        printf("What is your username? ");
        scanf(" %s", user);

        printf("Please create a password: ");
        scanf(" %s", password);

        // This loop goes through each character of the password and
        // tests
        // whether it is a digit, upppercase letter, then lowercase
        // letter.

        for (i = 0; i < strlen(password) ; i++ )
        {
           if (isdigit(password[i]))
           {
              hasDigit = 1;
              continue;
           }
           if (isupper(password[i]))
           {
              hasUpper = 1;
              continue;
           }
           if (islower(password[i]))
```

```
        {
            hasLower = 1;
        }
    }


    /* The if portion will only execute if all three variables
below are 1, and the variables will only equal 1 if the appropriate
characters were each found */
  if ((hasDigit) && (hasUpper) && (hasLower))
            {
            printf("\n\nExcellent work, %s,\n", user);
            printf("Your password has upper and lowercase ");
            printf("letters and a number.");
  } else
  {
            printf("\n\nYou should consider a new password, %s,\n",
                user);
            printf("One that uses upper and lowercase letters ");
            printf("and a number.");
        }


    return(0);


}
```

Anyone creating a password these days gets a lecture about the need for a variety of letters, numbers, and, in some cases, characters in their password to make it difficult for hackers to crack their code. This program uses the functions listed in this chapter to check that a password has each of the three types of characters in an entered password by looping through the password character by character and testing each of the three types. If a specific character is one of those three types, a variable flag is set to 1 (TRUE in C parlance), and then the loop moves on.

In the case of the first two tests, after the variable flag (hasDigit or hasUpper) is set to 1, a continue statement starts the next version of the loop—after the character has been determined to be a digit, there is no need to run the next two tests (after all, it can't be more than one category, right?), so for efficiency's sake, skipping the subsequent tests makes sense. The last if code section does not need a continue statement because it is already at the end of the loop.

After all the characters in the password string have been tested, an `if` statement checks whether all three conditions were met. If so, it prints a congratulatory message. If not, it prints a different message.

 TIP Some passwords today also ask for at least one non-letter, non-number character (such as $, !, *, &, and so on). You could further refine this code to check for those by putting an `else` at the end of the final `islower` test. After all, if a character fails the first three tests, then it fits in this last category.

Case-Changing Functions

C has two important character-changing functions (also called *character-mapping functions*) that return their arguments changed a bit. Unlike `isupper()` and `islower()`, which only *test* character values and return a `true` or `false` result of the test, `toupper()` and `tolower()` return their arguments converted to a different case. `toupper()` returns its parentheses argument as uppercase. `tolower()` returns its parentheses argument as lowercase.

The following program segment prints `yes` or `no`, depending on the user's input. Without the `toupper()` function, you need an extra test to execute your plan:

```
if ((userInput == 'Y') || (userInput == 'y'))
        { printf("yes\n"); }
else
        { printf("no\n"); }
```

The next set of statements uses the `toupper()` function to streamline the `if` statement's logical test for lowercase letters:

```
if (toupper(userInput) == 'Y') // only need to test for upper case
        { printf("yes\n"); }
else
        { printf("no\n"); }
```

String Functions

The `string.h` header file contains descriptions for more functions than just `strcpy()` and `strlen()`. This section explains the `strcat()` function that lets you merge two character arrays, as long as the arrays hold strings. `strcat()` stands for *string concatenation*.

strcat() takes one string and appends it to—that is, adds it onto the end of—another string. This code fragment shows what happens with strcat():

```
char first[25] = "Katniss";
char last[25] = " Everdeen";
strcat(first, last); //Adds last to the end of first
printf("I am $s\n", first);
```

Here is the output of this code:

```
I am Katniss Everdeen
```

strcat() requires two string arguments. strcat() tacks the second string onto the end of the first one. The space appears before the last name only because the last array is initialized with a space before the last name in the second line.

 WARNING You are responsible for making sure that the first array is large enough to hold *both* strings. If you attempt to concatenate a second string to the end of another string, and the second string is not defined with enough characters to hold the two strings, strange and unpredictable results can happen.

Because the second argument for strcat() is not changed, you can use a string literal in place of a character array for the second argument, if you like.

The puts() and gets() functions provide an easy way to print and get strings. Their descriptions are in stdio.h, so you don't have to add another header file for puts() and gets(). puts() sends a string to the screen, and gets() gets a string from the keyboard. The following program demonstrates gets() and puts(). As you look through it, notice that neither printf() nor scanf() is required to input and print strings.

```
// Example program #2 from Chapter 19 of Absolute Beginner's Guide
// to C, 3rd Edition
// File Chapter19ex2.c


/* This program asks a user for their hometown and the two-letter
abbreviation of their home state. It then uses string concatenation
to build a new string with both town and state and prints it using
puts. */


// stdio.h is needed for puts() and gets()
// string.h is needed for strcat()
```

```c
#include <stdio.h>

main()
{

        char city[15];
        // 2 chars for the state abbrev. and one for the null zero
        char st[3];
        char fullLocation[18] = "";

        puts("What town do you live in? ");
        gets(city);

        puts("What state do you live in? (2-letter abbreviation)");
        gets(st);

        /* Concatenates the strings */
        strcat(fullLocation, city);
        strcat(fullLocation, ", "); //Adds a comma and space between
                                    // the city
        strcat(fullLocation, st); //and the state abbreviation

        puts("\nYou live in ");
        puts(fullLocation);
        return(0);
}
```

 TIP strcat() has to be used three times: once to add the city, once for the comma, and once to tack the state onto the end of the city.

Here is the output from a sample run of this program:

```
What town do you live in?
Gas City
What state do you live in? (2-letter abbreviation)
IN


You live in
Gas City, IN
```

`puts()` automatically puts a newline at the end of every string it prints. You don't have to add a \n at the end of an output string unless you want an extra blank line printed.

 TIP   `gets()` converts the Enter keypress to a null zero to ensure that the data obtained from the keyboard winds up being a null-terminated string instead of an array of single characters.

One of the most important reasons to use `gets()` over `scanf()` is that you can ask the user for strings that contain embedded spaces, such as a full name (first and last name). `scanf()` cannot accept strings with spaces; `scanf()` stops getting user input at the first space. Using the name of the city from the code example, Gas City, with a `scanf()` statement would have caused data-entry issues. This is the value of `gets()`. So if you went back to the favorite movie program in Chapter 15, "Looking for Another Way to Create Loops," and replaced the `scanf()` statement with `gets()`, you could allow the user to type in titles with more than one word.

THE ABSOLUTE MINIMUM

The goal of this chapter was to show you some built-in character and string functions that help you test and change strings. The string functions presented in this chapter work on both string literals and arrays. The character functions test for digits and letters, and convert uppercase and lowercase characters to their opposites. Key concepts from this chapter include:

- Use C's built-in character-testing and character-mapping functions so your programs don't have to work as hard to determine the case of character data.

- Use gets() to get strings and puts() to print strings.

- Use gets() when you must get strings that might contain spaces. Remember that scanf() cannot grab strings with spaces.

- Use strcat() to merge two strings.

- Don't concatenate two strings with strcat() unless you're positive that the first character array can hold the strings after they're merged.

- Don't put a newline inside the puts() string unless you want an extra line printed. puts() automatically adds a newline to the end of strings.

IN THIS CHAPTER

- Practicing your math
- Doing more conversions
- Getting into trig and other really hard stuff
- Getting random

20

ADVANCED MATH (FOR THE COMPUTER, NOT YOU!)

This chapter extends your knowledge of built-in functions to the numeric functions. C helps you do math that the C operators can't do alone. More than anything else, the C built-in numeric functions supply routines that you don't have to write yourself.

A lot of C's built-in math functions are highly technical—not that their uses are difficult, but their purposes might be. Unless you need trigonometric and advanced math functions, you might not find a use for many of the functions described in this chapter.

TIP Some people program in C for years and never need many of these functions. You should read this chapter's material to get an idea of what C can accomplish so you'll know what's available if you ever do need these powerful functions.

Practicing Your Math

All the functions this chapter describes require the use of the `math.h` header file. Be sure to include `math.h` along with `stdio.h` if you use a math function. The first few math functions are not so much math functions as they are numeric functions. These functions convert numbers to and from other numbers.

The `floor()` and `ceil()` functions are called the *floor* and *ceiling* functions, respectively. They "push down" and "push up" nonintegers to their next-lower or next-higher integer values. For example, if you wanted to compute how many dollar bills were in a certain amount of change (that includes dollars and cents), you could use `floor()` on the amount. The following code does just that:

```
change = amtPaid - cost; //These are all floating-point values
dollars = floor(change);
printf("The change includes %f dollar bills.\n", dollars);
```

 WARNING Although `ceil()` and `floor()` convert their arguments to integers, each function returns a `float` value. That's why the `dollars` variable was printed using the `%f` conversion code.

The `ceil()` function (which is the opposite of `floor()`) finds the next-highest integer. Both `ceil()` and `floor()` work with negative values, too, as the following few lines show:

```
lowVal1 = floor(18.5);  // Stores 18.0
lowVal2 = floor(-18.5);  // Stores -19.0
hiVal1 = ceil(18.5); // Stores 19.0
hiVal2 = ceil(-18.5); // Stores =18.0
```

 NOTE The negative values make sense when you think about the direction of negative numbers. The next integer *down* from −18.5 is −19. The next integer *up* from −18.5 is −18.

See, these functions aren't so bad, and they come in handy when you need them.

Doing More Conversions

Two other numeric functions convert numbers to other values. The `fabs()` function returns the floating-point *absolute value*. When you first hear about absolute value, it sounds like something you'll never need. The absolute value of a number, whether it is negative or positive, is the positive version of the number. Both of these `printf()` functions print 25:

```
printf("Absolute value of 25.0 is %.0f.\n", fabs(25.0));
printf("Absolute value of -25.0 is %.0f.\n", fabs(-25.0));
```

 NOTE   The floating-point answers print without decimal places because of the `.0` inside the `%f` conversion codes.

Absolute values are useful for computing differences in ages, weights, and distances. For example, the difference between two people's ages is always a positive number, no matter how you subtract one from the other.

Two additional mathematical functions might come in handy, even if you don't do heavy scientific and math programming. The `pow()` function raises a value to a power, and the `sqrt()` function returns the square root of a value.

 TIP   You can't compute the square root of a negative number. The `fabs()` function can help ensure that you don't try to do so by converting the number to a positive value before you compute the square root.

Perhaps a picture will bring back fond high school algebra memories. Figure 20.1 shows the familiar math symbols used for `pow()` and `sqrt()`.

If a C programmer does this:	A mathematician does this:
`x = pow(4, 6);`	$x = 4^{6 \times 6 \times 6 \times 6 \times 6 \times 6}$
`x = sqrt(value);`	$x = \sqrt{value}$

FIGURE 20.1

Looking at the math symbols for `pow()` *and* `sqrt()`.

The following code prints the value of 10 raised to the third power and the square root of 64:

```
printf("10 raised to the third power is %.0f.\n", pow(10.0, 3.0));
printf("The square root of 64 is %.0f.\n", sqrt(64));
```

Here is the output of these `printf()` functions:

```
10 raised to the 3rd power is 1000.
The square root of 64 is 8.
```

Getting into Trig and Other Really Hard Stuff

Only a handful of readers will need the trigonometric and logarithmic functions. If you know you won't, or if you hope you won't, go ahead and skip to the next section. Those of you who need them now won't require much explanation, so not much is given.

Table 20.1 explains the primary trigonometric functions. They each require an argument expressed in radians.

TABLE 20.1   C Trigonometric Functions

Function	Description
`cos(x)`	Returns the cosine of the angle x
`sin(x)`	Returns the sine of the angle x
`tan(x)`	Returns the tangent of the angle x
`acos(x)`	Returns the arc cosine of the angle x
`asin(x)`	Returns the arc sine of the angle x
`atan(x)`	Returns the arc tangent of the angle x

Again, it's unlikely you will need these functions, unless you want to relearn trigonometry (or have a child or relative taking the class and want to check their homework), but it's good to know the capabilities of your programming language.

 TIP   If you want to supply an argument in degrees instead of radians, you can convert from degrees to radians with this formula:

```
radians = degrees * (3.14159 / 180.0);
```

Table 20.2 shows the primary log functions.

TABLE 20.2 C Logarithmic Functions

Function	Description
e^{x}p(x)	Returns e, the base of the natural logarithm, raised to a power specified by x (e^x).
log(x)	Returns the natural logarithm of the argument x, mathematically written as ln(x). x must be positive.
log$_{10}$(x)	Returns the Base10 logarithm of the argument x, mathematically written as log10(x). x must be positive.

The following program uses the math functions described in this chapter:

```
// Example program #1 from Chapter 20 of Absolute Beginner's Guide
// to C, 3rd Edition
// File Chapter20ex1.c


/* This program demonstrates the math functions from the C math.h
library, so that you can get your homework right thanks to some
quick-and-easy programming. */


#include <stdio.h>
#include <string.h>
#include <math.h>



main()
{

    printf("It's time to do your math homework!\n");

    printf("Section 1: Square Roots\n");
    printf("The square root of 49.0 is %.1f\n", sqrt(49.0));
    printf("The square root of 149.0 is %.1f\n", sqrt (149.0));
    printf("The square root of .149 is %.2f\n", sqrt (.149));

    printf("\n\nSection 2: Powers\n");
    printf("4 raised to the 3rd power is %.1f\n", pow(4.0, 3.0));
    printf("7 raised to the 5th power is %.1f\n", pow(7.0, 5.0));
```

```
    printf("34 raised to the 1/2 power is %.1f\n", pow(34.0, .5));

    printf("\n\nSection 3: Trigonometry\n");
    printf("The cosine of a 60-degree angle is %.3f\n",
        cos((60*(3.14159/180.0))));
    printf("The sine of a 90-degree angle is %.3f\n",
        sin((90*(3.14159/180.0))));
    printf("The tangent of a 75-degree angle is %.3f\n",
        tan((75*(3.14159/180.0))));
    printf("The arc cosine of a 45-degree angle is %.3f\n",
        acos((45*(3.14159/180.0))));
    printf("The arc sine of a 30-degree angle is %.3f\n",
        asin((30*(3.14159/180.0))));
    printf("The arc tangent of a 15-degree angle is %.3f\n",
        atan((15*(3.14159/180.0))));

    printf("\nSection 4: Log functions\n");
    printf("e raised to 2 is %.3f\n", exp(2));
    printf("The natural log of 5 is %.3f\n", log(5));
    printf("The base-10 log of 5 is %.3f\n", log10(5));

    return(0);
}
```

Here is the output. Does C compute these values faster than you can with pencil and paper?

```
It's time to do your math homework!
Section 1: Square Roots
The square root of 49.0 is 7.0
The square root of 149.0 is 12.2
The square root of .149 is 0.39



Section 2: Powers
4 raised to the 3rd power is 64.0
7 raised to the 5th power is 16807.0
34 raised to the 1/2 power is 5.8
```

```
Section 3: Trigonometry
The cosine of a 60-degree angle is 0.500
The sine of a 90-degree angle is 1.000
The tangent of a 75-degree angle is 3.732
The arc cosine of a 45-degree angle is 0.667
The arc sine of a 30-degree angle is 0.551
The arc tangent of a 15-degree angle is 0.256


Section 4: Log functions
e raised to 2 is 7.389
The natural log of 5 is 1.609
The base-10 log of 5 is 0.699
```

Getting Random

For games and simulation programs, you often need to generate random values. C's built-in `rand()` function does just that. It returns a random number from 0 to 32767. The `rand()` function requires the `stdlib.h` (*standard library*) header file. If you want to narrow the random numbers, you can use `%` (the modulus operator) to do so. The following expression puts a random number from 1 to 6 in the variable `dice`:

```
dice = (rand() % 5) + 1;   /* From 1 to 6 */
```

 NOTE Because a die can have a value from 1 to 6, the modulus operator returns the integer division remainder (0 through 5), and then a 1 is added to produce a die value.

You must do one crazy thing if you want a *truly* random value.

To *seed* the random number generator means to give it an initial base value from which the `rand()` function can offset with a random number. Use `srand()` to seed the random number generator. The number inside the `srand()` parentheses must be different every time you run the program, unless you want to produce the same set of random values.

The trick to giving `srand()` a different number each run is to put the exact time of day inside the `srand()` parentheses. Your computer keeps track of the time of day, down to hundredths of a second. So first declare a time variable, using the `time_t` declaration, and then send its address (using the `&` character at the front of the variable name) to the `srand()` function.

NOTE You might always want a different set of random numbers produced each time a program runs. Games need such randomness. However, many simulations and scientific studies need to repeat the same set of random numbers. `rand()` will always do that if you don't seed the random number generator.

You must include `time.h` before seeding the random number generator with the time of day, as done here.

The bottom line is this: If you add the two weird-looking time statements, `rand()` will always be random and will produce different results every time you run a program.

As always, the best way to understand these types of functions is to see an example. The following code uses the `rand()` function to roll two dice and present the result. Then the user gets to decide whether a second roll of the dice is going to be higher, lower, or the same as the previous roll:

```
// Example program #2 from Chapter 20 of Absolute Beginner's Guide
// to C, 3rd Edition
// File Chapter19ex2.c


/* This program rolls two dice and presents the total. It then asks
the user to guess if the next total will be higher, lower, or equal.
It then rolls two more dice and tells the user how they did. */

#include <stdio.h>
#include <string.h>
#include <time.h>
#include <ctype.h>



main()
{

        int dice1, dice2;
        int total1, total2;
        time_t t;
        char ans;

        // Remember that this is needed to make sure each random number
        // generated is different
```

```
    srand(time(&t));



    // This would give you a number between 0 and 5, so the + 1
    // makes it 1 to 6

    dice1 = (rand() % 5) + 1;
    dice2 = (rand() % 5) + 1;
    total1 = dice1 + dice2;
    printf("First roll of the dice was %d and %d, ", dice1, dice2);
    printf("for a total of %d.\n\n\n", total1);

    do {
        puts("Do you think the next roll will be ");
        puts("(H)igher, (L)ower, or (S)ame?\n");
        puts("Enter H, L, or S to reflect your guess.");

        scanf(" %c", &ans);
        ans = toupper(ans);
        } while ((ans != 'H') && (ans != 'L') && (ans != 'S'));

    // Roll the dice a second time to get your second total

    dice1 = (rand() % 5) + 1;
    dice2 = (rand() % 5) + 1;
    total2 = dice1 + dice2;

    // Display the second total for the user

    printf("\nThe second roll was %d and %d, ", dice1, dice2);
    printf("for a total of %d.\n\n", total2);

    // Now compare the two dice totals against the user's guess
    // and tell them if they were right or not.

    if (ans == 'L')
```

```
    {
        if (total2 < total1)
        {
            printf("Good job! You were right!\n");
            printf("%d is lower than %d\n", total2, total1);
        }
        else
        {
            printf("Sorry! %d is not lower than %d\n\n", total2,
                    total1);
        }
    }
else if (ans == 'H')
    {
        if (total2 > total1)
        {
            printf("Good job! You were right!\n");
            printf("%d is higher than %d\n", total2, total1);
        }
        else
        {
            printf("Sorry! %d is not higher than %d\n\n", total2,
                    total1);
        }
    }
else if (ans == 'S')
    {
        if (total2 == total1)
        {
            printf("Good job! You were right!\n");
            printf("%d is the same as %d\n\n", total2, total1);
        }
        else
        {
            printf("Sorry! %d is not the same as %d\n\n",
                    total2, total1);
```

```
            }
        }

    return(0);
}
```

Not bad—you're not even two-thirds of the way through the book, and you can call yourself a game programmer! The program is a simple guessing game for users to predict how a second roll will total when compared to the original roll. The program gives the users one chance and then terminates after comparing the results and telling the user how successful that guess was. However, a simple do-while loop encompassing the entire program could change this so that users could keep playing as long as they want until they choose to quit. Why not try adding that loop?

THE ABSOLUTE MINIMUM

The goal of this chapter was to explain built-in math functions that can make numeric data processing easier. C contains a rich assortment of integer functions, numeric conversion functions, time and date functions, and random number–generating functions.

You don't have to understand every function in this chapter at this time. You might write hundreds of C programs and never use many of these functions. Nevertheless, they are in C if you need them.

- Use the built-in numeric functions when you can so that you don't have to write code to perform the same calculations.

- Many of the numeric functions, such as floor(), ceil(), and fabs(), convert one number to another.

- Be sure to seed the random number generator with the time of day if you want random numbers with rand() to be different every time you run a program.

- Don't feel that you must master the trig and log functions if you don't need them now. Many C programmers never use them.

- Don't use an integer variable to hold the return value from this chapter's math functions (unless you typecast the function return values); they return float or double values even though some, like ceil(), produce whole-number results.

21

DEALING WITH ARRAYS

The really nice thing about this chapter is that it covers absolutely nothing new. You've already worked with arrays throughout the book when storing strings in character arrays. This chapter simply hones that concept of arrays and demonstrates that you can create an array of any data type, not just the `char` data type.

As you know, an array of characters is just a list of characters that has a name. Similarly, an array of integers is just a list of integers that has a name, and an array of floating-point values is just a list of floating-point values that has a name. Instead of referring to each of the array elements by a different name, you refer to them by the array name and distinguish them with a subscript enclosed in brackets.

Reviewing Arrays

All arrays contain values called *elements*. An array can contain *only* elements that are of the same type. In other words, you can't have an array that has a floating-point value, a character value, and an integer value.

You define arrays almost the same way you define regular non-array variables. To define a regular variable, you only have to specify its data type next to the variable name:

```
int i;     /* Defines a non-array variable */
```

To define an array, you must add brackets ([]) after the name and specify the maximum number of elements you will ever store in the array:

```
int i[25];  /* Defines the array */
```

If you want to initialize a character array with an initial string, you know that you can do this:

```
char name[6] = "Italy";  /* Leave room for the null! */
```

 WARNING After you define an array to a certain size, don't try to store more elements than were allowed in the original size. After defining `name` as just done, the `strcpy()` function *lets* you store a string longer than `Italy` in name, but the result would be disastrous because other data in memory could be overwritten unintentionally. If another variable happened to be defined immediately after `name`, that other variable's data will be overwritten if you try to store a too-long string in `name`.

If the initial array needs to be larger than the initial value you assign, specify a larger array size when you define the array, like this:

```
char name[80] = "Italy";  /* Leaves lots of extra room */
```

Doing this makes room for a string much longer than `Italy` if you want to store a longer string in name. For example, you might want to use `gets()` to get a string from the user that could easily be longer than `Italy`.

Make your arrays big enough to hold enough values, but don't overdo it. Don't make your arrays larger than you think you'll really need. Arrays can consume a large amount of memory, and the more elements you reserve, the less memory you have for your program and other variables.

You can initialize an array one element at a time when you define an array by enclosing the array's data elements in braces and following the array name with an equals sign. For example, the following statement both defines an integer array *and* initializes it with five values:

```
int vals[5] = {10, 40, 70, 90, 120};
```

As a review, Figure 21.1 shows what `vals` looks like in memory after the definition. The numbers in brackets indicate subscripts. No null zero is at the end of the array because null zeroes terminate only strings stored in character arrays.

The `vals` array

10	vals[0]
40	vals[1]
70	vals[2]
90	vals[3]
120	vals[4]

FIGURE 21.1

After defining and initializing the `vals` *array.*

 NOTE   The first subscript of all C arrays begins at 0.

The following statement defines and initializes two arrays, a floating-point array and a double floating-point array. Because C is free-form, you can continue the initialization list over more than one line, as is done for `annualSal`.

```
float money[10] = {6.23, 2.45, 8.01, 2.97, 6.41};
double annualSal[6] = {43565.78, 75674.23, 90001.34,
                        10923.45, 39845.82};
```

You also can define and initialize a character array with individual characters:

```
char grades[5] = {'A', 'B', 'C', 'D', 'F'};
```

Because a null zero is not in the last character element, `grades` consists of individual characters, but not a string. If the last elements were initialized with `'\0'`, which represents the null zero, you could have treated `grades` as a string and printed it with `puts()`, or `printf()` and the `%s` conversion code. The following name definition puts a string in `name`:

```
char italCity[7] = {'V', 'e', 'r', 'o', 'n', 'a', '\0'};
```

You have to admit that initializing such a character array with a string is easier to do like this:

```
char italCity[7] = "Verona";   /* Automatic null zero */
```

We should be getting back to numeric arrays, which are the primary focus of this chapter. Is there a null zero at the end of the following array named nums?

```
int nums[4] = {5, 1, 3, 0};
```

There is *not* a null zero at the end of nums! Be careful—nums is not a character array, and a string is not being stored there. The zero at the end of the array is a regular numeric zero. The bit pattern (that's fancy computer lingo for the internal representation of data) is exactly like that of a null zero. But you would never treat nums as if there were a string in nums because nums is defined as an integer numeric array.

WARNING   Always specify the number of subscripts when you define an array. This rule has one exception, however: If you assign an initial value or set of values to the array *at the time you define the array*, you can leave the brackets empty:

```
int ages[5] = {5, 27, 65, 40, 92};   // Correct

int ages[];   // Incorrect

int ages[] = {5, 27, 65, 40, 92};   // Correct
```

NOTE   sizeof() returns the number of bytes you *reserved* for the array, *not* the number of elements in which you have stored a value. For example, if floating-point values consume 4 bytes on your computer, an 8-element floating-point array will take a total of 32 bytes of memory, and 32 is the value returned if you apply sizeof() to the array after you define the array.

If you want to zero out every element of an array, you can do so with a shortcut that C provides:

```
float amount[100] = {0.0};   /* Zeroes-out all of the array */
```

If you don't initialize an array, C won't either. Until you put values into an array, you have no idea exactly what's in the array. The only exception to this rule is that most C compilers zero out all elements of an array if you initialize at least one of the array's values when you define the array. The previous clue works because one value was stored in amount's first element's position and C filled in the rest with zeroes. (Even if the first elements were initialized with 123.45, C would have filled the remaining elements with zeroes.)

Putting Values in Arrays

You don't always know the contents of an array at the time you define it. Often array values come from a disk file, calculations, or a user's input. Character arrays are easy to fill with strings because C supplies the strcpy() function. You can fill other types of arrays a single element at a time. No shortcut function, such as strcpy(), exists to put a lot of integers or floating-point values in an array.

The following code defines an array of integers and asks the user for values that are stored in that array. Unlike regular variables that all have different names, array elements are easy to work with because you can use a loop to count the subscripts, as done here:

```c
int ages[3];

for (i = 0; i < 3; i++)
{
        printf("What is the age of child #%d? ", i+1);
        scanf(" %d", &ages[i]); // Gets next age from user
}
```

Now let's use a simple program that combines both methods of entering data in an array. This program keeps track of how many points a player scored in each of 10 basketball games. The first six scores are entered when the array is initialized, and then the user is asked for the player's scores for games 7–10. After all the data is entered, the program loops through the 10 scores to compute average points per game:

```c
// Example program #1 from Chapter 21 of Absolute Beginner's Guide
// to C, 3rd Edition
// File Chapter21ex1.c

/* This program creates an array of 10 game scores for a basketball
player.
```

The scores from the first six games are in the program and the scores From the last four are inputted by the user. */

```c
#include <stdio.h>


main()
{

    int gameScores[10] = {12, 5, 21, 15, 32, 10};
    int totalPoints = 0;
    int i;
    float avg;

    // Only need scores for last 4 games so the loop will cover
    // array elements 6-9
    for (i=6; i < 10; i++)
    {
        // Add one to the array number as the user won't think
        // of the first game as game 0, but game 1
        printf("What did the player score in game %d? ", i+1);
        scanf(" %d", &gameScores[i]);
    }

    // Now that you have all 10 scores, loop through the scores
    // to get total points in order to calculate an average.

    for (i=0; i<10; i++)
    {
        totalPoints += gameScores[i];
    }

    // Use a floating-point variable for the average as it is
    // likely to be between two integers
```

```
    avg = ((float)totalPoints/10);

    printf("\n\nThe Player's scoring average is %.1f.\n", avg);

    return(0);
}
```

A sample run through the program follows:

```
What did the player score in game 7? 21
What did the player score in game 8? 8
What did the player score in game 9? 11
What did the player score in game 10? 14


The Player's scoring average is 14.9
```

So this program is designed to show you two different ways you can add values to a variable array. It's a bit impersonal, so if you wanted, you could add a string array for the player's name at the beginning of the program; then the prompts for the individual game scores and the final average could incorporate that name. In the next two chapters, you learn how to search an array, as well as sort the data in the array, in case you want to list the player's scoring from best to worst.

 WARNING Don't make the same mistake we made. The first time we ran the program, we got a scoring average of 42,000 per game (which we are fairly certain would be a record for an individual player). Why did this happen? When we defined the variable totalPoints, we did not set it to 0 initially, and as we've reminded you throughout the book (but did not apply to our own program), you cannot assume that, just because you define a variable, it is initially empty or 0.

THE ABSOLUTE MINIMUM

The goal of this chapter was to teach you how to store data in lists called *arrays*. An array is nothing more than a bunch of variables. Each variable has the same name (the array name). You distinguish among the variables in the array (the array *elements*) with a numeric *subscript*. The first array element has a subscript of 0, and the rest count up from there.

Arrays are characterized by brackets that follow the array names. The array subscripts go inside the brackets when you need to refer to an individual array element. Key concepts from this chapter include:

- Use arrays to hold lists of values of the same data type.

- Refer to the individual elements of an array with a subscript.

- Write `for` loops if you want to "step through" every array element, whether it be to initialize, print, or change the array elements.

- In an array, don't use more elements than defined subscripts.

- Don't use an array until you have initialized it with values.

22

SEARCHING ARRAYS

You bought this book to learn C as painlessly as possible—and that's what has been happening. (You knew that *something* was happening, right?) Nevertheless, you won't become an ace programmer if you aren't exposed a bit to searching and sorting values. Complete books have been written on searching and sorting techniques, and the next two chapters present only the simplest techniques. Be forewarned, however, that before you're done, this chapter and the next one might raise more questions than they answer.

You'll find that this and the next chapter are a little different from a lot of the others. Instead of teaching you new C features, these chapters demonstrate the use of C language elements you've been learning throughout this book. These chapters focus on arrays. You will see applications of the array concepts you learned in Chapter 21, "Dealing with Arrays." After these chapters strengthen your array understanding, Chapter 25, "Arrays and Pointers," explains a C alternative to arrays that sometimes comes in handy.

Filling Arrays

As Chapter 21 mentioned, your programs use several means to fill arrays. Some arrays, such as the day counts in each of the 12 months, historical temperature readings, and last year's sales records, are known in advance. You might initialize arrays with such values when you define the arrays or when you use assignment statements.

You will also be filling arrays with values that your program's users enter. A customer order-fulfillment program, for example, gets its data only as customers place orders. Likewise, a scientific lab knows test values only after the scientists gather their results.

Other data values come from disk files. Customer records, inventory values, and school transcript information is just too voluminous for users to enter each time a program is run.

In reality, your programs can and will fill arrays using a combination of all three of these methods:

- Assignment
- User data entry
- Disk files

This book has to keep the programs simple. Until you learn about disk files, you'll see arrays filled with assignment statements and possibly simple user data entry (and *you'll* be the user!).

 NOTE At this point, it's important for you to concentrate on what you do with arrays after the arrays get filled with values. One of the most important things to do is *find* values that you put in the arrays.

Finders, Keepers

Think about the following scenario: Your program contains an array that holds customer ID numbers and an array that holds the same number of customer balances. Such arrays are often called *parallel arrays* because the arrays are in synch—that is, element number 14 in the customer ID array contains the customer number that owes a balance found in element 14 of the balance array.

The customer balance program might fill the two arrays from disk data when the program first starts. As a customer places a new order, it's your program's job to find that customer balance and stop the order if the customer owes more than $100 already (the deadbeat!).

In a nutshell, here is the program's job:

1. Ask for a customer ID number (the key).

2. Search the array for a customer balance that matches the key value.

3. Inform you if the customer already owes more than $100.

The following program does just that. Actually, the program maintains a list of only 10 customers because you're not yet ready to tackle disk input (but you're almost there!). The program initializes the arrays when the arrays are first defined, so maintaining only 10 array element pairs (the customer ID and the corresponding balance arrays) keeps the array definitions simple.

Study this program before typing it in and running it. See if you can get the gist of the program from the code and comments. Following this code listing is an explanation.

```
// Example program #1 from Chapter 22 of Absolute Beginner's Guide
// to C, 3rd Edition
// File Chapter22ex1.c


/* This program takes an ID number from the user and then checks the
ID against a list of customers in the database. If the customer
exists, it uses that array element to check their current balance,
and warns the user if the balance is more than 100 */


#include <stdio.h>

main()
{

    int ctr; // Loop counter
    int idSearch; // Customer to look for (the key)
    int found = 0; // Will be 1 (true) if customer is found


    // Defines the 10 elements in the two parallel arrays
```

```c
int custID[10] = {313, 453, 502, 101, 892,
                  475, 792, 912, 343, 633};
float custBal[10] = {0.00, 45.43, 71.23, 301.56, 9.08,
                     192.41, 389.00, 229.67, 18.31, 59.54};

/* Interact with the user looking for a balance. */
printf("\n\n*** Customer Balance Lookup ***\n");
printf("What customer number do you need to check? ");
scanf(" %d", &idSearch);

/* Search to see that the customer ID exists in the array */
for (ctr=0; ctr<10; ctr++)
{
    if (idSearch == custID[ctr])
    {
        found = 1;
        break;
    }
}

if (found)
{
    if (custBal[ctr] > 100.00)
    {
        printf("\n** That customer's balance is $%.2f.\n",
                custBal[ctr]);
        printf(" No additional credit.\n");
    }
    else
    {
        printf("\n** The customer's credit is good!\n");
    }
}
else
{
    printf("** You must have typed an incorrect customer ID.");
```

```
        printf("\n   ID %3d was not found in list.\n", idSearch);
    }

    return(0);
}
```

This program's attempted customer search has three possibilities:

- The customer's balance is less than $100.

- The customer's balance is too high (more than $100).

- The customer's ID is not even in the list.

Here are three runs of the program showing each of the three possibilities:

```
*** Customer Balance Lookup ***
What customer number do you need to check? 313


** The customer's credit is good!


***Customer Balance Lookup ***
What customer number do you need to check? 891
** You must have typed an incorrect customer ID.

   ID 891 was not found in list.


***Customer Balance Lookup***
What customer number do you need to check? 475


** That customer's balance is $192.41.
No additional credit
```

The first part of the program defines and initializes two arrays with the customer ID numbers and matching balances. As you know, when you first define arrays, you can use the assignment operator, =, to assign the array's data.

After printing a title and asking for a customer ID number, the program uses a `for` loop to step through the parallel arrays looking for the user's entered customer ID. If it discovers the ID, a `found` variable is set to `true` (1) for later use. Otherwise, `found` remains `false` (0).

TIP   The `found` variable is often called a *flag* variable because it flags (signals) to the rest of the program whether the customer ID was or was not found.

The program's `for` loop might end without finding the customer. The code following the `for` loop would have no way of knowing whether the `for`'s break triggered an early `for` loop exit (meaning that the customer was found) or whether the `for` ended normally. Therefore, the `found` variable lets the code following the `for` loop know whether the `for` found the customer.

When the `for` loop ends, the customer is found (or not found). If found, the following two conditions are possible:

- The balance is already too high.

- The balance is okay for more credit.

No matter which condition is the true condition, the user is informed of the result. If the customer was not found, the user is told that and the program ends.

How was that for a *real-world* program? Too difficult, you say? Look it over once or twice more. You'll see that the program performs the same steps (albeit in seemingly more detail) that you would follow if you were scanning a list of customers by hand.

NOTE   What's *really* important is that if there were a thousand, or even 10,000 customers, and the arrays were initialized from a disk file, the same search code would work! The amount of data doesn't affect the logic of this program (only the way the arrays are initialized with data).

Here's a second program that shows the value of linked arrays. Returning to the basketball player from the last chapter, this program has three arrays: one for scoring, one for rebounding, and one for assists. The program searches through the scoring totals, finds the game in which the player scored the most points, and then prints the player's total in all three categories in that particular game:

```
// Example program #2 from Chapter 22 of Absolute Beginner's Guide
// to C, 3rd Edition
// File Chapter22ex2.c


/* This program fills three arrays with a player's total points,
rebounds, and assists It loops through the scoring array and finds
the game with the most points. Once it knows that information, it
prints the totals from all three categories from that game */
```

```c
#include <stdio.h>

main()
{
    int gameScores[10] = {12, 5, 21, 15, 32, 10, 6, 31, 11, 10};
    int gameRebounds[10] = {5, 7, 1, 5, 10, 3, 0, 7, 6, 4};
    int gameAssists[10] = {2, 9, 4, 3, 6, 1, 11, 6, 9, 10};
    int bestGame = 0; //The comparison variable for best scoring
                      //game
    int gmMark = 0; // This will mark which game is the best scoring
                    // game
    int i;

    for (i=0; i<10; i++)
    {
        // if loop will compare each game to the current best total
        // if the current score is higher, it becomes the new best
        // and the counter variable becomes the new flag gmMark

        if (gameScores[i] > bestGame)
        {
            bestGame = gameScores[i];
            gmMark = i;
        }
    }

    // Print out the details of the best scoring game
    // Because arrays start at 0, add 1 to the game number

    printf("\n\nThe Player's best scoring game totals:\n");
    printf("The best game was game #%d\n", gmMark+1);
    printf("Scored %d points\n", gameScores[gmMark]);
    printf("Grabbed %d rebounds\n", gameRebounds[gmMark]);
    printf("Dished %d assists\n", gameAssists[gmMark]);

    return(0);
}
```

TIP If you are keeping track of multiple variables tied to one object (such as one player's different stats from a single game in this code example), a structure can help tie things together nicely. You learn about structures in Chapter 27, "Setting Up Your Data with Structures."

Both example programs in this chapter use a *sequential search* because the arrays (customer ID and gameScores) are searched from beginning to end until a match is found. You'll learn about more advanced searches as your programming skills improve. In the next chapter, you'll see how sorting an array helps speed some array searches. You'll also check out advanced search techniques called *binary searches* and *Fibonacci searches*.

THE ABSOLUTE MINIMUM

The goal of this chapter was to show you how to find values in arrays. You saw how to find array values based on a *key*. The key is a value that the user enters. You'll often search through parallel arrays, as done here. One array (the key array) holds the values for which you'll search. If the search is successful, other arrays supply needed data and you can report the results to the user. If the search is unsuccessful, you need to let the user know that also. Key concepts from this chapter include:

- Filling arrays is only the first step; after they're filled, your program must interact with the data.

- Until you learn more about searches, use a sequential search because it is the easiest search technique to master.

- Don't forget that a match might not be found. Always assume that your search value might not be in the list of values and include the code needed to handle an unfound value.

23

ALPHABETIZING AND ARRANGING YOUR DATA

Sorting is the computer term given to ordering lists of values. Not only must you be able to find data in arrays, but you often need to arrange array data in a certain order. Computers are perfect for sorting and alphabetizing data, and arrays provide the vehicles for holding sorted data.

Your programs don't always hold array data in the order you want to see that data. For example, students don't enroll based on alphabetical last name, even though most colleges print lists of students that way. Therefore, after collecting student data, the school's computer programs must somehow arrange that data in last name order for reports.

This chapter explains the easiest of computer sorting techniques, called the *bubble sort*.

Putting Your House in Order: Sorting

If you want to alphabetize a list of letters or names, or put a list of sales values into *ascending* order (ascending means from low to high, and *descending* means from high to low), you should use a sorting routine. Of course, the list of values that you sort will be stored in an array because array values are so easily rearranged by their subscripts.

Think about how you'd put a deck of cards in order if you threw the cards up in the air and let them fall. You would pick them up, one by one, looking at how the current card fit in with the others in your hand. Often you would rearrange some cards that you already held. The same type of process is used for sorting an array; often you have to rearrange values that are in the array.

Several computer methods help in sorting values. This chapter teaches you about the *bubble sort*. The bubble sort isn't extremely efficient compared to other sorts, but it's the easiest to understand. The name *bubble sort* comes from the nature of the sort. During a sort, the lower values "float" up the list each time a pass is made through the data. Figure 23.1 shows the process of sorting five numbers using a bubble sort.

The next program sorts a list of 10 numbers. The numbers are randomly generated using `rand()`. The bubble sort routine is little more than a nested `for` loop. The inner loop walks through the list, swapping any pair of values that is out of order down the list. The outer loop causes the inner loop to run several times (one time for each item in the list).

An added bonus that is common to many improved bubble sort routines is the testing to see whether a swap took place during any iteration of the inner loop. If no swap took place, the outer loop finishes early (via a `break` statement). Therefore, if the loop is sorted to begin with, or if only a few passes are needed to sort the list, the outer loop doesn't have to finish all its planned repetitions.

Before sorting: 50
                      32
                      93
                       2
                      74

During first pass, C compares the first value
to the second. Because 32 is less than 50, they
switch places: 32
                      50
                      93
                       2
                      74

It then compares 32 and 93 and leaves them
where they are. Next, C compares 32 and 2. Because
2 is the lesser value, 32 and 2 switch places:
                       2
                      50
                      93
                      32
                      74

Finally, it compares 2, the new first value in
the list, to 74 and leaves them.

After first pass: 2
                      50
                      93
                      32
                      74

During second pass, C compares the second value, 50,
to 93 and leaves them. It then compares 50 to 32 and
switches them: 2
                      32
                      93
                      50
                      74

C then compares the second value, 32, to 74 and
leaves them.

After second pass: 2
                      32
                      93
                      50
                      74

This process continues until all the numbers
have been sorted.

After third pass: 2
                      32
                      50
                      93
                      74

After fourth pass: 2
                      32
                      50
                      74
                      93   (sorted)

FIGURE 23.1

During each pass, the lower values "float" to the top of the array.

```c
// Example program #1 from Chapter 23 of Absolute Beginner's Guide
// to C, 3rd Edition
// File Chapter23ex1.c

/* This program generates 10 random numbers and then sorts them */

#include <stdio.h>
#include <stdlib.h>
#include <time.h>

main()
{

    int ctr, inner, outer, didSwap, temp;
    int nums[10];
    time_t t;

    // If you don't include this statement, your program will always
    // generate the same 10 random numbers

    srand(time(&t));

    // The first step is to fill the array with random numbers
    // (from 1 to 100)



    for (ctr = 0; ctr < 10; ctr++)
    {
        nums[ctr] = (rand() % 99) + 1;
    }

    // Now list the array as it currently is before sorting
    puts("\nHere is the list before the sort:");
    for (ctr = 0; ctr < 10; ctr++)
    {
        printf("%d\n", nums[ctr]);
```

```c
    }

    // Sort the array

    for (outer = 0; outer < 9; outer++)
    {
        didSwap = 0; //Becomes 1 (true) if list is not yet ordered
        for (inner = outer; inner < 10; inner++)
        {
            if (nums[inner] < nums[outer])
            {
                temp = nums[inner];
                nums[inner] = nums[outer];
                nums[outer] = temp;
                didSwap = 1;
            }
        }
        if (didSwap == 0)
        {
            break;
        }
    }

    // Now list the array as it currently is after sorting
    puts("\nHere is the list after the sort:");
    for (ctr = 0; ctr < 10; ctr++)
    {
        printf("%d\n", nums[ctr]);
    }



    return(0);
}
```

The output from this sorting program is as follows:

```
Here is the list before the sort
64
17
1
34
9
5
58
5
6
70

Here is the list after the sort
1
5
5
6
9
17
34
58
64
70
```

 NOTE   Your output might be different than that shown in the preceding example because rand() produces different results between compilers. The important thing to look for is the set of 10 random values your program generates, which should be sorted upon completion of the program.

Here is the swapping of the variables inside the inner loop:

```
temp = nums[inner];
nums[inner] = nums[outer];
nums[outer] = temp;
```

In other words, if a swap needs to take place (the first of the two values being compared is higher than the second of the two values), the program must swap `nums[inner]` with `nums[outer]`.

You might wonder why an extra variable, `temp`, was needed to swap two variables' values. A natural (and incorrect) tendency when swapping two variables might be this:

```
nums[inner] = nums[outer];   /* Does NOT swap the */
nums[outer] = nums[inner];   /* two values        */
```

The first assignment wipes out the value of `nums[inner]` so that the second assignment has nothing to assign. Therefore, a third variable is required to swap any two variables.

 TIP If you wanted to sort the list in descending order, you would only have to change the less-than sign (<) to a greater-than sign (>) right before the swapping code.

If you wanted to alphabetize a list of characters, you could do so by testing and swapping character array values, just as you've done here. In Chapter 25, "Arrays and Pointers," you learn how to store lists of string data that you can sort.

Faster Searches

Sometimes sorting data speeds your data searching. In the last chapter, you saw a program that searched a customer ID array for a matching user's value.

If a match was found, a corresponding customer balance (in another array) was used for a credit check. The customer ID values were not stored in any order.

The possibility arose that the user's entered customer ID might not have been found. Perhaps the user entered the customer ID incorrectly, or the customer ID was not stored in the array. Every element in the entire customer ID array had to be searched before the programmer could realize that the customer ID was not going to be found.

However, if the arrays were sorted in customer ID order before the search began, the program would not always have to look at each array element before deciding that a match couldn't be made. If the customer ID array were sorted and the user's customer ID were passed when looking through a search, the program would know right then that a match would not be found. Consider the following list of unsorted customer IDs:

```
313
532
178
902
422
562
```

Suppose the program had to look for the customer ID 413. With an unsorted array, a program would have to match the ID 413 to each element in the array.

If the arrays contained hundreds or thousands of values instead of only six, the computer would take longer to realize unmatched searches because each search would require that each element be looked at. However, if the values were always sorted, a program would not always have to scan through the entire list before realizing that a match would not be found. Here is the same list of values sorted numerically, from low to high customer IDs:

```
178
313
422
532
562
902
```

A sorted list makes the search faster. Now if you search for customer ID 413, your program can stop searching after looking at only three array values. 422 is the third element, and because 422 is greater than 413, your program can stop searching. It can stop searching because 422 comes after 413.

NOTE In extreme cases, searching a sorted array is not necessarily faster than sorting using an unsorted array. For instance, if you were searching within the previous list for customer ID 998, your program would have to search all six values before realizing that 998 was not in the list.

The following program is a combination of the customer ID searching program shown in the previous chapter and the sorting routine shown in this chapter. The customer ID values are sorted, and then the user is asked for a customer ID to find. The program then determines whether the customer's balance is less than $100. However, if the ID is not in the list, the program terminates the search early. Keep in mind that having only 10 array values makes this program seem like overkill, but if there were tens of thousands of customers, the code would not be different.

```
// Example program #2 from Chapter 23 of Absolute Beginner's Guide
// to C, 3rd Edition
// File Chapter23ex2.c

/* This program searches a sorted list of customer IDs in order to
get credit totals */

#include <stdio.h>

main()
{

    int ctr; // Loop counter
    int idSearch; // Customer to look for (the key)
    int found = 0; // 1 (true) if customer is found

    /* Defines the 10 elements in each of the parallel arrays */
    int custID[10] = {313, 453, 502, 101, 892,
                      475, 792, 912, 343, 633};
    float custBal[10] = {  0.00, 45.43, 71.23, 301.56, 9.08,
                          192.41, 389.00, 229.67, 18.31, 59.54};
    int tempID, inner, outer, didSwap, i; // For sorting
    float tempBal;

    // First, sort the arrays by customer ID */
    for (outer = 0; outer < 9; outer++)
    {
        didSwap = 0; // Becomes 1 (true) if list is not yet ordered
        for (inner = outer; inner < 10; inner++)
        {
            if (custID[inner] < custID[outer])
            {
                tempID = custID[inner]; // Must switch both arrays
                tempBal = custBal[inner]; // or they are no longer
                                          // linked
                custID[inner] = custID[outer];
```

```
                custBal[inner] = custBal[outer];
                custID[outer] = tempID;
                custBal[outer] = tempBal;
                didSwap = 1; // True because a swap took place
            }
        }
        if (didSwap == 0)
        {
            break;
        }
    }

    /* Interact with the user looking to find a balance */
    printf("\n\n*** Customer Balance Lookup ***\n");
    printf("What is the customer number? ");
    scanf(" %d", &idSearch);

    // Now, look for the ID in the array
    for (ctr=0; ctr<10; ctr++)
    {
        if (idSearch == custID[ctr]) // Do they match?
        {
            found = 1; //Yes, match flag is set to TRUE
            break; //No need to keep looping
        }
        if (custID[ctr] > idSearch) // No need to keep searching
        {
            break;
        }
    }

    // Once the loop has completed, the ID was either found
    // (found = 1) or not

    if (found)
    {
```

```
        if (custBal[ctr] > 100)
        {
            printf("\n** That customer's balance is $%.2f.\n",
                    custBal[ctr]);
            printf("No additional credit.\n");


        }
        else // Balance is less than $100.00
        {
            printf("\n**The customer's credit is good!\n");
        }
    }
    else // The ID was not found
    {
        printf("** You have entered an incorrect customer ID.");
        printf("\n ID %3d was not found in the list.\n", idSearch);
    }
    return(0);
}
```

 NOTE   Other than the Draw Poker game in Appendix B, "The Draw Poker Program," the preceding program is this book's hardest to understand. Mastering this program puts you at a level above that of *absolute beginner*. Congratulations, and hats off to you when you master the logic presented here. See, programming in C isn't difficult after all!

Before seeing this program, you mastered both array searching and array sorting. This program simply puts the two procedures together. About the only additional job this program does is keep the two parallel arrays in synch during the search. As you can see from the body of the search code, when customer ID elements are swapped (within the custID array), the corresponding (via the subscript) element in the customer balance array is searched.

An early search termination could take place because of the following:

```
if (custID[ctr] > idSearch)  // No need to keep searching
{
    break;
}
```

When there are several thousand array elements, such an `if` saves a lot of processing time.

Keeping arrays sorted is not always easy or efficient. For instance, you don't want your program sorting a large array every time you add, change, or delete a value from the array. After storing several thousand values in an array, sorting the array after adding each value takes too much time, even for fast computers. Advanced ways of manipulating arrays ensure that you always insert items in sorted order. (However, such techniques are way beyond the scope of this book.) You're doing well without complicating things too much here.

THE ABSOLUTE MINIMUM

The goal of this chapter was to familiarize you with the bubble sort method of ordering and alphabetizing values in arrays. You don't need any new C commands to sort values. Sorting is one of the primary array advantages. It shows that arrays are a better storage method than separately named variables. The array subscripts let you step through the array and swap values, when needed, to sort the array.

Key concepts from this chapter include:

- Use an ascending sort when you want to arrange array values from low to high.

- Use a descending sort when you want to arrange array values from high to low.

- The nested `for` loop, such as the one you saw in this chapter, is a perfect statement to produce a bubble sort.

- Don't swap the values of two variables unless you introduce a third temporary variable to hold the in-between value.

- Sorting routines doesn't have to be hard; start with the one listed in this chapter, and adapt it to your own needs.

- Don't forget to keep your arrays sorted. You'll speed up searching for values.

IN THIS CHAPTER

- Working with memory addresses
- Defining pointer variables
- Using the dereferencing *

24

SOLVING THE MYSTERY OF POINTERS

Pointer variables, often called *pointers*, let you do much more with C than you can with programming languages that don't support pointers. When you first learn about pointers, you'll probably ask, "What's the point?" (Even after you master them, you might ask the same thing!) Pointers provide the means for the true power of C programming. This book exposes the tip of the pointer iceberg. The concepts you learn here will form the foundation of your C programming future.

Memory Addresses

Inside your computer is a bunch of memory. The memory holds your program as it executes, and it also holds your program's variables. Just as every house has a different address, every memory location has a different address. Not coincidentally, the memory locations have their own *addresses* as well. As with house addresses, the memory addresses are all unique; no two are the same. Your memory acts a little like one big hardware array, with each address being a different subscript and each memory location being a different array element.

When you define variables, C finds an unused place in memory and attaches a name to that memory location. That's a good thing. Instead of having to remember that an order number is stored at memory address 34532, you only have to remember the name orderNum (assuming that you named the variable orderNum when you defined the variable). The name orderNum is *much* easier to remember than a number.

Defining Pointer Variables

As with any other type of variable, you must define a pointer variable before you can use it. Before going further, you need to learn two new operators. Table 24.1 shows them, along with their descriptions.

TABLE 24.1   The Pointer Operators

Operator	Description
&	Address-of operator
*	Dereferencing operator

You've seen the * before. How does C know the difference between multiplication and dereferencing? The context of how you use them determines how C interprets them. You've also seen the & before scanf() variables. The & in scanf() is the address-of operator. scanf() requires that you send it the address of non-array variables.

The following shows how you would define an integer and a floating-point variable:

```
int num;
float value;
```

To define an integer pointer variable and a floating-point pointer variable, you simply insert an *:

```
int * pNum;   /* Defines two pointer variables */
float * pValue;
```

NOTE   There's nothing special about the names of pointer variables. Many C programmers like to preface pointer variable names with a p, as done here, but you can name them anything you like. The p simply reminds you they are pointer variables, not regular variables.

All data types have corresponding pointer data types—there are character pointers, long integer pointers, and so on.

Pointer variables hold addresses of other variables. That's their primary purpose. Use the address-of operator, &, to assign the address of one variable to a pointer. Until you assign an address of a variable to a pointer, the pointer is uninitialized and you can't use it for anything.

The following code defines an integer variable named age and stores 19 in age. Then a pointer named pAge is defined and initialized to point to age. The address-of operator reads just like it sounds. The second line that follows tells C to put the address of age into pAge.

```
int age = 19;        /* Stores a 19 in age */
int * pAge = &age; /* Links up the pointer */
```

You have no idea exactly what address C will store age at. However, whatever address C uses, pAge will hold that address. When a pointer variable holds the address of another variable, it essentially *points* to that variable. Assuming that age is stored at the address 18826 (only C knows exactly where it is stored), Figure 24.1 shows what the resulting memory looks like.

Address   Memory   Variable name

18826	19 age
20886	18826 pAge

FIGURE 24.1

The variable pAge *points to* age *if* pAge *holds the address of* age.

WARNING   Just because you define two variables back to back doesn't mean that C stores them back to back in memory. C *might* store them together, but it also might not.

WARNING   *Never* try to set the address of one type of variable to a pointer variable of a different type. C lets you assign the address of one type of variable only to a pointer defined with the same data type.

The * isn't part of a pointer variable's name. You use the * *dereferencing operator* for several things, but in the pointer definition, the * exists only to tell C that the variable is a pointer, not a regular variable. The following four statements do *exactly the same thing* as the previous two statements. Notice that you don't use * to store the address of a variable in a pointer variable unless you are also defining the pointer at the same time.

```
int age; // Defines a regular integer
int * pAge; // Defines a pointer to an integer
age = 19; //Stores 19 in age
pAge = &age; // Links up the pointer
```

Using the Dereferencing *

As soon as you link up a pointer to another variable, you can work with the other value by *dereferencing* the pointer. Programmers never use an easy word when a hard one will do just as well (and confuse more people). Dereferencing just means that you use the pointer to get to the other variable. When you dereference, use the * dereferencing operator.

In a nutshell, here are two ways to change the value of age (assuming that the variables are defined as described earlier):

```
age = 25;
```

and

```
*pAge = 25;   /* Stores 25 where pAge points */
```

This assignment tells C to store the value 25 at the address pointed to by pAge. Because pAge points to the memory location holding the variable age, 25 is stored in age.

Notice that you can use a variable name to store a value or dereference a pointer that points to the variable. You also can use a variable's value in the same way. Here are two ways to print the contents of age:

```
printf("The age is %d.\n", age);
```

and

```
printf("The age is %d.\n", *pAge);
```

The dereferencing operator is used when a function works with a pointer variable that it is sent. In Chapter 32, "Returning Data from Your Functions," you'll learn how to pass pointers to functions. When a function uses a pointer variable that is sent from another function, you must use the dereferencing operator before the variable name everywhere it appears.

The true power of pointers comes in the chapters that discuss functions, but getting you used to pointers still makes sense. Here's a simple program that declares integer, float, and character variables, as well as pointer versions of all three:

```
// Example program #1 from Chapter 24 of Absolute Beginner's Guide
// to C, 3rd Edition
// File Chapter24ex1.c
```

```
/* This program demonstrates pointers by declaring and initializing
both regular and pointer variables for int, float, and char types
and then displays the values of each. */

#include <stdio.h>


main()
{

    int kids;
    int * pKids;
    float price;
    float * pPrice;
    char code;
    char * pCode;

    price = 17.50;
    pPrice = &price;

    printf("\nHow many kids are you taking to the water park? ");
    scanf(" %d", &kids);

    pKids = &kids;

    printf("\nDo you have a discount ticket for the park?");
    printf("\nEnter E for Employee Discount, S for Sav-More ");
    printf("Discount, or N for No Discount: ");
    scanf(" %c", &code);

    pCode = &code;

    printf("\nFirst let's do it with the variables:\n");
    printf("You've got %d kids...\n", kids);
    switch (code) {
    case ('E') :
```

```
    printf("The employee discount saves you 25%% on the ");
    printf("$%.2f price", price);
    printf("\nTotal ticket cost: $%.2f", (price*.75*kids));
    break;
case ('S') :
    printf("The Sav-more discount saves you 15%% on the ");
    printf("$%.2f price", price);
    printf("\nTotal ticket cost: $%.2f", (price*.85*kids));
    break;
default : // Either entered N for No Discount or
          // an invalid letter
    printf("You will be paying full price of ");
    printf("$%.2f for your tickets", price);
}
                // Now repeat the same code, but use dereferenced
                // pointers and get the same results
printf("\n\n\nNow let's do it with the pointers:\n");
printf("You've got %d kids...\n", *pKids);
switch (*pCode) {
case ('E') :
    printf("The employee discount saves you 25%% on the ");
    printf("$%.2f price", *pPrice);
    printf("\nTotal ticket cost: $%.2f",
        (*pPrice * .75 * *pKids));
break;
case ('S') :
    printf("The Sav-more discount saves you 15%% on the ");
    printf("$%.2f price", *pPrice);
    printf("\nTotal ticket cost $%.2f",
        (*pPrice * .85 * *pKids));
break;
    default : // Either entered N for No Discount or
              // an invalid letter
    printf("You will be paying full price of ");
    printf("$%.2f for your tickets", *pPrice);
```

```
        }

    return(0);
}
```

Here's a sample run of the program:

```
How many kids are you taking to the water park? 3

Do you have a discount ticket for the park?
Enter E for Employee Discount, S for Sav-More Discount, and N for No
Discount: S

First let's do it with the variables:
You've got 3 kids…
The Sav-More discount saves you 15% on the $17.50 price
Total ticket cost: $44.63

Now let's do it with the pointers:
You've got 3 kids…
The Sav-More discount saves you 15% on the $17.50 price
Total ticket cost: $44.63
```

There's nothing too ground-breaking or complicated in this program. It's more to get you used to using pointers, including declaring, setting, and referencing pointers of all kinds. Again, when you use functions that take and return data, you will find yourself in need of pointers constantly.

THE ABSOLUTE MINIMUM

The goal of this chapter was to introduce you to pointer variables. A pointer variable is nothing more than a variable that holds the location of another variable. You can refer to the pointed-to variable by its name or by dereferencing the pointer.

Pointers have many uses in C, especially in advanced C programming. As you'll learn in the next chapter, arrays are nothing more than pointers in disguise. Because pointers offer more flexibility than arrays, many C programmers stop using arrays when they master pointers. Key concepts from this chapter include:

- Get comfortable with memory addresses because they form the basis of pointer usage.

- Use the & to produce the address of a variable.

- Use the * to define a pointer variable and to dereference a pointer variable. *pAge and age reference the same memory location, as long as you've made pAge point to age.

- Don't try to make a pointer variable of one data type point to a variable of a different data type.

- Don't worry about the *exact* address that C uses for variable storage. If you use &, C takes care of the rest.

- Don't forget to use * when dereferencing your pointer, or you'll get the wrong value.

- Don't get too far ahead. You will fully appreciate pointers only after programming in C for a while. At this point (pun not intended!), pointers will not seem to help at all. The only thing you might feel a little better about is knowing what the & inside scanf() really means.

IN THIS CHAPTER

- Understanding that array names are pointers
- Getting down in the list
- Working with characters and pointers
- Being careful with string lengths
- Creating arrays of pointers

25

ARRAYS AND POINTERS

This chapter teaches how C's array and pointer variables share a lot of principles. As a matter of fact, an array is a special kind of pointer. Because of their similarities, you can use pointer notation to get to array values, and you can use array notation to get to pointed-at values.

Perhaps the most important reason to learn how arrays and pointers overlap is for character string handling. By combining pointer notation (using the dereferencing operation) and array notation (using subscripts), you can store lists of character strings and reference them as easily as you reference array values of other data types.

Also, after you master the *heap*—a special place in memory that the next chapter introduces you to—you'll see that pointers are the only way to get to heap memory, where you put data values.

Array Names Are Pointers

An array name is nothing more than a pointer to the first element in that array. The array name is not exactly a pointer *variable*, though. Array names are known as *pointer constants.* The following statement defines an integer array and initializes it:

```
int vals[5] = {10, 20, 30, 40, 50};
```

You can reference the array by subscript notation. That much you know already. However, C does more than just attach subscripts to the values in memory. C sets up a pointer to the array and names that point to vals. You can never change the contents of vals; it is like a fixed pointer variable whose address C locks in. Figure 25.1 shows you what C really does when you define and initialize vals.

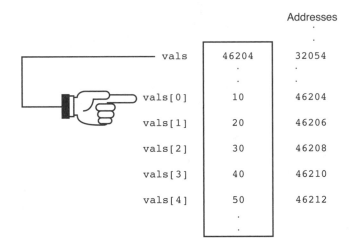

FIGURE 25.1

The array name is a pointer to the first value in the array.

Because the array name is a pointer (that can't be changed), you can print the first value in the array like this:

```
printf("The first value is %d.\n", vals[0]);
```

But more important for this chapter, you can print the first array value like this, too:

```
printf("The first value is %d.\n", *vals);
```

As you'll see in a moment, this is also equivalent and accesses vals[0]:

```
printf("The first value is %d.\n", *(vals+0));
```

WARNING The fact that an array is a fixed constant pointer is why you can't put just an array name on the left side of an equals sign. You can't change a constant. (Remember, though, that C relaxes this rule only when you first define the array because C has yet to fix the array at a specific address.)

Getting Down in the List

Because an array name is nothing more than a pointer to the *first* value in the array, if you want the second value, you only have to add 1 to the array name and dereference *that* location. This set of `printf()` lines

```
printf("The first array value is %d.\n", vals[0]);
printf("The second array value is %d.\n", vals[1]);
printf("The third array value is %d.\n", vals[2]);
printf("The fourth array value is %d.\n", vals[3]);
printf("The fifth array value is %d.\n", vals[4]);
```

does *exactly* the same as this set:

```
printf("The first array value is %d.\n", *(vals + 0));
printf("The second array value is %d.\n", *(vals +1));
printf("The third array value is %d.\n", *(vals + 2));
printf("The fourth array value is %d.\n", *(vals + 3));
printf("The fifth array value is %d.\n", *(vals + 4));
```

If `vals` is a pointer constant (and it is), and the pointer constant holds a number that is the address to the array's first element, adding 1 or 2 (or whatever) to `vals` before dereferencing `vals` adds 1 or 2 to the address `vals` points to.

TIP If you're wondering about the importance of all this mess, hang tight. In a moment, you'll see how C's pointer notation lets you make C act *almost* as if it has string variables.

As you might remember, integers usually take more than 1 byte of memory storage. The preceding `printf()` statements appear to add 1 to the address inside `vals` to get to the next dereferenced memory location, but C helps you out here. C adds one `int` size when you add 1 to an `int` pointer (and one `double` size when you add 1 to a double pointer, and so on). The expression `*(vals + 2)` tells C that you want the *third integer* in the list that `vals` points to.

Characters and Pointers

The following two statements set up almost the same thing in memory. The only difference is that, in the second statement, pName is a pointer *variable*, not a pointer constant:

```
char name[] = "Andrew B. Mayfair";   /* name points to A */
char * pName = "Andrew B. Mayfair"; /* pName points to A */
```

Because pName is a pointer variable, you *can* put it on the left side of an equals sign! Therefore, you don't always have to use strcpy() if you want to assign a character pointer a new string value. The character pointer will only point to the first character in the string. However, %s and all the string functions work with character pointers just as easily as with character arrays (the two are the same thing) because these functions know to stop at the null zero.

To put a different name in the name array, you have to use strcpy() or assign the string one character at a time—but to make pName point to a different name, you get to do this:

```
pName = "Theodore M. Brooks";
```

 TIP The only reason string assignment works is that C puts all your program's string literals into memory somewhere and then *replaces* them in your program with their addresses. C is not really putting Theodore M. Brooks into pName because pName can hold only addresses. C is putting the *address* of Theodore M. Brooks into pName.

You now have a way to assign strings new values without using strcpy(). It took a little work to get here, but aren't you glad you made it? If so, settle down—there's just one catch (isn't there always?).

Be Careful with Lengths

It's okay to store string literals in character arrays as just described. The new strings that you assign with = can be shorter or longer than the previous strings. That's nice because you might recall that you can't store a string in a character array that is longer than the array you reserved initially.

You must be extremely careful, however, *not* to let the *program* store strings longer than the first string you point to with the character pointer. This is a little complex, but keep following along—because this chapter stays as simple and short as possible. Never set up a character pointer variable like this:

```
main()
{
char * name = "Tom Roberts";
/* Rest of program follows… */
```

and then later let the user enter a new string with `gets()` like this:

```
gets(name); /* Not very safe */
```

The problem with this statement is that the user might enter a string longer than `Tom Roberts`, the first string assigned to the character pointer. Although a character pointer can point to strings of any length, the `gets()` function, along with `scanf()`, `strcpy()`, and `strcat()`, doesn't know that it's being sent a character pointer. Because these functions might be sent a character array that can't change location, they map the newly created string directly over the location of the string in name. If a string longer than `name` is entered, other data areas could be overwritten.

 WARNING Yes, this is a little tedious. You might have to read this section again later after you get more comfortable with pointers and arrays.

If you want to have the advantage of a character pointer—that is, if you want to be able to assign string literals to the pointer and still have the safety of arrays so you can use the character pointer to get user input—you can do so with a little trick.

If you want to store user input in a string pointed to by a pointer, first reserve enough storage for that input string. The easiest way to do this is to reserve a character array and then assign a character pointer to the beginning element of that array:

```
char input[81]; // Holds a string as long as 80 characters
char *iptr = input; // Also could have done char *iptr = &input[0]
```

Now you can input a string by using the pointer as long as the string entered by the user is not longer than 81 bytes long:

```
gets(iptr);  /* Makes sure that iptr points to the string typed by
the user */
```

You can use a nice string-input function to ensure that entered strings don't get longer than 81 characters, including the null zero. Use `fgets()` if you want to limit the number of characters accepted from the user. `fgets()` works like `gets()`, except that you specify a length argument. The following statement shows `fgets()` in action:

```
fgets(iptr, 81, stdin);  /*Gets up to 80 chars and adds null zero */
```

The second value is the maximum number of characters you want to save from the user's input. Always leave one for the string's null zero. The pointer `iptr` can point to a string as long as 81 characters. If the user enters a string less than 81 characters, `iptr` points to that string with no problem. However, if the user goes wild and enters a string 200 characters long, `iptr` points only to the first 80, followed by a null zero at the 81st position that `fgets()` added, and the rest of the user's input is ignored.

 TIP   You can use `fgets()` to read strings from data files. The third value of `fgets()` can be a disk file pointer, but you'll learn about disk pointers later in the book. For now, use `stdin` as the third value you send to `fgets()` so that `fgets()` goes to the keyboard for input and not somewhere else.

You also can assign the pointer string literals using the assignment like this:

```
iptr = "Mary Jayne Norman";
```

Arrays of Pointers

If you want to use a bunch of pointers, create an array of them. An array of pointers is just as easy to define as an array of any other kind of data, except that you must include the * operator after the data type name. The following statements reserve an array of 25 integer pointers and an array of 25 character pointers:

```
int * ipara[25];   /* 25 pointers to integers */
char * cpara[25]; /* 25 pointers to characters */
```

The array of characters is most interesting because you can store a list of strings in the array. More accurately, you can *point* to various strings. The following program illustrates two things: how to initialize an array of strings at definition time and how to print them using a `for` loop:

 NOTE   Actually, the program does a bit more than that. It also gets you to rate the nine strings (in this case, movie titles) that you've seen on a scale of 1 to 10 and then reuses our friendly bubble sort routine—but instead of going small to big, the sort reorders your list from highest rating to lowest. There's nothing wrong with going back and mixing in previously learned concepts when trying new lessons—that's how you start to build robust and interesting programs!

```
// Example program #1 from Chapter 25 of Absolute Beginner's Guide
// to C, 3rd Edition
```

```c
// File Chapter25ex1.c

/* This program declares and initializes an array of character
pointers and then asks for ratings associated  */

#include <stdio.h>


main()
{

        int i;
        int ctr = 0;
        char ans;

//Declaring our array of 9 characters and then initializing them
        char * movies[9] = {"Amour", "Argo",
                                    "Beasts of the Southern Wild",
                                    "Django Unchained",
                                    "Les Miserables",
                                    "Life of Pi", "Lincoln",
                                    "Silver Linings Playbook",
                                    "Zero Dark Thirty"};
  int movieratings[9]; // A corresponding array of 9 integers
                    // for movie ratings

        char * tempmovie = "This will be used to sort rated movies";
        int outer, inner, didSwap, temprating; // for the sort loop

        printf("\n\n*** Oscar Season 2012 is here! ***\n\n");
        printf("Time to rate this year's best picture nominees:");

        for (i=0; i< 9; i++)
        {
            printf("\nDid you see %s? (Y/N): ", movies[i]);
            scanf(" %c", &ans);
```

```c
            if ((toupper(ans)) == 'Y')
            {
                printf("\nWhat was your rating on a scale ");
                printf("of 1-10: ");
                scanf(" %d", &movieratings[i]);
                ctr++; // This will be used to print only movies
                        // you've seen
                continue;
            }
            else
            {
                movieratings[i] = -1;
            }
        }


    // Now sort the movies by rating (the unseen will go
    // to the bottom)

    for (outer = 0; outer < 8; outer++)
    {
        didSwap = 0;
        for (inner = outer; inner < 9; inner++)
        {
            if (movieratings[inner] > movieratings[outer])
            {
                tempmovie = movies[inner];
                temprating = movieratings[inner];
                movies[inner] = movies[outer];
                movieratings[inner] = movieratings[outer];
                movies[outer] = tempmovie;
                movieratings[outer] = temprating;
                didSwap = 1;
            }
        }
        if (didSwap == 0)
        {
            break;
```

```
        }
    }

    // Now to print the movies you saw in order
    printf("\n\n** Your Movie Ratings for the 2012 Oscar ");
    printf("Contenders **\n");
    for (i=0; i < ctr; i++)
    {
        printf("%s  rated a %d!\n", movies[i], movieratings[i]);
    }
    return(0);
}
```

Here is a sample output from this program:

```
*** Oscar Season 2012 is here! ***

Time to rate this year's best picture nominees:
Did you see Amour? (Y/N): Y
What was your rating on a scale of 1-10: 6

Did you see Argo? (Y/N): Y
What was your rating on a scale of 1-10: 8

Did you see Beasts of the Southern Wild? (Y/N): N

Did you see Django Unchained? (Y/N): Y
What was your rating on a scale of 1-10: 7

Did you see Les Miserables? (Y/N): Y
What was your rating on a scale of 1-10: 7

Did you see Life of Pi? (Y/N): N

Did you see Lincoln? (Y/N): Y
What was your rating on a scale of 1-10: 6

Did you see Silver Linings Playbook? (Y/N): Y
```

```
What was your rating on a scale of 1-10: 9

Did you see Zero Dark Thirty? N

** Your Movie Ratings for the 2012 Oscar Contenders **
Silver Linings Playbook rated a 9.
Argo rated a 8.
Les Miserables rated a 7.
Django Unchained rated a 7.
Lincoln rated a 6.
Amour rated a 6.
```

Figure 25.2 shows how the program sets up the `movies` array in memory. Each element is nothing more than a character pointer that contains the address of a different person's name. It's important to understand that `movies` does not hold strings—just pointers to strings.

FIGURE 25.2

The `movies` array contains pointers to strings.

See, even though there is no such thing as a string array in C (because there are no string variables), storing character pointers in `movies` makes the program act as though `movies` is a string array.

The program then loops through the nine movies in the array and asks the user whether he or she saw each one. If the answer is `Y` (or `y` after it is converted with the `toupper()` function), the program goes on to ask for an integer rating of 1 to 10. It also increments a counter (`ctr`) so the program will eventually know how many movies were seen. If the answer is `N` (or any character other than `Y` or `y`), the rating of `-1` is assigned to that movie, so it will fall to the bottom during the movie sort.

After the movies are all rated, a bubble sort is used to rate the movies best to worst. Isn't it nice to know that you can use your sort routine on string arrays? The sorted array is now ready to be printed. However, the `for` loop iterates only `ctr` times, meaning that it will not print the names of movies you didn't see.

THE ABSOLUTE MINIMUM

The goal of this chapter was to get you thinking about the similarities between arrays and pointers. An array name is really just a pointer that points to the first element in the array. Unlike pointer variables, an array name can't change. This is the primary reason an array name can't appear on the left side of an equals sign.

Using pointers allows more flexibility than arrays. You can directly assign a string literal to a character pointer variable, whereas you must use the `strcpy()` function to assign strings to arrays. You'll see many uses for pointer variables throughout your C programming career. Key concepts from this chapter include:

- Use character pointers if you want to assign string literals directly.

- Use either array subscript notation or pointer dereferencing to access array and pointer values.

- Don't use a built-in function to fill a character pointer's location unless that character pointer was originally set up to point to a long string.

MAXIMIZING YOUR COMPUTER'S MEMORY

Absolute beginners to C aren't the only ones who might find this chapter's concepts confusing at first. Even advanced C programmers get mixed up when dealing with the heap. The *heap* is the collection of unused memory in your computer. The memory left over—after your program, your program's variables, and your operating system's workspace—comprises your computer's available heap space, as Figure 26.1 shows.

Many times you'll want access to the heap, because your program will need more memory than you initially defined in variables and arrays. This chapter gives you some insight into why and how you want to use heap memory instead of variables.

You don't assign variable names to heap memory. The only way to access data stored in heap memory is through pointer variables. Aren't you glad you learned about pointers already? Without pointers, you couldn't learn about the heap.

Your operating system
Your C program
Your variables
Heap

FIGURE 26.1

The heap is unused memory.

NOTE The free heap memory is called free heap or unallocated heap memory. The part of the heap in use by your program at any one time is called the allocated heap. Your program might use varying amounts of heap space as the program executes. So far, no program in this book has used the heap.

Thinking of the Heap

Now that you've learned what the heap is—the unused section of contiguous memory—throw out what you've learned! You'll more quickly grasp how to use the heap if you think of the heap as just one big heap of free memory stacked up in a pile. The next paragraph explains why.

You'll be allocating (using) and deallocating (freeing back up) heap memory as your program runs. When you request heap memory, you don't know exactly from where on the heap the new memory will come. Therefore, if one statement in your program grabs heap memory, and then the very next statement also grabs another section of heap memory, that second section of the heap might not physically reside right after the first section you allocated.

Just as when scooping dirt from a big heap, one shovel does not pick up dirt granules that were right below the last shovel of dirt. Also, when you throw the shovel of dirt back onto the heap, that dirt doesn't go right back where it was. Although this analogy might seem to stretch the concept of computer memory, you'll find that you'll understand the heap much better if you think of the heap of memory like you think of the heap of dirt: You have no idea exactly where the memory you allocate and deallocate will come from or go back to. You know only that the memory comes and goes from the heap.

If you allocate 10 bytes of heap memory at once, those 10 bytes will be contiguous. The important thing to know is that the next section of heap memory you allocate will not necessarily follow the first, so you shouldn't count on anything like that.

Your operating system uses heap memory along with your program. If you work on a networked computer or use a multitasking operating environment such as Windows, other tasks might be grabbing heap memory along with your program. Therefore, another routine might have come between two of your heap-allocation statements and allocated or deallocated memory.

You have to keep track of the memory you allocate. You do this with pointer variables. For instance, if you want to allocate 20 integers on the heap, you use an integer pointer. If you want to allocate 400 floating-point values on the heap, you use a floating-point pointer. The pointer always points to the first heap value of the section you just allocated. Therefore, a single pointer points to the start of the section of heap you allocate. If you want to access the memory after the first value on the heap, you can use pointer notation or array notation to get to the rest of the heap section you allocated. (See, the last chapter's pointer/array discussion really does come in handy!)

But *Why* Do I Need the Heap?

Okay, before learning exactly how you allocate and deallocate heap memory, you probably want more rationalization about why you even need to worry about the heap. After all, the variables, pointers, and arrays you've learned about so far have sufficed nicely for program data.

The heap memory does not always replace the variables and arrays you've been learning about. The problem with the variables you've learned about so far is that you must know in advance exactly what kind and how many variables you will want. Remember, you must define all variables before you use them. If you define an array to hold 100 customer IDs, but the user has 101 customers to enter, your program can't just expand the array at runtime. Some programmers (like you) have to change the array definition and recompile the program before the array can hold more values.

With the heap memory, however, you don't have to know in advance how much memory you need. Similar to an accordion, the heap memory your program uses can grow or shrink as needed. If you need another 100 elements to hold a new batch of customers, your program can allocate that new batch at runtime without needing another compilation.

WARNING This book doesn't try to fool you into thinking that this chapter can answer all your questions. Mastering the heap takes practice—and, in reality, programs that really need the heap are beyond the scope of this book. Nevertheless, when you finish this chapter, you'll have a more solid understanding of how to access the heap than you would get from most books because of the approach that's used.

Commercial programs such as spreadsheets and word processors must rely heavily on the heap. After all, the programmer who designs the program cannot know exactly how large or small a spreadsheet or word processing document will be. Therefore, as you type data into a spreadsheet or word processor, the underlying program allocates more data. The program likely does not allocate the data 1 byte at a time as you type because memory allocation is not always extremely efficient when done 1 byte at a time. More than likely, the program allocates memory in chunks of code, such as 100-byte or 500-byte sections.

So why can't the programmers simply allocate huge arrays that can hold a huge spreadsheet or document instead of messing with the heap? For one thing, memory is one of the most precious resources in your computer. As we move into networked and windowed environments, memory becomes even more precious. Your programs can't allocate huge arrays for those rare occasions when a user might need that much memory. Your program would solely use all that memory, and other tasks could not access that allocated memory.

NOTE The heap enables your program to use only as much memory as it needs. When your user needs more memory (for instance, to enter more data), your program can allocate the memory. When your user is finished using that much memory (such as clearing a document to start a new one in a word processor), you can deallocate the memory, making it available for other tasks that might need it.

How Do I Allocate the Heap?

You must learn only two new functions to use the heap. The `malloc()` (for memory allocate) function allocates heap memory, and the `free()` function deallocates heap memory.

TIP Be sure to include the `stdlib.h` header file in all the programs you write that use `malloc()` and `free()`.

We might as well get to the rough part. `malloc()` is not the most user-friendly function for newcomers to understand. Perhaps looking at an example of `malloc()` is the best place to start. Suppose you were writing a temperature-averaging program for a local weather forecaster. The more temperature readings the user enters, the more accurate the correct prediction will be. You decide that you will allocate 10 integers to hold the first 10 temperature readings. If the user wants to enter more, your program can allocate another batch of 10, and so on.

You first need a pointer to the 10 heap values. The values are integers, so you need an integer pointer. You need to define the integer pointer like this:

```
int * temps;   /* Will point to the first heap value */
```

Here is how you can allocate 10 integers on the heap using `malloc()`:

```
temps = (int *) malloc(10 * sizeof(int));   /* Yikes! */
```

That's a lot of code just to get 10 integers. The line is actually fairly easy to understand when you see it broken into pieces. The `malloc()` function requires only a single value: the number of bytes you want allocated. Therefore, if you wanted 10 bytes, you could do this:

```
malloc(10);
```

The problem is that the previous description required not 10 bytes, but 10 integers. How many bytes of memory do 10 integers require? 10? 20? The answer, of course, is that it depends. Only `sizeof()` knows for sure.

Therefore, if you want 10 integers allocated, you must tell `malloc()` that you want 10 sets of bytes allocated, with each set of bytes being enough for an integer. Therefore, the previous line included the following `malloc()` function call:

```
malloc(10 * sizeof(int))
```

This part of the statement told `malloc()` to allocate, or set aside, 10 contiguous integer locations on the heap. In a way, the computer puts a fence around those 10 integer locations so that subsequent `malloc()` calls do not intrude on this allocated memory. Now that you've mastered that last half of the `malloc()` statement, there's not much left to understand. The first part of `malloc()` is fairly easy.

`malloc()` always performs the following two steps (assuming that enough heap memory exists to satisfy your allocation request):

1. Allocates the number of bytes you request and makes sure no other program can overwrite that memory until your program frees it

2. Assigns your pointer to the first allocated value

Figure 26.2 shows the result of the previous temperature `malloc()` function call. As you can see from the figure, the heap of memory (shown here as just that, a heap) now contains a fenced-off area of 10 integers, and the integer pointer variable named `temps` points to the first integer. Subsequent `malloc()` function calls will go to other parts of the heap and will not tread on the allocated 10 integers.

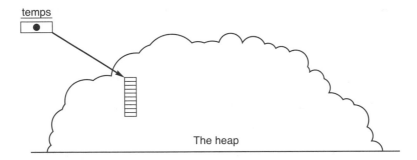

FIGURE 26.2

After allocating the 10 integers.

What do you do with the 10 integers you just allocated? Treat them like an array! You can store data by referring to `temps[0]`, `temps[1]`, and so on. You know from the last chapter that you access contiguous memory using array notation, even if that memory begins with a pointer. Also remember that each set of allocated memory will be contiguous, so the 10 integers will follow each other just as if you allocated temps as a 10-integer array.

The `malloc()` allocation still has one slight problem. We still have to explain the left portion of the temperature `malloc()`. What is the `(int *)` for?

The `(int *)` is a typecast. You've seen other kinds of typecasts in this book. To convert a float value to an int, you place `(int)` before the floating-point value, like this:

```
aVal = (int)salary;
```

The `*` inside a typecast means that the typecast is a pointer typecast. `malloc()` always returns a character pointer. If you want to use `malloc()` to allocate integers, floating points, or any kind of data other than `char`, you have to typecast the `malloc()` so that the pointer variable that receives the allocation (such as `temps`) receives the correct pointer data type. `temps` is an integer pointer; you should not assign `temps` to `malloc()`'s allocated memory unless you typecast `malloc()` into an integer pointer. Therefore, the left side of the previous `malloc()` simply tells `malloc()` that an integer pointer, not the default character pointer, will point to the first of the allocated values.

NOTE Besides defining an array at the top of `main()`, what have you gained by using `malloc()`? For one thing, you can use the `malloc()` function anywhere in your program, not just where you define variables and arrays. Therefore, when your program is ready for 100 `double` values, you can allocate those 100 `double` values. If you used a regular array, you would need a statement like this toward the top of `main()`:

```
doublemyVals[100];  /* A regular array of 100 doubles */
```

Those 100 `double` values would sit around for the life of the program, taking up memory resources from the rest of the system, even if the program only needed the 100 double values for only a short time. With `malloc()`, you need to define only the pointer that points to the top of the allocated memory for the program's life, not the entire array.

If There's Not Enough Heap Memory

In extreme cases, not enough heap memory might exist to satisfy `malloc()`'s request. The user's computer might not have a lot of memory, another task might be using a lot of memory, or your program might have previously allocated everything already. If `malloc()` fails, its pointer variable points to a null value, `0`. Therefore, many programmers follow a `malloc()` with an `if`, like this:

```
temps = (int *) malloc(10 * sizeof(int));
if (temps == 0)
{
        printf("Oops! Not Enough Memory!\n");
        exit(1); // Terminate the program early
}
// Rest of program would follow...
```

If `malloc()` works, `temps` contains a valid address that points to the start of the allocated heap. If `malloc()` fails, the invalid address of `0` is pointed to (heap memory never begins at address zero) and the error prints onscreen.

TIP Programmers often use the not operator, `!`, instead of testing a value against `0`, as done here. Therefore, the previous `if` test would more likely be coded like this:

```
if (!temps)     /* Means, if not true */
```

Freeing Heap Memory

When you're done with the heap memory, give it back to the system. Use `free()` to do that. `free()` is a lot easier than `malloc()`. To free the 10 integers allocated with the previous `malloc()`, use `free()` in the following manner:

```
free(temps);   /* Gives the memory back to the heap */
```

If you originally allocated 10 values, 10 are freed. If the `malloc()` that allocated memory for temps had allocated 1,000 values, all 1,000 would be freed. After freeing the memory, you can't get it back. Remember, `free()` tosses the allocated memory back onto the heap of memory—and after it's tossed, another task might grab the memory (remember the dirt heap analogy). If you use `temps` after the previous `free()`, you run the risk of overwriting memory and possibly locking up your computer, requiring a reboot.

If you fail to free allocated memory, your operating system reclaims that memory when your program ends. However, forgetting to call `free()` defeats the purpose of using heap memory in the first place. The goal of the heap is to give your program the opportunity to allocate memory at the point the memory is needed and deallocate that memory when you're finished with it.

Multiple Allocations

An array of pointers often helps you allocate many different sets of heap memory. Going back to the weather forecaster's problem, suppose the forecaster wanted to enter historical temperature readings for several different cities. But the forecaster has a different number of readings for each different city.

An array of pointers is useful for such a problem. Here is how you could allocate an array of 50 pointers:

```
int * temps[50];   /* 50 integer pointers */
```

The array will not hold 50 integers (because of the dereferencing operator in the definition); instead, the array holds 50 pointers. The first pointer is called `temps[0]`, the second pointer is `temps[1]`, and so on. Each of the array elements (each pointer) can point to a different set of allocated heap memory. Therefore, even though the 50 pointer array elements must be defined for all of `main()`, you can allocate and free the data pointed to as you need extra memory.

Consider the following section of code that the forecaster might use:

```
for (ctr = 0; ctr < 50; ctr++)
{
        puts("How many readings for the city?")
        scanf(" %d", &num);


// Allocate that many heap values
        temps[ctr] = (int *)malloc(num * sizeof(int));


// This next section of code would ask for each temperature
// reading for the city
}


// Next section of code would probably be calculations related
// to the per-city data entry


// Don't forget to deallocate the heap memory when done
for (ctr = 0; ctr < 50; ctr++)
{
        free(temps[ctr]);
}
```

Of course, such code requires massive data entry. The values would most likely come from a saved file instead of from the user. Nevertheless, the code gives you insight into the advanced data structures available by using the heap. Also, real-world programs aren't usually of the 20-line variety you often see in this book. Real-world programs, although not necessarily harder than those here, are usually many pages long. Throughout the program, some sections might need extra memory, whereas other sections do not. The heap lets you use memory efficiently.

Figure 26.3 shows you what the heap memory might look like while allocating the temps array memory (after the first 4 of the 50 malloc() calls). As you can see, temps belongs to the program's data area, but the memory each temps element points to belongs to the heap. You can free up the data temps points to when you no longer need the extra workspace.

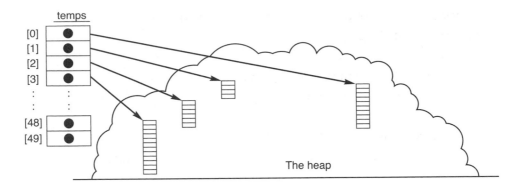

FIGURE 26.3

Each temps *element points to a different part of the heap.*

This has been a long chapter with some complicated material, but you're almost finished! We just need to close the chapter with a program that uses both malloc() and free(), as well as shows you how a small computer program written by you can deal with massive amounts of data.

```c
// Example program #1 from Chapter 26 of Absolute Beginner's Guide
// to C, 3rd Edition
// File Chapter26ex1.c


/* The program looks for a number of random integers, allocates an
array and fills it with numbers between 1 and 500 and then loops
through all the numbers and figures out the smallest, the biggest,
and the average. It then frees the memory. */


#include <stdio.h>
#include <stdlib.h>
#include <time.h>


main()
{

    int i, aSize;

    int * randomNums;
```

```c
    time_t t;

    double total = 0;
    int biggest, smallest;
    float average;

    srand(time(&t));

    printf("How many random numbers do you want in your array? ");
    scanf(" %d", &aSize);

    // Allocate an array of integers equal to the number of
    // elements requested by the user

    randomNums = (int *) malloc(aSize * sizeof(int));

    // Test to ensure that the array allocated properly

    if (!randomNums)
    {
        printf("Random array allocation failed!\n");
        exit(1);
    }
    // Loops through the array and assigns a random
    // number between 1 and 500 to each element

    for (i = 0; i < aSize; i++)
    {
        randomNums[i] = (rand() % 500) + 1;
    }

    // Initialize the biggest and smallest number
    // for comparison's sake

    biggest = 0;
    smallest = 500;
```

```
// Loop through the now-filled array
// testing for the random numbers that
// are biggest, smallest, and adding all
// numbers together to calculate an average

for (i = 0; i < aSize; i++)
{
    total += randomNums[i];
    if (randomNums[i] > biggest)
    {
        biggest = randomNums[i];
    }
    if (randomNums[i] < smallest)
    {
        smallest = randomNums[i];
    }
}

average = ((float)total)/((float)aSize);
printf("The biggest random number is %d.\n", biggest);
printf("The smallest random number is %d.\n", smallest);
printf("The average of the random numbers is %.2f.\n", average);

// When you use malloc, remember to then use free

free(randomNums);

return(0);
}
```

This program has a minimum of user interaction and looks only for the number of random numbers to create. It's an excellent way to test how much memory is on your computer by vastly increasing the size of your random number array. I was able to create an array of 12 million elements without triggering the `malloc` failure section. In fact, when writing this program originally, my `total` variable failed before the `malloc` did. `total` was originally an `int`, and when I set the array to 10 million values, the sum total of the random numbers was bigger than the allowed maximum for an `int` variable. My average calculation was thus wrong. (It seemed wrong—after all, how could the average of numbers between 1 and 500 be –167!) When that variable was increased to a `double`, I was able to build even bigger arrays of random numbers.

Another interesting fact is that, with a small number of elements, your largest, smallest, and average numbers can fluctuate, but the more elements are in your array, the more likely you will get a small of 1, a big of 500, and an average right in the middle.

THE ABSOLUTE MINIMUM

`malloc()` allocates heap memory for your programs. You access that heap via a pointer variable, and you can then get to the rest of the allocated memory using array notation based on the pointer assigned by the `malloc()`. When you are done with heap memory, deallocate that memory with the `free()` function. `free()` tosses the memory back to the heap so other tasks can use it. Key concepts in this chapter include:

- Use `malloc()` and `free()` to allocate and release heap memory.

- Tell `malloc()` exactly how large each allocation must be by using the `sizeof()` operator inside `malloc()`'s parentheses.

- Allocate only the pointer variables at the top of your function along with the other variables. Put the data itself on the heap when you need data values other than simple loop counters and totals.

- If you must track several chunks of heap memory, use an array of pointers. Each array element can point to a different amount of heap space.

- Check to make sure `malloc()` worked properly. `malloc()` returns a 0 if the allocation fails.

- Don't always rely on regular arrays to hold a program's data. Sometimes a program needs data for just a short time, and using the heap makes better use of your memory resources.

SETTING UP YOUR DATA WITH STRUCTURES

Arrays and pointers are nice for lists of values, but those values must all be of the same data type. Sometimes you have different data types that must go together and be treated as a whole.

A perfect example is a customer record. For each customer, you have to track a name (character array), balance (double floating-point), address (character array), city (character array), state (character array), and zip code (character array or long integer). Although you would want to be able to initialize and print individual items within the customer record, you would also want to access the customer record as a whole, such as when you would write it to a customer disk file (as explained in the next chapter).

The C *structure* is the vehicle by which you group data such as would appear in a customer record *and* get to all the individual parts, called *members*. If you have many occurrences of that data and many customers, you need an array of structures.

NOTE Other programming languages have equivalent data groupings called *records*. The designers of C wanted to call these data groupings *structures*, however, so that's what they are in C.

Many times, a C structure holds data that you might store on 3x5 cards in a cardfile. Before personal computers, companies maintained a cardfile box with cards that contained a customer's name, balance, address, city, state, and zip code, like the customer structure just described. Later in this chapter, you'll see how C structures are stored in memory, and you'll see even more similarities to the cardfile cards.

Defining a Structure

The first thing you must do is tell C exactly what your structure will look like. When you define variables of built-in data types such as an int, you don't have to tell C what an int is—C already knows. When you want to define a structure, however, you must first tell C exactly what your structure looks like. Only then can you define variables for that structure.

Try to view a structure as just a group of individual data types. The entire structure has a name and can be considered a single value (such as a customer) taken as a whole. The individual members of the structure are built-in data types, such as int and char arrays, that could represent an age and a name. You can access the individual members if you want to.

Not only is a structure like a cardfile, but you also can see that a structure is a lot like a paper form with blanks to fill in. A blank form, such as one you might fill out when applying for a credit card, is useless by itself. If the credit card company prints 10,000 forms, that doesn't mean it has 10,000 customers. Only when someone fills out the form is there a customer, and only when you define a variable for the structure you describe does C give memory space to a structure variable.

To define an int variable, you only have to do this:

```
int i;
```

You don't first have to tell C what an int is. To define a structure variable, you must first define what the structure looks like and assign a data type name, such as customer, to C. After defining the structure's format, you can define a variable.

The struct statement defines the look (or layout) of a structure. Here is the format of struct:

```
struct [structure tag] {
```

```
    member definition;
    member definition;
    ...
    member definition;
};
```

Again, the `struct` defines only the layout, or the *look*, of a structure. The *structure tag* is a name you give to that particular structure's look, but the *structure tag* has nothing to do with a structure variable name you might create later. After you define the format of a structure, you can define variables.

The *member definitions* are nothing more than regular built-in data type definitions such as `int age;` in the previous example. Instead of defining variables, though, you are defining *members*, essentially giving a name to that particular part of the structure.

 WARNING You *can* define a variable at the same time as the `struct` declaration statement, but most C programmers don't do so. If you want to define a variable for the structure at the same time you declare the structure format itself, insert one or more variable names before the `struct` statement's closing semicolon.

Structures are a lot to absorb. The following example will aid your understanding.

Let's say you're writing a program to track a simple retail computer inventory. You need to track a computer manufacturer and model, amount of disk space (in megabytes), amount of memory space (in megabytes), quantity, cost, and retail price.

First, you must use `struct` to define a structure. Here is a good candidate:

```
struct invStruct {
    char manuf[25]; // Manufacturer name
    char model[15]; // Model code
    int diskSpace; // Disk size in Gigabytes
    int memSpace; // Memory Space in Gigabytes
    int ports; // The number of USB ports on the system
    int quantity; // Number in inventory
    float cost; // Cost of computer
    float price; // Retail price of computer
};
```

Figure 27.1 shows you what this structure format looks like.

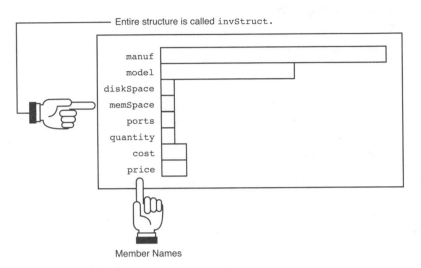

FIGURE 27.1

The format of the invStruct *structure.*

The previous structure definition does *not* define eight variables! The previous structure definition defines a single structure data type. Remember, you don't have to tell C what an integer looks like before defining an integer variable; you *must*, however, tell C what an invStruct looks like before defining variables for that structure data type. The previous struct statement tells C what the user's invStruct is supposed to look like. After C learns the structure's format, C can define variables that take on the format of that structure when the user is ready to define variables.

If you create a structure that you might use again sometime, consider putting it in its own header file, or in a header file along with other common structures. Use #include to pull that header file into any source code that needs it. If you ever need to change the structure definition, you have to look in only one place to change it: in its header file.

Often a programmer puts structure declarations, such as the previous one for invStruct, before main() and then defines variables for that structure in main() and in any other functions below main(). To create variables for the structure, you must do the same thing you do when you create variables for any data type: Put the structure name before a variable list. Because there is no data type named invStruct, you must tell C that invStruct is a struct name. You can define three structure variables like this:

```
#include "c:\cprogramming files\inv.h"
main()
{
        struct invStruct item1, item2, item3;
        // Rest of program would follow...
```

Now you can put data into three variables. These variables are structure variables named item1, item2, and item3. If you wanted to define 500 structure variables, you would use an array:

```
#include "c:\cprogramming files\inv.h"
main()
{
        struct invStruct items[500];
        // Rest of program would follow...
```

Remember, the structure definition must go in the INV.H header file if you take this approach. Otherwise, you must place the structure definition directly inside the program before the structure variables, like this:

```
struct invStruct {
    char manuf[25]; // Manufacturer name
    char model[15]; // Model code
    int diskSpace; // Disk size in Gigabytes
    int memSpace; // Memory Space in Gigabytes
    int ports; // The number of USB ports on the system
    int quantity; // Number in inventory
    float cost; // Cost of computer
    float price; // Retail price of computer
};
main()
{
        struct invStruct items[500];
        // Rest of program would follow...
```

As long as the struct definition appears before main(), you can define invStruct structure variables throughout the rest of the program in any function you write. (The last part of this book explains how to write programs that contain more functions than main().)

Perhaps you will need pointers to three structures instead of structure variables. Define them like this:

```
main()
{
        struct invStruct *item1, *item2,*item3;
        // Rest of program would follow
```

`item1`, `item2`, and `item3` now can point to three structure variables. You can then reserve heap memory for the structures instead of using actual variables. (`sizeof()` works for structure variables to allow for heap structure data.) The following three statements reserve three heap structure areas and make `item1`, `item2`, and `item3` point to those three heap values:

```
item1 = (struct invStruct *)malloc(sizeof(invStruct));

item2 = (struct invStruct *)malloc(sizeof(invStruct));

item3 = (struct invStruct *)malloc(sizeof(invStruct));
```

Putting Data in Structure Variables

A new operator, the *dot operator*, lets you put data in a structure variable's individual members. Here is the format of the dot operator:

```
structureVariableName.memberName
```

To the left of the dot is always the name of a structure variable, such as `item1` or `employee[16]`. To the right of the dot operator is always the name of a member from that structure, such as `quantity`, `cost`, or `name`. The dot operator puts data only in named structure variables. If you want to put data in a heap structure pointed to by a structure pointer variable, you must use the *structure pointer operator*, `->`.

The following program defines an array of three structure variables using a `bookInfo` structure tag shown that is defined in the `bookInfo.h` header file presented first. The user is asked to fill the structure variables, and then the program prints them. In the next couple chapters, you'll see how to output the structure variables to a disk file for long-term storage.

The first file is the header file containing the structure definition:

```
// Example program #A from Chapter 27 of Absolute Beginner's Guide
// to C, 3rd Edition
// File bookinfo.h
```

```
// This header file defines a structure for information about a book
struct bookInfo {
     char title[40];
     char author[25];
     float price;
     int pages;
};
```

And now the .c program file:

```
// Example program #1 from Chapter 27 of Absolute Beginner's Guide
// to C, 3rd Edition
// File Chapter27ex1.c


/* The program gets the bookInfo structure by including bookInfo.h
and asks the user to fill in three structures and then prints them.
*/


//First include the file with the structure definition
#include "bookinfo.h"
#include <stdio.h>



main()
{
    int ctr;
    struct bookInfo books[3]; // Array of three structure variables

    // Get the information about each book from the user

    for (ctr = 0; ctr < 3; ctr++)
    {
        printf("What is the name of the book #%d?\n", (ctr+1));
        gets(books[ctr].title);
        puts("Who is the author? ");
        gets(books[ctr].author);
        puts("How much did the book cost? ");
        scanf(" $%f", &books[ctr].price);
```

```
        puts("How many pages in the book? ");
        scanf(" %d", &books[ctr].pages);
     getchar(); //Clears last newline for next loop
  }


  // Print a header line and then loop through and print the info

  printf("\n\nHere is the collection of books: \n");
  for (ctr = 0; ctr < 3; ctr++)
  {
     printf("#%d: %s by %s", (ctr+1), books[ctr].title,
           books[ctr].author);
     printf("\nIt is %d pages and costs $%.2f", books[ctr].pages,
           books[ctr].price);
     printf("\n\n");
  }
  return(0);

}
```

If you stored the structures on the heap, you couldn't use the dot operator because the dot operator requires a variable name. Use -> to store data in heap structures. -> requires a pointer on the left and a member name on the right. Here is an equivalent program to the previous one, except that the heap and -> are used instead of structure variables and the dot operator.

```
// Example program #2 from Chapter 27 of Absolute Beginner's Guide
// to C, 3rd Edition
// File Chapter27ex2.c

/* The program again looks to fill three book structures with info,
but it uses a pointer array this time. */

//First include the file with the structure definition
#include "bookinfo.h"
#include <stdio.h>
#include <stdlib.h>

main()
```

```c
{
    int ctr;
    struct bookInfo * books[3]; // Array of three structure variables

    // Get the information about each book from the user

    for (ctr = 0; ctr < 3; ctr++)
    {
        books[ctr] = (struct bookInfo*)malloc(sizeof
                            (struct bookInfo));
        printf("What is the name of the book #%d?\n", (ctr+1));
        gets(books[ctr]->title);
        puts("Who is the author? ");
        gets(books[ctr]->author);
        puts("How much did the book cost? ");
        scanf(" $%f", &books[ctr]->price);
        puts("How many pages in the book? ");
        scanf(" %d", &books[ctr]->pages);
        getchar(); //Clears newline input to keep things clean for
                    // next round
    }

    // Print a header line and then loop through and print the info

    printf("\n\nHere is the collection of books: \n");
    for (ctr = 0; ctr < 3; ctr++)
    {
        printf("#%d: %s by %s", (ctr+1), books[ctr]->title,
            books[ctr]->author);
        printf("\nIt is %d pages and costs $%.2f", books[ctr]->pages,
            books[ctr]->price);
        printf("\n\n");
    }
    return(0);
}
```

THE ABSOLUTE MINIMUM

This chapter's goal was to teach you about structures. A *structure* is an aggregate variable data type. Whereas an array must hold values that are all the same data type, a structure can hold several values of different data types.

Before using a structure variable, you must tell C exactly what the structure looks like with a `struct` statement. The `struct` statement lets C know how many members are in the structure and the data types of each member. A structure variable is like a group of more than one variable of different data types. Key concepts in this chapter include:

- Define structures when you want to group items of different data types.

- Declare a structure before defining a structure variable.

- Use the dot operator to access individual data members within a structure variable.

- Use the `->` (the *structure pointer operator*) to access individual data members within a structure pointed to by a pointer variable.

- Don't use member names as variables. Member names exist only so you can work with an individual part of a structure.

- Don't forget to add a semicolon to the end of all structure definitions.

- Don't intermix the dot operator and the structure pointer operator. Remember that a structure variable must appear before the dot operator, and a structure *pointer* variable must appear before the `->` operator.

IN THIS CHAPTER

- Storing information in disk files
- Opening a file
- Using sequential files

28

SAVING SEQUENTIAL FILES TO YOUR COMPUTER

None of the programs you've seen so far has been able to store data for very long. Think about this for a moment: If you defined an integer variable, put a 14 in it, and then turned off the computer (believe me now and try it later), that variable would no longer have 14 in it. If you turned your computer back on and tried to find the value in the variable, you couldn't find it—no way.

This chapter explains how to save data to your disk. When the data is on your disk, it will be there until you change or erase it. Data on your disk is just like music on a tape. You can turn off the tape deck, and the tape will hold the music until you change it. There's no good reason why a user should enter data, such as historical sales records, more than once.

NOTE Files are critical to computer data programs. How useful would a word processor be without files?

Disk Files

Disks hold data in *files*. You already understand the concept of files if you've saved a C program to a disk file. Files can hold either programs or data. Your programs must be loaded from disk into memory before you can run them. You also must load data from the disk file into variables before you can work with the data. The variables also hold data before the data goes to a disk file.

Two types of files exist: *sequential-access files* and *random-access files*. Their types determine how you can access them. If you work with a sequential-access file, you have to read or write the file in the order of the data. In a random-access file, you can jump around, reading and writing any place in the file.

TIP A sequential file is like a video tape, and a random-access file is like a DVD or Blu-Ray. You have to watch a movie in sequence on a tape (or fast-forward through it in order), whereas you can skip to different chapters on a DVD or a Blu-Ray.

All disk files have names that conform to the same naming rules as filenames on your operating system. Before you can use a disk file, whether to create, read, or change the data in the file, you must *open* the file.

As with a filing cabinet, you can't use a disk file without opening the file. Instead of pulling out a drawer, your computer attaches something called a *file pointer* to the file and makes sure that the disk is properly set up to hold the file you specify.

Opening a File

To open a file, you must use the `fopen()` function, whose description is included along with `printf()`'s in `stdio.h`. Before seeing `fopen()`, you have to understand the concept of a file pointer.

NOTE The concept of a file pointer is easy to understand. A regular pointer holds the address of data in a variable. A file pointer holds the disk location of the disk file you're working with.

You must specify a special statement to define a file pointer. As with any variable, you can name file pointers anything you want. Suppose you want to open an employee file. Before the `fopen()`, you must define a file pointer variable. If you called the file pointer `fptr`, here is how you would define a file pointer:

```
FILE * fptr;  /* Defines a file pointer named fptr */
```

WARNING Most C programmers define their file pointers before `main()`. This makes the file pointer *global*, which is a fancy term meaning that the entire program can use the file. (Most other kinds of variables are *local*, not global.) Because part of the file pointer statement is in upper case, `FILE` is defined someplace with `#define`. `FILE` is defined in `stdio.h`, which is the primary reason you should include the `stdio.h` header file when your program uses the disk for data.

After you define a file pointer, you can connect that pointer to a file with `fopen()`. After you specify `fopen()`, you can use the file throughout the rest of the program. Here is the way to open a file named `C:\cprograms\cdata.txt`.

TIP If you don't have a `C:` drive, change the `C:` in these examples to a different drive letter. In fact, if you want to put your files in a specific folder but are not sure of the path, right-click a file in that folder and select Properties from the menu. You should see the directory path of the folder, which you can then use in your `fopen()` statement.

```
#include <stdio.h>
FILE *fptr; // Defines a file pointer
main()
{
        fptr = fopen("c:\cprograms\cdata.txt", "w");
        // rest of program would follow
        fclose (fptr); // Always close files you've opened
```

For the rest of the program, you'll access the `cdata.txt` file via the file pointer, not via the filename. Using a file pointer variable is easier and less error prone than typing the filename and complete pathname to the file every time you must access the file.

WARNING Close your filing cabinet drawers when you're done with your files, or you'll hit your head! Close all open files when you're finished with them, or you could lose some data. `fclose()` is the opposite of `fopen()`. In its parentheses, `fclose()` requires a file pointer of the file you want to close.

If the file pointer equals 0, you know that an error happened. C returns a 0 from `fopen()` if an error occurs when you open a file. For example, if you attempt to open a file on a disk drive that doesn't exist, `fopen()` returns an error.

The `"w"` (the second argument in the previous code's `fopen()`) means *write*. The second argument of `fopen()` must be one of the string *mode* values in Table 28.1.

TABLE 28.1 The Basic `fopen()` Mode Strings

Mode	Description
`"w"`	Write mode that creates a new file whether it exists or not.
`"r"`	Read mode that lets you read an existing file. If the file doesn't exist, you get an error.
`"a"`	Append mode that lets you add to the end of a file or create the file if it doesn't already exist.

Using Sequential Files

You'll do only three things with a sequential file: create it, read it, and add to it (write to it). To write to a file, you can use `fprintf()`. `fprintf()` is easy because it's just a `printf()` with a file pointer at the beginning of its parentheses. The following program creates a file and writes some data to it using `fprintf()`:

```
// Example program #1 from Chapter 28 of Absolute Beginner's Guide
// to C, 3rd Edition
// File Chapter28ex1.c

/* The program takes the book info program from chapter 27 and
writes the info to a file named bookinfo.txt. */

//First include the file with the structure definition
#include "bookinfo.h"
#include <stdio.h>
#include <stdlib.h>
FILE * fptr;

main()
{
    int ctr;
    struct bookInfo books[3]; // Array of three structure variables
```

```
// Get the information about each book from the user

for (ctr = 0; ctr < 3; ctr++)
{
    printf("What is the name of the book #%d?\n", (ctr+1));
    gets(books[ctr].title);
    puts("Who is the author? ");
    gets(books[ctr].author);
    puts("How much did the book cost? ");
    scanf(" $%f", &books[ctr].price);
    puts("How many pages in the book? ");
    scanf(" %d", &books[ctr].pages);
    getchar(); //Clears last newline for next loop
}


// Remember when typing your filename path to double up the
// backslashes or C will think you are putting in a conversion
// character

fptr = fopen("C:\\users\\DeanWork\\Documents\\BookInfo.txt","w");

// Test to ensure that the file opened

if (fptr == 0)
{
    printf("Error--file could not be opened.\n");
    exit (1);
}


// Print a header line and then loop through and print the info
// to your file, but this time this printout will be in your
// file and not on the screen.

fprintf(fptr, "\n\nHere is the collection of books: \n");
for (ctr = 0; ctr < 3; ctr++)
{
```

```
        fprintf(fptr, "#%d: %s by %s", (ctr+1), books[ctr].title,
            books[ctr].author);
        fprintf(fptr, "\nIt is %d pages and cost $%.2f",
            books[ctr].pages, books[ctr].price);
        fprintf(fptr, "\n\n");
    }
    fclose(fptr); // Always close your files
    return(0);
}
```

If you ran this program and looked at the contents of the file named `bookinfo.txt` (just find the file and double-click it, and Notepad should open it), you would see the book info you entered. Here's what mine looked like:

```
Here is the collection of books:
#1: 10 Count Trivia by Dean Miller
It is 250 pages and costs $14.99


#2: Moving from C to C++ by Greg Perry
It is 600 pages and costs $39.99


#3: The Stand by Stephen King
It is 1200 pages and costs $24.99
```

Miller, Perry, and King—nice to see the three great authors of our time collected into one file! The nice thing about reusing the program from Chapter 27, "Setting Up Your Data with Structures," is that it shows how easily you can adapt what you've already learned (and programs that you've already written) to file work. All this took was declaring the file pointer, opening the file (and making sure it opened properly), and changing the `printf()` statements to `fprintf()` statements for any output you wanted to go to the file instead of the screen.

 WARNING Opening a file in "w" mode overwrites an existing file with the same name. So if you run the previous program twice, the file will have only your data from the second run. If you want to build on to the file and keep the previous data, you need to open the file in "a" mode.

Now that you can write data to a file, how would you go about getting that information? Use `fgets()` to read the contents of the file. `fgets()` is nothing more than a `gets()` that you can direct to a disk file. `fgets()` reads lines from a file into character arrays (or allocated heap memory pointed to with a character pointer).

TIP   Think of the *f* at the beginning of `fputs()` and `fgets()` as standing for *file*. `puts()` and `gets()` go to the screen and keyboard, respectively; `fputs()` and `fgets()` write and read their data from files.

Unlike `gets()`, `fgets()` requires that you specify a maximum length for the array you're reading into. You might read past the end of the file (producing an error) if you're not careful, so be sure to check for the location of the end of the file.

`fgets()` reads one line at a time. If you specify more characters to read in the `fgets()` than actually reside on the file's line you're reading, `fgets()` stops reading the line of data as long as the file's lines end with a newline character. The previous program that created the `bookinfo.txt` file always wrote \n at the end of each line so that subsequent `fgets()` functions could read the file line by line.

The following program loops through a file (in this case, the `bookinfo.txt` created in the last example) and prints the info on the screen.

```
// Example program #2 from Chapter 28 of Absolute Beginner's Guide
// to C, 3rd Edition
// File Chapter28ex2.c


/* The program takes the book info file from the first example of
chapter 28; also reads each line from the file and outputs it to the
screen. */

#include <stdio.h>
#include <stdlib.h>
FILE * fptr;

main()
{
    char fileLine[100]; // Will hold each line of input
    fptr = fopen("C:\\users\\DeanWork\\Documents\\BookInfo.txt","r");

    if (fptr != 0)
    {
        while (!feof(fptr))
        {
            fgets(fileLine, 100, fptr);
            if (!feof(fptr))
```

```
            {
                puts(fileLine);
            }
        }
    }
    else
    {
        printf("\nError opening file.\n");
    }
    fclose(fptr); // Always close your files
    return(0);
}
```

`feof()` returns a true condition if you just read the last line from the file. The `feof()` really isn't needed in the previous program because we know exactly what the `bookinfo.txt` contains. (We just created the file in an earlier program.) We know how many lines are in the files, but you should generally use `feof()` when reading from disk files. You often don't know exactly how much data the file contains because other people using other programs might have added data to the file.

 WARNING In the `fprintf()` function, the file pointer goes at the beginning of the function. In the `fgets()` function, the file pointer goes at the *end*. There's nothing like consistency!

You also can use an `fscanf()` to read individual numeric values from a data file if you wrote the values with a corresponding `fprintf()`.

You can add to a file by opening the file in append mode and outputting data to it. The following program adds the line `More books to come!` to the end of the book `info.txt` data file:

```
// Example program #3 from Chapter 28 of Absolute Beginner's Guide
// to C, 3rd Edition
// File Chapter28ex3.c


/* The program opens the existing book info file from the first
example of chapter 28, and adds a line to the end. */


#include <stdio.h>
#include <stdlib.h>
```

```
FILE * fptr;

main()
{
    fptr = fopen("C:\\users\\DeanWork\\Documents\\BookInfo.txt","a");

    if (fptr == 0)
    {
        printf("Error opening the file! Sorry!\n");
        exit (1);
    }


    // Adds the line at the end
    fprintf(fptr, "\nMore books to come!\n");

    fclose(fptr); // Always close your files
    return(0);
}
```

Here is what MYDATA.DAT now contains (notice the extra line):

```
Here is the collection of books:
#1: 10 Count Trivia by Dean Miller
It is 250 pages and costs $14.99

#2: Moving from C to C++ by Greg Perry
It is 600 pages and costs $39.99

#3: The Stand by Stephen King
It is 1200 pages and costs $24.99


More books to come!
```

THE ABSOLUTE MINIMUM

The goal of this chapter was to show you how to create, read, and write sequential files. Your C program must open a file before data can be written to or read from the file. When your program is done with a file, the program should close the file.

When reading from a file, you must check for the end-of-file condition to ensure that you don't try to read past the end of the file. The `feof()` function is a built-in C function that you use to check for the end of the file. Key concepts from this chapter include:

- Store long-term data in data files.

- Open a file with `fopen()` before you use the file.

- Always close a file with `fclose()` when you're done.

- Don't read from a file without checking for `feof()` because you might have previously read the last line in the file.

- Don't use the filename when you open a file. Use the file pointer that you connected to the file with `fopen()`.

- Don't forget that the file pointer goes at the *beginning* of `fprintf()` and that `fputs()` requires a file pointer at the *end* of its argument list.

SAVING RANDOM FILES TO YOUR COMPUTER

This chapter shows you how to skip around in a file, reading and writing data as you go. The preceding chapter introduced methods you can use to write, read, or append data to a file. The problem is, when you open a sequential file for reading, you can *only* read it.

Sometimes you might want to read a customer structure from disk and change the customer's balance. You certainly wouldn't want to have to create a new file just so you could write that one change. Instead, you would want to read the customer information into a variable, change it, and then write it back to disk exactly where it first resided. As Figure 29.1 shows, random files let you skip around in the file, reading and writing at any point you access.

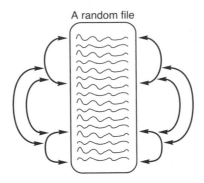

FIGURE 29.1

Random files let you read and write data in any order.

The physical layout of a file doesn't define the type of file (whether random or sequential). You can create a file sequentially and then read and change it randomly. To C, a file is just a stream of bytes, and the way you access it isn't linked to any format of the file.

Opening Random Files

To read or write a file randomly, you must open the file randomly. Table 29.1 lists the modes that access random files. As you can see, the cornerstone of random-access files is the use of the plus sign combined with the access modes you learned about in the previous chapter.

TABLE 29.1 The Random-Access `fopen()` Modes

Mode	Description
`"r+"`	Opens an existing file for both reading and writing
`"w+"`	Opens a new file for writing and reading
`"a+"`	Opens a file in append mode (the file pointer points to the end of the file), but lets you move back through the file, reading and writing as you go

NOTE As with sequential files, the access mode is a string that appears as the last argument of `fopen()`. You close open random files with `fclose()`, just as you do with sequential files.

All three modes let you read and write to the file. The access mode you choose depends on what you want to do *first* to the file. If the file exists and you want to access the file randomly, use the r+ mode. If you want to create the file, use w+. (If the file already exists, C overwrites the existing version.) If you want to add to the end of a file but optionally "back up" and read and write existing data, use a+.

Here is a sample fopen() statement that opens a new file for writing and reading:

```
fptr = fopen("C:\\Users\DeanWork\\letters.txt", "w+");
```

As with sequential files, the fptr variable must be a file pointer variable. The double backslash is needed if you specify a pathname. Remember that fopen() returns a zero if the open fails.

 TIP   You can store the filename in a character array and use the character array name in place of an actual string literal for the filename.

Moving Around in a File

Use the fseek() function to move around in a file. After you open a file, C initializes the file pointer to point to the next place in the file you can read or write. fseek() moves the file pointer so that you can read and write at places that would normally not be pointed at using sequential access. Here is the format of fseek():

```
fseek(filePtr, longVal, origin);
```

The *filePtr* is the file pointer used in the fopen() function that used a random-access mode. The *longVal* is a longint variable or literal that can be either positive or negative. The *lonqVal* is the number of bytes to skip forward or backward in the file. The *origin* is always one of the values shown in Table 29.2. *origin* tells fseek() where to start seeking.

TABLE 29.2   origin **Values That Can Appear in** fseek()

Origin	Description
SEEK_SET	Beginning of file
SEEK_CUR	Current position in file
SEEK_END	End of file

The *origin* value tells C the position *from where* you want to access the random file next. After you position the file pointer with fseek(), you can use file input and output functions to write and read to and from the file. If you position the file pointer at the end of the file (using SEEK_END) and then write data, new data goes to the end of the file. If you position the file pointer over existing data (using SEEK_SET and SEEK_CUR) and then write new data, the new data replaces the existing data.

 WARNING Use fseek() for random-access files only. Sequential files can be accessed only in the order of the data.

Table 29.2's values are in uppercase, which implies that they're defined somewhere. They're defined in stdio.h using #define directives.

The following program opens a file for random-access mode, writes the letters A through Z to the file, and then rereads those letters backward. The file doesn't have to be reopened before the reading begins because of the random-access mode "w+".

```
// Example program #1 from Chapter 29 of Absolute Beginner's Guide
// to C, 3rd Edition
// File Chapter29ex1.c

/* The program opens a file named letters.txt and prints A through Z
into the file
It then loops backward through the file printing each of the letters
    from Z to A. */

#include <stdio.h>
#include <stdlib.h>
FILE * fptr;

main()
{
    char letter;
    int i;

    fptr = fopen("C:\\users\\deanwork\\documents\\letters.txt",
                "w+");

    if (fptr == 0)
    {
        printf("There was an error while opening the file.\n");
        exit(1);
```

```
    }

    for (letter = 'A'; letter <= 'Z'; letter++)
    {
        fputc(letter, fptr);
    }

    puts("Just wrote the letters A through Z");

    // Now read the file backwards

    fseek(fptr, -1, SEEK_END); // Minus 1 byte from the end
    printf("Here is the file backwards:\n");
    for (i = 26; i > 0; i--)
    {
        letter = fgetc(fptr);
        // Reads a letter, then backs up 2
        fseek(fptr, -2, SEEK_CUR);
        printf("The next letter is %c.\n", letter);
    }

    fclose(fptr); // Again, always close your files

    return(0);
}
```

 TIP   As you can see, `fputc()` is a great function for outputting individual characters to a file. `fgetc()` reads individual characters from a file. `fputc()` and `fgetc()` are to `putc()` and `getc()` what `fputs()` and `fgets()` are to `puts()` and `gets()`.

So far, you might not see a purpose for random-access files. Random access offers you the advantage of writing data to a file and then rereading the same data without closing and opening the file. Also, `fseek()` lets you position the file pointer any number of bytes from the beginning, middle, or end of the file.

Assuming that the file of letters still resides on the disk from the last program, this next program asks the user which position he or she wants to change. The program then positions the file pointer with `fseek()` and writes an * at that point before using `fseek()` to return to the beginning of the file and printing it again.

```c
// Example program #2 from Chapter 29 of Absolute Beginner's Guide
// to C, 3rd Edition
// File Chapter29ex2.c

/* The program opens the file created in the first program of the
chapter and changes one of the letters to an *. It then prints the new
list with the altered list of letters.*/

#include <stdio.h>
#include <stdlib.h>
FILE * fptr;

main()
{
    char letter;
    int i;

    fptr = fopen("C:\\users\\deanwork\\documents\\letters.txt", "r+");

    if (fptr == 0)
    {
        printf("There was an error while opening the file.\n");
        exit(1);
    }

    printf("Which # letter would you like to change (1-26)? ");
    scanf(" %d", &i);

    // Seeks that position from the beginning of the file
    fseek(fptr, (i-1), SEEK_SET); // Subtract 1 from the position
                                  // because array starts at 0

    // Write an * over the letter in that position
    fputc('*', fptr);

    // Now jump back to the beginning of the array and print it out
```

```
    fseek(fptr, 0, SEEK_SET);
    printf("Here is the file now:\n");
    for (i = 0; i < 26; i++)
    {
        letter = fgetc(fptr);
        printf("The next letter is %c.\n", letter);
    }


    fclose(fptr); // Again, always close your files
    return(0);
}
```

The program prints the contents of the file after the * is written at the position indicated by the user. Here is a sample session:

```
The next letter is A.
The next letter is B.
The next letter is C.
The next letter is D.
The next letter is E.
The next letter is F.
The next letter is G.
The next letter is *.
The next letter is I.
The next letter is J.
The next letter is K.
The next letter is L.
The next letter is M.
The next letter is N.
The next letter is O.
The next letter is P.
The next letter is Q.
The next letter is R.
The next letter is S.
The next letter is T.
The next letter is U.
The next letter is V.
The next letter is W.
```

```
The next letter is X.
The next letter is Y.
The next letter is Z.
```

As you can see, the eighth position of the alphabetical file, the letter H, now contains an asterisk. The rest of the file remains unchanged.

NOTE If you ran this program a second time and changed a different letter (say, the 15th position of the alphabet, the O), your file would print with asterisks instead of H and O because the change to the H is now permanent in the letters.txt file. You could run the program 26 times and replace every letter if you wanted.

THE ABSOLUTE MINIMUM

The goal of this chapter was to explain how random-access files work. When you open a file in random-access mode, you can read and write to that file in any order you need to. The fseek() function is the built-in function that skips around the file from position to position.

Being able to change the contents of a file is important when you want to update file data. Often you will want to change a person's address, change an inventory item's quantity, and so on without rewriting the entire file as you would have to if you used sequential file processing. Key concepts from this chapter include:

- Use a plus sign in the fopen() mode string if you need to change data in a file.

- Remember that fseek() moves a file pointer all around a random file so that you can read or write from the beginning, middle, or end.

- Don't forget to close a file when you are done with it.

- Don't attempt to work with a file if the fopen() fails (by returning a zero).

ORGANIZING YOUR PROGRAMS WITH FUNCTIONS

Typical computer programs are not the 20- to 30-line variety that you see in textbooks. In the "real world," computer programs are much longer—but long programs contain lots of code that can get in the way while learning new concepts. That's why, until this point, you've seen fairly short programs that contain all their code in main().

If you were to put an entire long program in main(), you would spend a lot of time trying to find anything specific if you later needed to change it. This chapter is the first of three chapters that explore ways to partition your programs into sections via multiple functions. Categorizing your code by breaking it into sections makes programs easier to write and also easier to maintain.

People have to write, change, and fix code. The clearer you make the code by writing lots of functions that do individual tasks, the faster you can get home from your programming job and relax! As you'll see, separate functions let you focus on code that needs changing.

Form Follows C Functions

C was designed to force you to think in a modular style through the use of functions. A C program isn't just one long program. It's made up of many routines named, as you know, *functions*. One of the program's functions (the one always required and usually listed first) is named `main()`.

If your program does a lot, break it into several functions. Each function should do one primary task. For instance, if you were writing a C program to assign an ID number to a new employee, get the person's contact information, and then add him or her to the payroll, you *could* write all of this in one big function—all in `main()`—as the following program outline shows:

```
main()
{
        // Not a working program, just an outline…

    …

        // First section of code that assigns an ID number to an
        // employee

    …

        // Next section of code has the user input basic contact info

    …

        // Final section of code adds the employee to the payroll
        // system

    …

        return(0);

}
```

This program does *not* offer a good format for the tasks you want accomplished because it's too sequential. All the code appears in `main()`, even though several distinct tasks need to be done. This program might not require many lines of code, but it's much better to get in the habit of breaking every program into distinct tasks.

 NOTE Breaking programs into smaller functions is called *structured programming.*

Don't use `main()` to do everything. In fact, you should use `main()` to do very little except call each of the other functions. A better way to organize this program would be to write separate functions for each task the program is to do. Of course, not every function should be a single line, but make sure each function acts as a building block and performs only a single task.

Here is a better outline for the program just described:

```
main()
{
        assignID(); // Sets up a unique ID for the new employee
        buildContact(); // Enters the employee's basic contact info
        payrollAdd(); // Adds the new employee to the payroll system
        return 0;
}
/* Second function, one that sets an ID for the new employee
assignID()*/
{
        // Block of C code to set up a unique ID for the
        // new employee
        return;
}


/* Next function—the contact building function */
buildContact()
{
        // Block of code to input the employee's
        // home address, phone number, birth date,
        // and so on
        return;
}


/* Fourth function to add employee to the payroll */
payrollAdd()
{
        // Code to set the new employee's salary,
        // benefits, and other info in the
        // payroll system
        return;
}
```

NOTE Even though this program outline is longer than the previous one, this one is better organized and, therefore, easier to maintain. The only thing main() does is control the other functions by showing an overview of how they're called.

Each separate function does its thing and then returns to main(), where main() calls the next function until there are no more functions. main() then returns to your operating system. main() acts almost like a table of contents for the program. With adequate comments, main() lets you know exactly what functions contain code you need to change.

TIP A good rule of thumb is that a function should not take more lines than will fit on a single screen. If the function is longer than that, you're probably making it do too much. In high school, didn't you *hate* to read literature books with l-o-n-g chapters? You'll also dislike working on programs with long functions.

Any function can call any other function. For example, if you wanted buildContact() to print the complete contact info after it was entered, you might have buildContact() call another function named printContact(). printContact() would then return to buildContact() when it finishes. Here is the outline of such a code:

```c
main()
{
        assignID(); // Sets up a unique ID for the new employee
        buildContact(); // Enters the employee's basic contact info
        payrollAdd(); // Adds the new employee to the payroll system
        return 0;
}
/* Second function, one that sets an ID for the new employee
assignID()*/
{
        // Block of C code to set up a unique ID for the
        // new employee
        return;
}


/* Next function—the contact building function */
buildContact()
```

```
{
        // Block of code to input the employee's
        // home address, phone number, birth date,
        // and so on
        printContact();
        return;
}


/* Fourth function to add employee to the payroll */
payrollAdd()
{
        // Code to set the new employee's salary,
        // benefits, and other info in the
        // payroll system
        return;
}


/* Fifth function to print an entire contact onscreen */
printContact()
{
        // Code to print the contact
        return; // Returns to buildContact(), not to main()
}
```

 NOTE   Look at all the functions in the Draw Poker game in Appendix B, "The Draw Poker Program." The program is only a few pages long, but it contains several functions. Look through the code and see if you can find a function that calls another function located elsewhere in the program.

The entire electronics industry has learned something from the programming world. Most electronic components today, such as televisions, computers, and phones, contain a lot of boards that can be removed, updated, and replaced without affecting the rest of the system. In a similar way, you'll be able to change certain workings of your programs: If you write well-structured programs by using functions, you can then change only the functions that need changing without having to mess with a lot of unrelated code.

Local or Global?

The program outline explained in the preceding section needs more code to work. Before being able to add code, you need to take a closer look at variable definitions. In C, all variables can be either *local* or *global*. All the variables you have seen so far have been local. Most of the time, a local variable is safer than a global variable because a local variable offers itself on a *need-to-know access*. That is, if a function needs a variable, it can have access to another function's local variables through a variable-passing process described in the next chapter.

If a function doesn't need to access another function's local variable, it can't have access. Any function can read, change, and zero out global variables, so they don't offer as much safety.

The following rules describe the difference between local and global variables:

- A variable is *global* only if you define the variable (such as `int i;`) before a function name.

- A variable is *local* only if you define it after an opening brace. A function always begins with opening braces. Some statements, such as `while`, also have opening braces, and you can define local variables within those braces as well.

 TIP   An opening and closing brace enclose what is known as a *block*.

Given these rules, it should be obvious that `l1` and `l2` are local variables and that `g1` and `g2` are global variables in the following program:

```
// Example program #1 from Chapter 30 of Absolute Beginner's Guide
// to C, 3rd Edition
// File Chapter30ex1.c


/* The program is a simple demonstration of the difference between
global variables and local variables. */


#include <stdio.h>
int g1 = 10;


main()
{
    float l1;
```

```
    l1 = 9.0;

    printf("%d %.2f\n", g1, l1); // prints the 1st global and first
                                 //      local variable
    prAgain(); // calls our first function
    return 0;
}


float g2 = 19.0;

prAgain()
{
    int l2 = 5;

    // Can't print l1--it is local to main
    printf("%d %.2f %d\n", l2, g2, g1);
    return;
}
```

TIP   You might not yet completely understand the `return 0;` statement. To make matters worse, `return` by itself is used at the end of the `prAgain()` function. You'll find a detailed description for `return` in the next two chapters.

The variable g2 is global because it's defined before a function (`prAgain()`).

Local variables are usable *only* within their own block of code. Therefore, `l1` could never be printed or changed in `prAgain()` because `l1` is local to `main()`. Conversely, `l2` could never be used in `main()` because `l2` is visible only to `prAgain()`. The variable `g1` is visible to the entire program. `g2` is visible only from its point of definition *down*.

TIP   All global variables are known from their points of definition *down* in the source file. Don't define a global variable in the middle of a program (as is done in the preceding program) because its definition can be too hard to find during debugging sessions. You should limit (or eliminate) the use of globals. If you use them at all, define all of them before `main()`, where they are easy to find (such as if you need to change them or look at their defined data types).

The program outline shown earlier has a problem. If you use only local variables (and you should always try to), the user ID created in `assignID()` cannot be used in `buildContact()` or `addPayroll()`. Stay tuned—the next chapter shows you the solution.

 WARNING If you compile the previous program and receive a compiler warning about a call to a function without a prototype, ignore the warning for now. Chapter 32, "Returning Data from Your Functions," answers your questions.

THE ABSOLUTE MINIMUM

The goal of this chapter was to teach you the building-block approach to writing C programs. Long programs can become unwieldy unless you break them into several separate functions. One long `main()` function is analogous to a long book without chapter divisions. Break your long programs into separate functions, and have each function perform a single, separate task in the program.

When you divide your programs into several functions, you have to consider how variables are used throughout the code. Local variables are defined inside a function and are usable only in that function. The opposite of a local variable is a global variable, whose value is usable in all functions after its definition. Global variables are frowned upon. Local variables are safer because you can limit their access to only functions that need to use them. In the next chapter, you learn how to share local variables between functions. Key concepts from this chapter include:

- Define local variables after a block's opening brace. Define global variables before a function begins.

- Local variables are safer than global variables, so use local variables as much as possible.

- Break your programs into lots of functions to ease maintenance and speed development time.

- Don't define global variables in the middle of a program. They're too hard to locate if you do.

- Don't start out using global variables. As your program grows, you might occasionally see the need for a global variable—add one then. (The next chapter talks more about using local variables in place of globals.)

PASSING VARIABLES TO YOUR FUNCTIONS

The preceding chapter left some questions unanswered. If multiple functions are good (they are), and if local variables are good (they are), then you must have a way to share local variables between functions that need to share them (there is a way). You don't want *all* functions to have access to *all* variables because not every function needs access to every variable. If full variable access between functions is needed, you might as well use global variables.

To share data from function to function, you must *pass* variables from function to function. When one function passes a variable to another function, only those two functions have access to the variable (assuming that the variable is local). This chapter explains how to pass variables between functions.

Passing Arguments

When you pass a variable from one function to another, you are *passing an argument* from the first function to the next. You can pass more than one variable at a time. The receiving function *receives the parameters* from the function that sent the variables.

 WARNING The words *variable*, *argument*, and *parameter* are sometimes used interchangeably when passing and receiving values. The name is not as important as understanding what is happening. Figure 31.1 helps explain these terms.

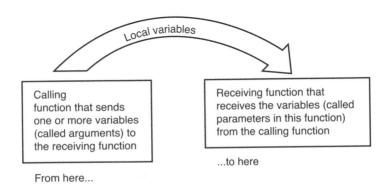

Local variables

Calling function that sends one or more variables (called arguments) to the receiving function

Receiving function that receives the variables (called parameters in this function) from the calling function

...to here

From here...

FIGURE 31.1

Getting the terms correct.

Methods of Passing Arguments

You pass arguments from a function to another function in two ways: *by value* and *by address*. Both of these methods pass arguments *to* a receiving function from a calling function. There is also a way to *return* a value from a function back to the calling function (see the next chapter).

All this talk of passing values focuses on the parentheses that follow function names. That's right, those empty parentheses have a use after all! The variables you want to pass go inside the parentheses of the function call and also in the receiving function, as you'll see in the next section.

 NOTE Yes, this passing values stuff is important! It's easy, though, as you'll see.

Passing by Value

Sometimes *passing by value* is called *passing by copy*. You'll hear these terms used interchangeably because they mean the same thing. Passing by value means that the *value* of the variable is passed to the receiving function, not the variable itself. Here is a program that passes a value from `main()` to `half()`:

```c
// Example program #1 from Chapter 31 of Absolute Beginner's Guide
// to C, 3rd Edition
// File Chapter31ex1.c

/* The program demonstrates passing a variable to a function by
value. */


#include <stdio.h>

main()
{
    int i;

    printf("Please enter an integer... ");
    scanf(" %d", &i);

    // Now call the half function, passing the value of i

    half(i);
    // Shows that the function did not alter i's value
    printf("In main(), i is still %d.\n", i);

    return(0); // Ends the program
}


/**************************************************************/

/* Sometimes putting dividers like the one above is a nice break
   between your different functions. */

half (int i)  // Recieves the value of i
```

```
{
    i = i / 2;
    printf("Your value halved is %d.\n", i);
    return; // Returns to main
}
```

Here is a sample of the program's output:

```
Please enter an integer… 28
Your value halved is 14.
In main(), i is still 28.
```

Study this first line of the `half()` function:

```
half(int i)   /* Receives value of i */
```

Notice that you must put the data type (int) inside the receiving function's parameter list. As Figure 31.2 shows, the contents of i are passed to `half()`. The i in `main()` is never changed *because only a copy of its value is passed.*

```
main( )
{
    int i;
    /* Prompt and input code go here*/
    half(i);      value of i
    return 0;
}
                        half(int i)
                        {
                            i = i / 2
                            printf( /*Rest of printf()*/
                            return;
                        }
```

FIGURE 31.2

The value of i is passed, not the variable i.

If you passed more than one variable separated by commas, all would have to have their data types listed as well, even if they were all the same type. Here is a function that receives three variables: a floating point, a character array, and an integer:

```
aFun(float x, char name[15], int age)   /* Receives three arguments */
```

WARNING Passing by value protects a variable. If the receiving function changes a passed-by-value variable, the calling function's variable is left unchanged. Therefore, passing by value is always safe because the receiving function can't change the passing function's variables—it can only use them.

If the previous program's receiving function called its parameter i2, the program would still work the way it does now. The i2 would be local to half(), whereas the i in main() would be local to main(). The i2 would be local to the half() function and distinct from main().

C uses the passing by value method for all non-array variables. Therefore, if you pass any variable that is not an array to a function, only a copy of that variable's value is passed. The variable is left unchanged in the calling function, no matter what the called function does with the value.

Passing by Address

When you pass an array to another function, the array is passed by address. Instead of a copy of the array being passed, the memory address of the array is passed. The receiving function then places its receiving parameter array *over* the address passed. The bottom line is that the receiving function works with the same address as the calling function. If the receiving function changes one of the variables in the parameter list, *the calling function's argument changes as well.*

The following program passes an array to a function. The function puts X throughout the array, and then main() prints the array. Notice that main() prints all Xs because the function changed the argument.

```
// Example program #2 from Chapter 31 of Absolute Beginner's Guide
// to C, 3rd Edition
// File Chapter31ex2.c

/* The program demonstrates passing an array to a function. */

#include <stdio.h>
#include <string.h>

main()
{
    char name[15] = "Michael Hatton";
    change(name);
```

```
        printf("Back in main(), the name is now %s.\n", name);

        return(0); // Ends the program
}


/******************************************************************/

/* Sometimes putting dividers like the one above is a nice break
   between your different functions. */

change(char name[15])  // Recieves the value of i
{
    // Change the string stored at the address pointed to by name

    strcpy(name, "XXXXXXXXXXXXXX");
    return; // Returns to main
}
```

This program produces the following output:

```
Back in main(), the name is now XXXXXXXXXXXXXX.
```

If you want to override the passing of non-arrays by value, you can force C to pass regular non-array variables by address. However, doing so looks really crazy! Here is a program, similar to the first one you saw in this chapter, that produces a different output:

```
// Example program #3 from Chapter 31 of Absolute Beginner's Guide
// to C, 3rd Edition
// File Chapter31ex3.c


/* The program demonstrates passing a variable to a function by
address. */

#include <stdio.h>

main()
{
```

```
    int i;

    printf("Please enter an integer... ");
    scanf(" %d", &i);

    // Now call the half function, passing the address of i

    half(&i);
    // Shows that the function did alter i's value
    printf("In main(), i is now %d.\n", i);

    return(0); // Ends the program
}


/**************************************************************/


/* Sometimes putting dividers like the one above is a nice break
   between your different functions. */

half (int *i)  // Receives the address of i
{
    *i = *i / 2;
    printf("Your value halved is %d.\n", *i);
    return; // Returns to main
}
```

Here is the output from the program:

```
Please enter an integer… 28
Your value halved is 14.
In main(), i is now 14.
```

It looks strange, but if you want to pass a non-array by address, precede it in the passing function with an & (address-of) symbol and then put a * (dereferencing) symbol in front of the variable *everywhere it appears* in the receiving function. If you think you're now passing a pointer to a function, you're exactly right.

NOTE Now scanf() is not so unfamiliar. Remember that you put an & before non-array variables but not before array variables that you pass to scanf(). When you call scanf(), you must pass it the address of variables so that scanf() can change the variables. Because strings are arrays, when you get a string from the keyboard, you don't put an address-of operator before the array name.

Here is a program that passes an integer i by value, a floating-point x by address, and an integer array by address (as all arrays should be passed):

```c
// Example program #4 from Chapter 31 of Absolute Beginner's Guide
// to C, 3rd Edition
// File Chapter31ex4.c

/* The program demonstrates passing multiple variables to a
function. */

#include <stdio.h>

// The following statement will be explained in Chapter 32
changeSome(int i, float *newX, int iAry[5]);

main()
{
    int i = 10;
    int ctr;
    float x = 20.5;

    int iAry[] = {10, 20, 30, 40, 50};

    puts("Here are main()'s variables before the function:");
    printf("i is %d\n", i);
    printf("x is %.1f\n", x);
    for (ctr = 0; ctr < 5; ctr++)
    {
        printf("iAry[%d] is %d\n", ctr, iAry[ctr]);
    }
```

```
    // Now call the changeSome function, passing the value of i
    // and the address of x (hence, the &)

    changeSome(i, &x, iAry);

    puts("\n\nHere are main()'s variables after the function:");
    printf("i is %d\n", i);
    printf("x is %.1f\n", x);
    for (ctr = 0; ctr < 5; ctr++)
    {
        printf("iAry[%d] is %d\n", ctr, iAry[ctr]);
    }

    return(0); // Ends the program
}


/**************************************************************/

changeSome (int i, float *newX, int iAry[5])
{
    // All variables are changes, but only the float and array
    // remain changed when the program returns to main()

    // changed when the program returns to main()
    int j;

    i = 47;
    *newX = 97.6; // Same location as x in main

    for (j = 0; j < 5; j++)
    {
        iAry[j] = 100 + 100*j;
    }
    return; // Returns to main
}
```

Here is the output from the program:

```
Here are main()'s variables before the function:
i is 10
x is 20.5
iAry[0] is 10
iAry[1] is 20
iAry[2] is 30
iAry[3] is 40
iAry[4] is 50

Here are main()'s variables after the function:
i is 10
x is 97.6
iAry[0] is 100
iAry[1] is 200
iAry[2] is 300
iAry[3] is 400
iAry[4] is 500
```

The next chapter finishes with the passing of values between functions by showing you how to return a value from one function to another. Also, you will finally understand the true use of stdio.h.

THE ABSOLUTE MINIMUM

The goal of this chapter was to show you how to share local variables between functions. When one function needs access to a local variable defined in another function, you must pass that variable. The parentheses after function names contain the variables you're passing and receiving.

Normally, you pass non-array variables *by value*, which means that the receiving function can use them but not affect their values in the calling function. Arrays are passed *by address*, which means that if the receiving function changes them, the array variables are also changed in the calling function. You can pass non-array variables by address by preceding them with the address-of operator, &, and receiving them with the dereference operator, *. Key concepts from this chapter include:

- Pass local variables from one function to another if you want the functions to share local variables.

- Pass variables by value if you want their values protected from the called function.

- Pass variables by address if you want their values changed by the called function.

- Place an & before non-array variables you want to pass by address. Leave off the & if you want to pass arrays.

- Don't pass an array variable by value; C has no way to do that.

IN THIS CHAPTER
- Returning values
- Using the `return` data type

32

RETURNING DATA FROM YOUR FUNCTIONS

This chapter isn't the end of your C learning—it's only the beginning. Sounds deep, doesn't it? This chapter completes the multiple-function picture by showing you how to return values from the called function to the calling function. It also explains function *prototypes*.

The bottom line is this: You will now understand why most programs in this book contain this line:

```
return 0;
```

You also will understand the true purpose of header files.

Returning Values

So far, you've seen how to send variables *to* functions. You're now ready to learn how to return a value. When a function is to return a value, use the `return` statement to return the value. C programmers often put parentheses after the `return` statement, with the return value inside those parentheses, such as `return (answer);`.

 NOTE If a function doesn't return a value, a `return` statement isn't needed because the function will return to the calling function automatically. Nevertheless, if you need to return a value, a `return` statement is required.

Although you can pass several arguments to functions, you can return *only one value* to the calling function. Figure 32.1 explains what is going on. This rule has no exceptions.

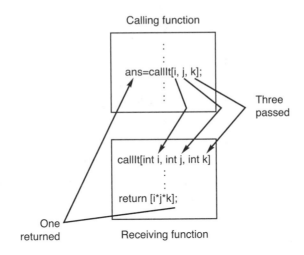

FIGURE 32.1

You can pass more than one value but return only one.

Although a single return value might seem limiting, it really isn't. Consider the built-in `sqrt()` function. You might remember from Chapter 20, "Advanced Math (For the Computer, Not You!)," that `sqrt()` returns the square root of whatever value is passed to it. `sqrt()` doesn't return several values—only one. As a matter of fact, none of the built-in functions returns more than a single value, and neither can yours.

NOTE   The gets'() function seems as if it returns more than one value because it returns a character string array. Remember, though, that an array name is nothing more than a pointer to the array's first position. Therefore, gets() actually returns a character pointer that points to the beginning of the string the user entered.

The following program contains a function that receives three floating-point values: test1, test2, and test3. The function named gradeAve() calculates the average of those three grades and then returns the answer.

```
// Example program #1 from Chapter 32 of Absolute Beginner's Guide
// to C, 3rd Edition
// File Chapter32ex1.c


/* The program demonstrates functions returning a value by passing
three floating-point numbers (grades) and calculating the average of
the three. */


#include <stdio.h>
float gradeAve(float test1, float test2, float test3);

main()
{
    float grade1, grade2, grade3;
    float average;

    printf("What was the grade on the first test? ");
    scanf(" %f", &grade1);

    printf("What was the grade on the second test? ");
    scanf(" %f", &grade2);

    printf("What was the grade on the third test? ");
    scanf(" %f", &grade3);

    //Pass the three grades to the function and return the average

    average = gradeAve(grade1, grade2, grade3);
```

```
    printf("\nWith those three test scores, the average is %.2f",
            average);

    return 0;
}


/****************************************************************/


float gradeAve(float test1, float test2, float test3)
// Receives the values of three grades
{
    float localAverage;

    localAverage = (test1+test2+test3)/3;

    return (localAverage); // Returns the average to main
}
```

Here is sample output from this program:

```
What was the grade on the first test? 95
What was the grade on the second test? 88
What was the grade on the third test? 91
With those three test scores, the average is 91.33.
```

 NOTE Notice that `main()` assigned the `gradeAve()` return value to `average`. `main()` had to do something with the value that was returned from `gradeAve()`.

You can put an expression after `return` as well as variables. This:

```
sales = quantity * price;
return (sales);
```

is identical to this:

```
return (quantity * price);
```

The `return` Data Type

At the beginning of the `gradeAve()` function, you see `float`. `float` is the data type of the returned value `localAverage`. You *must* put the return data type before any function name that returns a value. If the function returned a `long int`, `long int` would have to precede the function name.

If you don't specify a return data type, C assumes `int`. Therefore, C expects that every function without a return data type specified explicitly will return `int`. *Both* of these functions' first lines mean exactly the same thing to C:

```
int myFun(int a, float x, char c)
```

and

```
myFun(int a, float x, char c)   /* int is assumed */
```

TIP   Guess what? Even `main()` is assumed to return an `int` value unless you specify an overriding return data type. *That* is why you've seen `return 0;` at the end of most of these programs! Because `main()` has no specified return data type, `int` is assumed, and the `return 0;` ensures that an `int` is returned to your operating system.

If your function doesn't return a value, or if your function isn't passed a value, you can insert the keyword `void` for either the return data type or the parameter list or both. Therefore, the first line of a function that neither gets any value nor returns any value might look like this:

```
void doSomething(void)   /* Neither is passed nor returns */
```

WARNING   `main()` can't be of type `void` if you use strict American National Standards Institute (ANSI) C. It must be of type `int`. (However, most compilers—even those that promote themselves as ANSI C-compatible—enable you to specify `void` as `main()`'s return type.)

One Last Step: Prototype

Making a function work properly involves one last step. If a function returns any value other than `int`, you should *prototype* that function. Actually, you should prototype functions that return integers as well for clarity.

The word *prototype* means a model of something else. A prototype of a function is just a model of the actual function. At first, a C prototype seems like a total waste of time.

The reason functions that return `int` values don't need prototypes is that `int` is the default prototyped return value unless you specify a different return value. Therefore, these two prototypes *both* model the same function:

```
int aFunc(int x, float y);  /* 2 passed, one integer returned */
```

and

```
aFunc(int x, float y);  /* 2 passed, one integer returned */
```

Prototypes aren't required if you don't return a value or if you return an integer value, but they are *strongly recommended*. When you prototype, C ensures that you don't pass a `float` value to a function that expects to receive a `char`. Without the prototype, C tries to convert the `float` to a `char`, and a bad value is passed as a result.

To prototype a function, place an exact duplicate of the function's first line somewhere before `main()`. The prototype for `gradeAve()` appears right before `main()` in the program you saw earlier. The line is *not* a function call because it appears before `main()`. The line is not a function's actual first line because of the semicolon that follows all prototypes. The line is a function prototype. If your program calls 20 functions, you should have 20 prototypes.

Prototype every function in your programs—every function called by your code and even the built-in functions such as `printf()`. "Huh?" might be a good question at this point. You might wonder how you can prototype `printf()` when you didn't write it to begin with. The file `stdio.h` contains a prototype for `printf()`, `scanf()`, `getchar()`, and many other input and output functions. The prototype for `strcpy()` appears in `string.h`. You should find out the name of the header file when you learn a new built-in function so that you can use the `#include` directive to add the file to your program and make sure that each function is prototyped.

TIP `main()` needs no prototype as long as you place `main()` as the first function in the program. `main()` is known as a *self-prototyping* function because no other functions call `main()` before it appears in the code.

The following program does not work correctly because the `float` return type is not prototyped correctly. Remember, C assumes that an `int` is returned (even if you return a different data type) unless you override the return type in the prototype.

```c
#include <stdio.h>
compNet(float atomWeight, float factor);


main()
{
      float atomWeight, factor, netWeight;
      printf("What is the atomic weight? ");
      scanf(" %f", &atomWeight);
      printf("What is the factor? ");
      scanf(" %f", &factor);
      netWeight = compNet(atomWeight, factor);
      printf("The net weight is %.4f\n", netWeight);
      return 0;
}



/**************************************************************/


compNet(float atomWeight, float factor)
{
      float netWeight;

      netWeight = (atomWeight - factor) * .8;
      return(netWeight);
}
```

This shows the incorrect output:

```
What is the atomic weight? .0125
What is the factor? .98
The net weight is 0.0000
```

To fix the problem, you have to change the prototype to this:

```c
float compNet(float atomWeight, float factor);
```

You also have to change the compNet()'s definition line (its first line) to match the prototype:

```c
float compNet(float atomWeight, float factor)
```

Wrapping Things Up

Never pass or return a global variable if you use one. Global variables don't have to be passed. Also, the parameter lists in the calling function, receiving function, and prototype should match in both numbers and data types. (The names of the values don't have to match.)

You now know everything there is to know about passing parameters and returning values. Put on your official programmer's thinking cap and start your C compiler!

THE ABSOLUTE MINIMUM

The goal of this chapter was to round out your knowledge of functions by explaining prototypes and return values. When your program contains a lot of functions, prototype those functions somewhere before `main()`. The prototypes tell C what to expect. After you prototype, you can pass and return variables of any data type. (You can return `int`s only if you don't prototype.)

The prototype ensures that you don't inadvertently pass the wrong data types to functions. For example, if the prototype states that you'll pass two `float` values to a function, but you accidentally pass two `int` variables, C complains. C doesn't complain if you don't prototype, and you might get wrong results because of it.

Now that you know how to return values, you can write functions that mirror those that are built in, such as `sqrt()` and `rand()`. When you call a function, that function returns a value based on the function's code. A function can return a maximum of one value, just like functions that are built in. Key concepts from this chapter include:

- Place the return data type before a function name that returns a value.

- The return value appears after a `return` statement.

- In the calling function, do something with the return value. Print it or assign it to something. Calling a function that returns a value is useless if you do nothing with the return value.

- Use `void` as the return data type or in the parameter list if you neither return nor pass values to a function.

- Don't return more than one value from a function.

- Don't return a non-integer without a prototype. Better yet, prototype *all* functions except `main()`.

The ASCII Table

Dec	Hex	ASCII	Dec	Hex	ASCII
0	00	null	14	0E	♪
1	01	☺	15	0F	☼
2	02	☻	16	10	►
3	03	♥	17	11	◄
4	04	♦	18	12	↕
5	05	♣	19	13	‼
6	06	♠	20	14	¶
7	07	•	21	15	§
8	08	◘	22	16	▬
9	09	○	23	17	↨
10	0A	◙	24	18	↑
11	0B	♂	25	19	↓
12	0C	♀	26	1A	→
13	0D	♪	27	1B	←

Dec	Hex	ASCII	Dec	Hex	ASCII
28	1C	∟	59	3B	;
29	1D	↔	60	3C	<
30	1E	▲	61	3D	=
31	1F	▼	62	3E	>
32	20	space	63	3F	?
33	21	!	64	40	@
34	22	"	65	41	A
35	23	#	66	42	B
36	24	$	67	43	C
37	25	%	68	44	D
38	26	&	69	45	E
39	27	'	70	46	F
40	28	(	71	47	G
41	29	)	72	48	H
42	2A	*	73	49	I
43	2B	+	74	4A	J
44	2C	'	75	4B	K
45	2D	-	76	4C	L
46	2E	.	77	4D	M
47	2F	/	78	4E	N
48	30	0	79	4F	O
49	31	1	80	50	P
50	32	2	81	51	Q
51	33	3	82	52	R
52	34	4	83	53	S
53	35	5	84	54	T
54	36	6	85	55	U
55	37	7	86	56	V
56	38	8	87	57	W
57	39	9	88	58	X
58	3A	:	89	59	Y

Dec	Hex	ASCII	Dec	Hex	ASCII
90	5A	Z	121	79	y
91	5B	[	122	7A	z
92	5C	\	123	7B	{
93	5D	]	124	7C	¦
94	5E	^	125	7D	}
95	5F	–	126	7E	~
96	60	`	127	7F	Δ
97	61	a	128	80	Ç
98	62	b	129	81	ü
99	63	c	130	82	é
100	64	d	131	83	â
101	65	e	132	84	ä
102	66	f	133	85	à
103	67	g	134	86	å
104	68	h	135	87	ç
105	69	ı	136	88	ê
106	6A	j	137	89	ë
107	6B	k	138	8A	è
108	6C	l	139	8B	ï
109	6D	m	140	8C	î
110	6E	n	141	8D	ì
111	6F	o	142	8E	Ä
112	70	p	143	8F	Å
113	71	q	144	90	É
114	72	r	145	91	æ
115	73	s	146	92	Æ
116	74	t	147	93	ô
117	75	u	148	94	ö
118	76	v	149	95	ò
119	77	w	150	96	û
120	78	x	151	97	ù

Dec	Hex	ASCII	Dec	Hex	ASCII
152	98	ÿ	181	B5	╡
153	99	Ö	182	B6	╢
154	9A	Ü	183	B7	╖
155	9B	¢	184	B8	╕
156	9C	£	185	B9	╣
157	9D	¥	186	BA	║
158	9E	₧	187	BB	╗
159	9F	ƒ	188	BC	╝
160	A0	á	189	BD	╜
161	A1	í	190	BE	╛
162	A2	ó	191	BF	┐
163	A3	ú	192	C0	└
164	A4	ñ	193	C1	┴
165	A5	─	194	C2	┬
166	A6	ª	195	C3	├
167	A7	º	196	C4	─
168	A8	¿	197	C5	+
169	A9	⌐	198	C6	╞
170	AA	¬	199	C7	╟
171	AB	½	200	C8	╚
172	AC	¼	201	C9	╔
173	AD	¡	202	CA	╩
174	AE	«	203	CB	╦
175	AF	»	204	CC	╠
176	B0		205	CD	═
177	B1		206	CE	╬
178	B2		207	CF	╧
179	B3	│	208	D0	╨
180	B4	┤	209	D1	╤

Dec	Hex	ASCII	Dec	Hex	ASCII
210	D2	╥	239	EF	∩
211	D3	╨	240	F0	Å
212	D4	╞	241	F1	±
213	D5	╟	242	F2	≥
214	D6	╓	243	F3	≤
215	D7	╫	244	F4	⌠
216	D8	╪	245	F5	⌡
217	D9	┘	246	F6	÷
218	DA	┌	247	F7	≈
219	DB		248	F8	°
220	DC	▄	249	F9	•
221	DD	▌	250	FA	·
222	DE	▐	251	FB	√
223	DF	▀	252	FC	ⁿ
224	E0	α	253	FD	²
225	E1	β	254	FE	■
226	E2	Γ	255	FF	
227	E3	π			
228	E4	Σ			
229	E5	σ			
230	E6	μ			
231	E7	γ			
232	E8	Φ			
233	E9	θ			
234	EA	Ω			
235	EB	δ			
236	EC	∞			
237	ED	ø			
238	EE	∈			

B

THE DRAW POKER PROGRAM

Programming is not all work and no play, and the following Draw Poker game proves it! The game program provides a long example that you can study as you master C. Although the game is simple and straightforward, a lot happens in this program.

As with all well-written programs, this one is commented thoroughly. In fact, if you have read each chapter of this book, you will understand the programming of Draw Poker. One of the reasons the program is kept simple is to keep it compiler-independent. For your program, you might want to find out how your C compiler produces colors onscreen so that you can add pizazz to the game's display. Also, when you master enough of C to understand the program's inner workings, you'll want to explore graphics capabilities and actually draw the cards.

NOTE You can also experiment with changes to the program. For example, most draw poker programs pay out on a pair only if it is Jacks or better (that is, only a pair of Jacks, Queens, Kings, or Aces). How would you have to alter the analyzeHand() function to make that change?

```c
// Example poker program from Appendix B of Absolute Beginner's
// Guide to C, 3rd Edition
// File AppendixBpoker.c


/* This program plays draw poker. Users can play as often as they
want, betting between 1 and 5. They are dealt 5 cards and then get
to choose which cards to keep, and which cards to replace. The new
hand is then reviewed and the user's payout is set based on the
value of the hand. The user's new bankroll is displayed as they are
given
    the option to continue. */


// Header files

#include <stdio.h>
#include <time.h>
#include <ctype.h>
#include <stdlib.h>


// Two constants defined for determining whether hands are flushes
// or straights

#define FALSE 0
#define TRUE 1


// Function prototyping

void printGreeting();
int getBet();
char getSuit(int suit);
char getRank(int rank);
void getFirstHand(int cardRank[], int cardSuit[]);
```

```
void getFinalHand(int cardRank[], int cardSuit[], int finalRank[],
          int finalSuit[], int ranksinHand[],
          int suitsinHand[]);
int analyzeHand(int ranksinHand[], int suitsinHand[]);



main()
{
    int bet;
    int bank = 100;
    int i;
    int cardRank[5]; // Will be one of 13 values (Ace-King)
    int cardSuit[5]; // Will be one of 4 values (for Clubs, Diamonds,
                     // Hearts, Spades)
    int finalRank[5];
    int finalSuit[5];
    int ranksinHand[13]; // Used for evaluating the final hand
    int suitsinHand[4]; // Used for evaluating the final hand
    int winnings;
    time_t t;
    char suit, rank, stillPlay;


    // This function is called outside the do...while loop because
    // the greeting
    // only needs to be displayed once, while everything else in main
    // will run
    // multiple times, depending on how many times the user wants to
    // play.

    printGreeting();

    // Loop runs each time the user plays a hand of draw poker

    do {
        bet = getBet();
```

```c
    srand(time(&t));
    getFirstHand(cardRank, cardSuit);
    printf("Your five cards: \n");
    for (i = 0; i < 5; i++)
    {
        suit = getSuit(cardSuit[i]);
        rank = getRank(cardRank[i]);
        printf("Card #%d: %c%c\n", i+1, rank, suit);
    }

// These two arrays are used to figure out the value of
// the player's hand. However, they must be zeroed out
// in case the user plays multiple hands.

for (i=0; i < 4; i++)
{
    suitsinHand[i] = 0;
}

for (i=0; i < 13; i++)
{
    ranksinHand[i] = 0;
}



getFinalHand(cardRank, cardSuit, finalRank, finalSuit,
                        ranksinHand, suitsinHand);

printf("Your five final cards: \n");
for (i = 0; i < 5; i++)
{
    suit = getSuit(finalSuit[i]);
    rank = getRank(finalRank[i]);
    printf("Card #%d: %c%c\n", i+1, rank, suit);
}
```

```
        winnings = analyzeHand(ranksinHand,suitsinHand);
        printf("You won %d!\n", bet*winnings);
        bank = bank - bet + (bet*winnings);
        printf("\nYour bank is now %d.\n", bank);
        printf("\nDo you want to play again? ");
        scanf(" %c", &stillPlay);
    } while (toupper(stillPlay) == 'Y');


    return;
}
/***************************************************************/


// Print a quick greeting as well as tell the users the value of
// different winning hands

void printGreeting()
{
    printf("**************************************************\n");
    printf("\n\n\tWelcome to the Absolute Beginner's Casino\n\n");
    printf("\tHome of Video Draw Poker\n\n");
    printf("**************************************************\n");

    printf("Here are the rules:\n");
    printf("You start with 100 credits, and you make a bet from ");
    printf("1 to 5 credits.\n");
    printf("You are dealt 5 cards, and you then choose which ");
    printf("cards to keep ");
    printf("or discard.\n");
    printf("You want to make the best possible hand.\n");
    printf("\nHere is the table for winnings (assuming a ");
    printf("bet of 1 credit):");
    printf("\nPair\t\t\t\t1 credit");
    printf("\nTwo pairs\t\t\t2 credits");
    printf("\nThree of a kind\t\t\t3 credits");
    printf("\nStraight\t\t\t4 credits");
    printf("\nFlush\t\t\t\t5 credits");
```

```c
        printf("\nFull House\t\t\t8 credits");
        printf("\nFour of a Kind\t\t\t10 credits");
        printf("\nStraight Flush\t\t\t20 credits");
        printf("\n\nHave fun!!\n\n");
}


// Function to deal the first five cards

void getFirstHand(int cardRank[], int cardSuit[])
{
    int i,j;
    int cardDup;

    for (i=0; i < 5; i++)
        {
            cardDup = 0;
            do {
                // Card rank is one of 13 (2-10, J, Q, K, A)
                cardRank[i] = (rand() % 13);
                //  Card suit is one of 4
                //  (club, diamond, heart, spade)
                cardSuit[i] = (rand() % 4);

                // Loop that ensures each card is unique
                for (j=0; j < i; j++)
                {
                    if ((cardRank[i] == cardRank[j]) &&
                    (cardSuit[i] == cardSuit[j]))
                    {
                        cardDup = 1;
                    }
                }
            } while (cardDup == 1);
        }

}
```

```
// Function that changes the suit integer value to a character
// representing the suit

char getSuit(int suit)
{
    switch (suit)
    {
        case 0:
            return('c');
        case 1:
            return('d');
        case 2:
            return('h');
        case 3:
            return('s');
    }
}


// Function that changes the rank integer value to a character
// representing the rank

char getRank(int rank)
{
    switch (rank)
    {
        case 0:
            return('A');
        case 1:
            return('2');
        case 2:
            return('3');
        case 3:
            return('4');
        case 4:
            return('5');
        case 5:
```

```
                    return('6');
            case 6:
                    return('7');
            case 7:
                    return('8');
            case 8:
                    return('9');
            case 9:
                    return('T');
            case 10:
                    return('J');
            case 11:
                    return('Q');
            case 12:
                    return('K');
        }
    }


// Function to get the user's bet between 1 and 5

int getBet()
{
    int bet;

    do //Will keep running until the user enters 0-5
    {
        printf("How much do you want to bet? (Enter a number ");
        printf("1 to 5, or 0 to quit the game): ");
        scanf(" %d", &bet);

        if (bet >= 1 && bet <= 5)
        {
            return(bet);
        }
        else if (bet == 0)
        {
```

```
            exit(1);
        }
        else
        {
            printf("\n\nPlease enter a bet from 1-5 or ");
            printf("0 to quit the game.\n");
        }

    } while ((bet < 0) || (bet > 5));
}


// Last function reviews the final hand and determines the value of
// the hand.

int analyzeHand(int ranksinHand[], int suitsinHand[])
{
    int num_consec = 0;
    int i, rank, suit;
    int straight = FALSE;
    int flush = FALSE;
    int four = FALSE;
    int three = FALSE;
    int pairs = 0;


    for (suit = 0; suit < 4; suit++)
        if (suitsinHand[suit] == 5)
            flush = TRUE;
    rank = 0;
    while (ranksinHand[rank] == 0)
        rank++;
    for (; rank < 13 && ranksinHand[rank]; rank++)
        num_consec++;
    if (num_consec == 5) {
        straight = TRUE;
    }
```

```c
for (rank = 0; rank < 13; rank++) {
    if (ranksinHand[rank] == 4)
        four = TRUE;
    if (ranksinHand[rank] == 3)
        three = TRUE;
    if (ranksinHand[rank] == 2)
        pairs++;
}

if (straight && flush) {
    printf("Straight flush\n\n");
    return (20);
}
else if (four) {
    printf("Four of a kind\n\n");
    return (10);
}
else if (three && pairs == 1) {
    printf("Full house\n\n");
    return (8);
}
else if (flush) {
    printf("Flush\n\n");
    return (5);
}
else if (straight) {
    printf("Straight\n\n");
    return (4);
}
else if (three) {
    printf("Three of a kind\n\n");
    return (3);
}
else if (pairs == 2) {
    printf("Two pairs\n\n");
    return (2);
}
```

```
        else if (pairs == 1) {
            printf("Pair\n\n");
            return (1);
        }
        else {
            printf("High Card\n\n");
            return (0);
        }
    }


// This function looks through each of the five cards in the first hand
// and asks the user if they want to keep the card. If they say no,
// they get a replacement card.

void getFinalHand(int cardRank[], int cardSuit[], int finalRank[],
            int finalSuit[], int ranksinHand[],
            int suitsinHand[])
{
    int i, j, cardDup;
    char suit, rank, ans;

    for (i=0; i < 5; i++)
    {
        suit = getSuit(cardSuit[i]);
        rank = getRank(cardRank[i]);
        printf("Do you want to keep card #%d: %c%c?", i+1, rank, suit);
        printf("\nPlease answer (Y/N): ");
        scanf(" %c", &ans);
        if (toupper(ans) == 'Y')
        {
            finalRank[i] = cardRank[i];
            finalSuit[i] = cardSuit[i];
            ranksinHand[finalRank[i]]++;
            suitsinHand[finalSuit[i]]++;
            continue;
        }
```

```c
            else if (toupper(ans) == 'N')
            {
                cardDup = 0;
                do {
                    cardDup = 0;
                    finalRank[i] = (rand() % 13);
                    finalSuit[i] = (rand() % 4);

                    // First check your new card against the 5 original
                    // cards to avoid duplication
                    for (j=0; j < 5; j++)
                    {
                        if ((finalRank[i] == cardRank[j]) &&
                        (finalSuit[i] == cardSuit[j]))
                        {
                            cardDup = 1;
                        }
                    }
                     // Next, check the new card against any newly drawn
                     //  cards to avoid duplication
                    for (j=0; j < i; j++)
                    {
                        if ((finalRank[i] == finalRank[j]) &&
                        (finalSuit[i] == finalSuit[j]))
                        {
                            cardDup = 1;
                        }
                    }
                } while (cardDup == 1);
                ranksinHand[finalRank[i]]++;
                suitsinHand[finalSuit[i]]++;
            }
        }

    }
```

Index

U-V

updating variables, compound assignment operators, 85-86

uppercase letters, defined constant names, 61

vals arrays, 195

values
arrays, putting in, 197-199
passing arguments by, 295-297
returning, functions, 306-309

variables, 41-43, 294
char, 42
checking case, 172-176
counter, 84
data types, 42
decrementing, 119
defining, 44-45, 60
double, 42
flag, 206
float, 42
found, 206
global, 45, 290-292, 312
incrementing, 119
incrementing counter, 132
int, 42
local, 45, 290-292
naming, 43-44
nonarray, passing, 303
passing, 293-294
by address, 297-302
by value, 295-297
pointers, 221, 231
array names, 232-233
arrays of, 236, 239-241
characters, 234
constants, 232
defining, 222-224
dereferencing, 225, 228
heap memory, 243-244
memory addresses, 222
scanf() function, ampersands, 68-69
storing data in, 45-48
string, 49

structure, putting data in, 262-265

typecasting, 89

updating, compound assignment operators, 85-86

void keyword, 309

W-Z

while command, 124

while loops
repeating code, 124-129
terminating, 142-144

whitespace, 27-28

word processors, copying code from, 15

writing programs, requirements, 7-10

zeroes, terminating, strings, 50-51

FREE
Online Edition

Your purchase of *C Programming Absolute Beginner's Guide* includes access to a free online edition for 45 days through the **Safari Books Online** subscription service. Nearly every Que book is available online through **Safari Books Online**, along with thousands of books and videos from publishers such as Addison-Wesley Professional, Cisco Press, Exam Cram, IBM Press, O'Reilly Media, Prentice Hall, Sams, and VMware Press.

Safari Books Online is a digital library providing searchable, on-demand access to thousands of technology, digital media, and professional development books and videos from leading publishers. With one monthly or yearly subscription price, you get unlimited access to learning tools and information on topics including mobile app and software development, tips and tricks on using your favorite gadgets, networking, project management, graphic design, and much more.

Activate your FREE Online Edition at
informit.com/safarifree

STEP 1:   Enter the coupon code: MFQLMXA.

STEP 2:   New Safari users, complete the brief registration form.
Safari subscribers, just log in.

If you have difficulty registering on Safari or accessing the online edition,
please e-mail customer-service@safaribooksonline.com